A Manual Of Field Excavation

HANDBOOK FOR FIELD ARCHAEOLOGISTS

Editors
William G. Dever
H. Darrell Lance

With contributions by

Reuben G. Bullard
Daniel P. Cole
William G. Dever
John S. Holladay, Jr.
H. Darrell Lance
Joe D. Seger
Anita Walker
Robert B. Wright

HEBREW UNION COLLEGE—JEWISH INSTITUTE OF RELIGION
Cincinnati • New York • Los Angeles • Jerusalem
1978

+
913.031
M319

81021629

Copyright © 1978 by Hebrew Union College—Jewish Institute of Religion
Nelson Glueck School of Biblical Archaeology
American Office: 40 West 68th Street, New York NY 10023

Library of Congress Catalog Card Number 78-51085

All Rights Reserved

Printed in the United States of America

Preface

The purpose of this manual is to set down in written form a description of field archaeology as it was practiced at the Hebrew Union College/Harvard Semitic Museum Excavations at Gezer, Phase I, 1964-71. Our motivation stems in part from the fact that many of the concepts, methods, and procedures developed at Gezer have spread widely to other American excavations in Israel, Jordan, Cyprus, and even North Africa, through the medium of staff members who received their training at Gezer. We could rightly be accused of hypocrisy if we pretended distress at this state of affairs, and it is because much of the "Gezer Method" has been imitated in this way that we think that a larger audience might be interested in a full statement from us.

The authors were all members of the Core Staff at Gezer and have among them the accumulated experience of dozens of seasons at this and other sites. The authors did not collaborate in their writing; hence there are repetitions and even differences of opinion among the chapters. We have not attempted to edit out these differences, preferring to let each writer speak for himself or herself and to allow the reader the benefit of varied opinions and approaches.

This manual has a predecessor in Lance's Excavation Manual for Area Supervisors (Jerusalem: Hebrew Union College Biblical and Archaeological School, 1967; now out of print), which was the result of the experiences of the first seasons at Gezer and which after its publication in 1967 served as our basic statement of method and procedure. Improvements and changes were constant so that the present product represents our thinking and practice as of our last season in 1971. For Phase II of the excavations, the final seasons in 1972 and 1973, J. D. Seger wrote a new manual, Handbook for Field Operations (Jerusalem: Hebrew Union College Biblical and Archaeological School, 1971), which in some details represents an advance over the procedures described here and which we warmly commend to the reader.

Two self-imposed limitations must be acknowledged. (1) This is a manual in the literal sense, i.e., a "handbook" which covers practical procedures rather than attempting to deal with the general theory of field archaeology. (2) This manual is based upon our experiences with the problems encountered specifically at Bronze and Iron Age sites of ancient Palestine (principally modern Israel and Jordan) and thus may not be fully applicable in other areas. Even for this area, our present manual is too specific and detailed to serve as a substitute for excellent general introductions such as Sir Mortimer Wheeler's Archaeology from the Earth or Dame Kathleen Kenyon's Beginning in Archaeology.

Finally, we owe a special debt to those who introduced us to field problems and methods at Shechem in the early 1960's, particularly the late G. E. Wright; among others we mention Edward F. Campbell, Jr.,

Paul W. Lapp, Lawrence Toombs and Prescott Williams, from whose wide experience we profited. We also express appreciation to the Hebrew Union College - Jewish Institute of Religion for its sponsorship of the Gezer project and for its substantial contributions financially and otherwise. A special debt is owed to two officials of the HUC-JIR: the late President Nelson Glueck; and Dr. Paul M. Steinberg, Dean of the New York school and Director of the American office of the Jerusalem school (now the "Nelson Glueck School of Biblical Archaeology").

The ideas expressed here were field-tested over the years at Gezer, where the excavations were funded principally by the Smithsonian Institution through its program for administering U.S. counterpart funds (P.L. 480). The Harvard Semitic Museum contributed minor support. To these institutions and their administrators we express our warmest appreciation.

The publication of this manual has been made possible by the support of the President of the HUC-JIR, Dr. Alfred A. Gottschalk, and through the generosity of Mr. Richard J. Scheuer, Chairman of the Jerusalem School Committee of the HUC-JIR Board of Governors.

The Editors
Jerusalem, 1975

Postscript:

We are grateful to the contributors to this manual for being patient in the delay of its publication. We have not made any attempt to update the chapters, so that they represent the state of the art as it was understood when the manuscripts were being written by the various authors in 1972-73.

The Editors
Tucson and Rochester
November, 1977

TABLE OF CONTENTS

Chapter I

PRINCIPLES OF EXCAVATION

Anita Walker

"No-one goes anywhere without a porpoise." Lewis Carroll.

The aim of an archaeological project is the reconstruction of the life-ways of the people who lived at the site, the study of the processes of culture change and the testing of hypotheses set up by the project designer. It is impossible, or should be, to excavate unless the excavator has clearly in mind the kind of goals he wants to reach. Before setting trowel to ground, therefore, the archaeologist must first define his objectives and then derive a set of procedures to fulfill them, because the goals he sets will themselves condition the methods he uses to achieve them. Put bluntly, he tends to find what he knows to look for. If this remark sounds unduly harsh, its truth can be demonstrated by looking at almost any of the site reports in great Near Eastern excavations of the 1930's. Since the excavators of these sites were interested primarily in architecture, chronology, and political events, that is the kind of data they sought. On the other hand, since most of them were not much interested in (for instance) the economic history of their site, they did not collect data which would have allowed them (or later archaeologists) to reconstruct economic processes from their records.

It must never be forgotten that when excavation is completed, all that remains is a neat square hole with bedrock at the bottom. All subsequent interpretation about the site and its people will be based on the data collected in the course of excavation, whether those data are faunal remains, soil samples, artifacts, section-drawings, notebooks, plans or photographs. The limits of interpretation are set, then, in turn by methods used and the completeness of the records kept. Means and ends thus interact upon each other, and the means you use must be appropriate to the ends you choose. Since this is a how-to rather than a why-to book, a discussion of project design will not be treated here, but it should be understood that the theoretical design of why you are digging must precede any devising of specific procedures in the field. For discussion of the theory of archaeology and the formulation of explanatory models, consult:

Binford, Lewis, "Archaeology as Anthropology," American Antiquity 28 (1963), pp. 217-22.

Binford, Lewis, "A Consideration of Archaeological Research Design," American Antiquity 29 (1964), pp. 425-41.

Binford, Lewis and Sally Binford, eds., New Perspectives in Archaeology (Chicago: Aldine, 1968).

Clarke, D. L., Analytical Archaeology (London: Methuen, 1968).

Watson, Patty Jo, Steven A. LeBlanc and Charles Redman, Explanation in Archeology: An Explicitly Scientific Approach (New York: Columbia University Press, 1971).

I

ORGANIZATION OF PERSONNEL

Modern excavations are usually quite complex in their organization, since the multifarious tasks and skills required cannot be carried out except by a team.

The Director is responsible for the design of the project and ultimately responsible for overseeing all work in the field, interpreting data, and integrating all publication. In the field he will orchestrate the work, advise, consult, and challenge his supervisors with hard questions.

The field-work will be carried out by archaeologists and their teams aided by various specialists. Each work force is organized into teams of five or six people, each team in the charge of an "Area" Supervisor. Groups of three or four "Area" Supervisors will be responsible to a "Field" Supervisor, and the "Field" Supervisor will be responsible to the Director. At Gezer the work-force consisted almost entirely of student volunteers (mostly American), who made up in enthusiasm what they lacked in experience.

"Area" Supervisors are responsible for the supervision and book-keeping of all work done in their Areas. They work closely with their Field Supervisor, who in turn consults the Director on sticky points. The degree to which a Field Supervisor regulates and directs his Area Supervisors will depend on their experience. A nervous novice will find his Field Supervisor hovering over his shoulder and breathing hotly in his ear; a highly experienced Area Supervisor will plan strategy tactics for the day with his Field Supervisor who will check on and consult with him regularly to make sure everything is proceeding smoothly but will let the Area Supervisor work more independently in order to spend more time with less experienced personnel.

The excavating personnel will be helped by various roving consultants, such as the geologist, physical anthropologist, and paleobotanist. Some of these people may also be making their own data collections from the site and its environs to compare with excavated material.

At the dig-house there will be a back-up team of other personnel-- the Registrar, Conservationist, Photographer, Draftsman--some of whom will be called to the field when necessary.

The regulation of relationships between all personnel from Director to digger must depend on certain shared premises--that the excavated data is the <u>primary data</u>, that it is irreplaceable.

It is, therefore, incumbent upon all members of the team to give of their best and never wittingly to make mistakes which destroy or disturb the data or permit others to do so. These are tough standards to uphold and upholding them may lead to friction and hurt feelings if handled badly at any level, but acceptance of these principles for working is essential.

II

PRINCIPLES OF EXCAVATION METHOD: STRATIGRAPHY

Ideally, the records of an excavation should enable any observer to construct a three-dimensional model of all soil layers, features, artifacts, etc. in their precise topographic relationship. The closest way of achieving such a methodological ideal seems to be the procedures of stratigraphic excavation devised by Mortimer Wheeler,[1] introduced into Palestine by Kathleen Kenyon. Stratigraphic excavation involves the excavation of soil layers, etc., in the reverse order of their decomposition by close attention to the relationships of soils and features. To do this, it is necessary to work in small areas, to triangulate measurements, and most important to use vertical balks or sections to dig by. Balks tell you where you are going and record where you have been. In order to retain accuracy in reconstruction it will usually be necessary to survey the site first and mark it off in a grid of units small enough for controlled excavation. The grid size can vary; at Gezer the typical grid unit was six meters square, providing a five-meter square for digging with one meter balks between adjacent squares.

In excavating at Gezer, the basic recording unit was the _locus_. A locus can be defined as any material whose composition or stratigraphic position seems to mark it as discrete. Thus, soil layers and features are subsumed under the term _locus_ and each locus is given a number in sequence as it is encountered. This proved to be a useful and practical device both in defining layers etc., in digging and in recording. For instance, you come upon a line of rocks orientated north-south; since it may be something different from the soil layer you are digging, it should be given a separate locus number and treated separately. A second line of rocks appears on the other side of the square--it too receives its own locus number. Further excavation may show that these two lines of rocks are walls and join to form a corner, and are not actually separate but formed part of a single installation. The two separate wall loci can be later collapsed together in reconstructing the installation. It is better to overseparate than to underseparate. A distinctive soil which turns out to be a lens or pocket within another soil layer and not stratigraphically significant can be collapsed with its enclosing soil layer locus. But it is often not possible to separate _within_ a layer if it turns out later to be composed of two different

things. The history of feature construction and soil deposition must
be built up from the building blocks of different loci and their relationships. Thus a room may be excavated as a large number of loci:
each wall and each soil will have its own number. [See Chapter IV,
Part I below for a more detailed statement on the concept of locus as
used at Gezer.--Eds.]

III

PRINCIPLES OF EXCAVATION METHOD: CERAMIC TYPOLOGY

The second fundamental characteristic of the Gezer method, first
introduced in the excavations of G. Ernest Wright at Shechem, is the
daily analysis of the pottery from each locus under excavation. All
the pottery is looked at and dated immediately as soon as it is washed
and dried. This serves as a check upon the clear identification and
clean separation of loci in the process of excavation. Although there
is usually a greater or lesser amount of earlier pottery in any locus,
the locus is always dated by the latest pottery in it. If, for example, the latest pottery of a locus is consistently of one chronological
period, then stratigraphic separation of loci in the digging has proceeded correctly. But if sherds of a later chronological period appear
unaccountably (one expects earlier material the deeper one goes), then
something is awry in the stratigraphic separation. Two separate loci
are being mixed, and the cause of the intrusive late pottery must be
found and explained. Repeatedly at Gezer when this or a similar situation occurred, the Field and Area Supervisors would re-evaluate their
fieldwork, re-examine their balks and excavation areas, and find the
source of the unexpected pottery--an undiscovered pit, a terrace situation, etc. Once the source of contamination was identified, the
stratigraphical analysis was corrected, loci redefined, and the work
continued.

The use of pottery as a check upon stratigraphy is possible only if
the provenance of the pottery excavated can be determined with exacti-
tude. Therefore great care must be exercised in the gathering and
processing of pottery. The pottery from each digging operation is
placed in a bucket which is tagged and designated for that particular
operation. Only pottery from that individual operation is placed in
that bucket. Stray sherds are never allowed to collect in random piles
to be bucketed later. The earth from each digging operation is kept
confined within the designated limits of excavation so that pottery
from the loosened earth is not mixed with that from another locus. Any
sherd that falls from a balk or from the edge of the trench into the
area being excavated is discarded.

If a sherd even looks suspicious, e.g. if it is lying dry in the moist soil, it should be discarded rather than risk contamination. If a pottery bucket is knocked over and spilled, only those sherds should be replaced in the bucket which of certainty came from it. Workmen must be impressed with the importance of preventing contamination so that they will take care not to throw sherds carelessly into the wrong bucket. Or if they do, so that they will confess the mistake so that precautionary measures can be taken, e.g. writing "Possible contamination" on the basket tag. Buckets should not be filled too full lest they spill easily, and once the bucket is no longer in use it should be promptly taken from the square and away from the excavated area. [See Part IA of Chapter V for another statement on the gathering of pottery in the field.--Eds.]

IV

PROCEDURES OF FIELD EXCAVATION

Work in the field consists of the repetition of a small number of procedures in various permutations. No one can teach you which procedure to apply in every situation; that is something which comes only from experience and handling of the actual soil. This section does not attempt to be exhaustive. It merely tries to set out the general pattern of procedure and to give some things to consider while digging.

Let us assume that your area (5 x 5 m. with a one-meter balk or 4 x 4 m. with a one-meter balk or whatever) is neatly squared off with marked pegs and strings and that you have been given a datum set by transit, on the top of one of the nails set in the middle of the pegs. (All elevations in your square will be calculated from that datum, unless a transit is sited permanently near your area.) Paint the datum numbers on the side of the peg, write them on a pottery tag and attach it to the nail, and also write them in your notebook with a note on which peg it is. This will save you rechecking the datum every time. But if the peg is knocked or the nail bent at any time, have the datum reset or you will end up with a distorted reconstruction. Before you begin to dig, clean your area thoroughly with broom, dustpan, and brush. Sweep the balks clear of any small stones or sherds which could be kicked into the square.

A. Probe trenches.

The heart of the digging system is the probe trench (or test pit as it is sometimes called). So when you have cleaned your square of loose soil, tree roots, weeds, etc., lay out a probe against one of the main balks with nails and string. The size of the probe and its depth are matters of individual preference. There is one school of thought which favors a one-by-five-meter slice along a main balk dug to a depth of one meter (the maxi-probe). At the opposite end of the spectrum some favor a one-meter square taken down only so far as the first soil change (the mini-probe). There are points to be said in favor of both extremes.

The Small Shallow Probe

Pro: By going down only to the first soil change and then peeling back throughout the square, you end up with a square completely in phase, which can more easily be drawn and photographed.
Con: It is extremely difficult to interpret the balk of a very shallow trench, so that you are more dependent in this kind of probe on the appearance of your soil from the top.

The Deeper (and/or Larger)Probe

Pro: The deeper probe trench which usually involves several different soil layers provides balks which are much easier to "read", and therefore it is easier to trace out each separate layer from the probe trench throughout the square.
Con: The bigger and deeper the probe, the more cut-up the square will look, so that often photographs which are intended to show a square at one phase are complicated by the presence of the probe trench in one corner.

On balance, however, the writer recommends a moderate position, a one-meter-square probe trench taken down to a depth of as much as 50 cm. Such a probe gives enough exposure of layers in the balks to separate them clearly when moving into the rest of the square, yet does minimum aesthetic damage to the appearance of any one phase. Probes should be dug with small tools (but with all deliberate speed) since there is always danger, when digging blind from the top, of mixing up material. The different soils within a probe can be separated out and each given a designation as a layer within the locus number of the probe trench. When you begin to move out from the probe trench, each layer, as you trace it, in turn will receive a new locus number, and later the material from each layer of the artificial locus of the probe trench can be assimilated to its proper natural locus in the rest of the square so that all data is conserved.

Some proponents of the maxi-probe (one-meter-deep along the length of the main balk) eschew this method of following out each layer throughout the square and instead favor a kind of "running balk." In this strategy, once the initial probe is dug and layers separated within the probe and tagged in the balks of the probe, you simply lay off another one-by-five-meter probe parallel to your first and remove the layers, using balks of your original probe as your guide. You continue to do this until you reach the other side of the square, then come back and start again. A disadvantage of this technique is that you never see any one phase exposed all at one time, and photographing and planning a coherent phase would be difficult except as a kind of mosaic.

In working out from the probe trench you will encounter three main types of deposit: (1) soil layers, (2) installations originally built up, (3) installations originally dug down. [See also Chapter III, Section III below for a catalogue of the kinds of features and soil layers typical of the Palestinian tell.--Eds.]

B. Sedimentary deposits.

In tackling soil layers several things should be kept in mind. From the probe trench you know the thickness of your layer in the probe balk: be prepared for the fact that it may be thicker or thinner in the rest of the square or may peter out completely. The chances of the soil layer filling the entire square exactly, dead flat and an even 10 cm. thick, are remote. The actual contours of each soil layer must be followed, sloping upward or downward or sagging into depressions. However, within those natural contours, try to remove the soil evenly, preferably by scraping with a trowel or hand-picking. Do not get stuck in one spot and find that in your enthusiasm you have created an artificial depression in the soil layer. Some soil layers (fills, for example) can be quite thick (50 cm. or even more), but it is still advisable to remove your layer in small spits of not more than 5-10 cm., even if you use a pick. This is NOT advocating the pernicious practice of digging by completely artificial 10 cm. spits, but is a method of achieving a higher control within the natural soil layer. For example, a thick fill may suddenly become shallower over some other underlying layer. If you are digging in huge bites with large tools, you may easily dig through an underlying layer without perceiving it.

As you begin to dig a soil layer you will need to answer certain questions about it. First, its physical composition. What is it composed of? What particle-sizes make it up? (Use the Wentworth scale.) To what degree is it compacted? How are the various particles disposed --chaotically, suggesting a fill--in graded bedding, suggesting water-sorting--or in laminae, suggesting a surface build-up. A knife and pocket lens are a great help here. Pry up a chunk of soil and look at its cut section (a micro-balk). If the dig has a geologist, consult him frequently. Soil samples of each layer sent to a lab are useful, but they are no substitute for the presence of a geologist in the field. Packing and shipping a soil sample will usually destroy its fabric and disposition of particles as well as changing compaction as it dries out. The geologist who analyzes your sample in the lab will be able to tell you its raw composition, but much data valuable for the interpretation of the soil layer will have been lost.

Color can also be a useful clue in interpretation, but avoid meaningless terms like "greenish-grey" and "sandy-buff," and use a Munsell soil-color chart.[2]

The second group of questions about a soil layer concerns physical dimensions. What is the horizontal extent of this layer? Does it dip: if so, to what degree, and in what direction? Remember that each soil-layer is three-dimensional and record it that way.

The third set of questions is the most vital for articulating loci --the stratigraphic relationship of this layer to other loci. How does this layer relate to other layers and features? It is not enough to note simple juxtaposition of loci--the intelligent digger must always perceive the nature of the juncture. Does this soil layer run up against a wall, over a foundation trench, under another layer? Is it cut by later intrusions from above (pits, cisterns, burials, foundation trenches, etc.)?

The excavator should try to work out as he goes what loci were in use with the locus he is digging, keeping in mind that use. Surfaces may vary in their composition sufficiently to warrant being distinguished as separate loci, while both loci are part of the same use-phase and represent the same facility. Thus, for instance, a "floor" or walk-surface may be tamped earth in one part, heavily gravelled in another, plastered in a third. And yet all three loci, compositionally so different, may be part of the same courtyard.

C. Structures.

This category includes features intended to stand for the most part above ground (such as buildings, fortifications, standing stones, etc.). Usually any one square will contain only parts of large built features --half a room, a segment of a fortification--so that the excavator is concerned with the digging of short segments of walls, perhaps forming one or two corners or intersections, and their associated soil layers.

While many of the same kinds of questions which one must consider in dealing with soil layers apply to walls and other originally above-ground features, there are also different considerations. The excavator must try to discern as he digs the construction material and techniques (for instance, dressed or undressed stones, baked or unbaked mudbrick, or a combination of these). How many courses high is it (and remember that its extant height is probably not its original height)? On the other hand, it may still preserve its original width. Did it undergo several rebuildings, or was it in use with several phases of soil layers and surfaces? Examine most carefully the juncture of surface layers with walls and also the juncture of wall with wall. Do the walls bond together or merely abut? Bonded walls are almost certainly contemporary; abutting walls may or may not be, depending on other factors. Look very carefully for signs of a foundation trench. Most walls have foundation trenches, although sometimes the trenches may be cut into bedrock to receive the lowest courses; and occasionally small walls are merely set down onto existing surfaces without a prepared trench.

Stone Walls

When in the course of digging a soil layer, you begin to uncover the tops of rocks, particularly a line of rocks, you are clearly encountering something new! However, at this point, there is no way of knowing whether this line of rocks represents a curbing one row wide and one course high or the top-most extant remains of a fortification five meters high and fifteen meters wide. Never dig along the face of a possible wall, or you will sever all its stratigraphic connections. Before tackling a wall, you must first provide yourself with a preview of its history, preferably down to its foundation level. Unless the wall runs at right angles to two of the four main balks, (which is unlikely) you must devise a subsidiary balk, relating the wall to one of the main balks of the square. This can be done in several ways. First, measure off a narrow strip on either side of the wall at right angles to the wall (for the best angle in viewing the juncture of balk and wall) and extending to the main balks. Site your strip at a point along your wall where the subsidiary balk will form the least acute angle with a main balk. You can offset your strips on either side of the wall if they do not necessarily have to be in a straight line, so long as they relate each side of the wall to a main balk (Fig. 1).

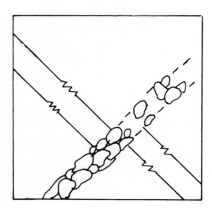 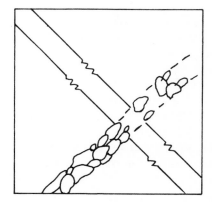

Figure 1

You can then excavate your strips as probe trenches and trim down the sides of the probes to form the subsidiary balks (Fig. 2a). The reverse procedure can also be useful: excavate on either side of the strips, reserving the strips as mini-balks (Fig. 2b). Instead of a double-edged strip, you can lay out a single line at 90° from the wall to a main balk and excavate up to the line, which will then form a subsidiary balk (Fig. 2c).

11

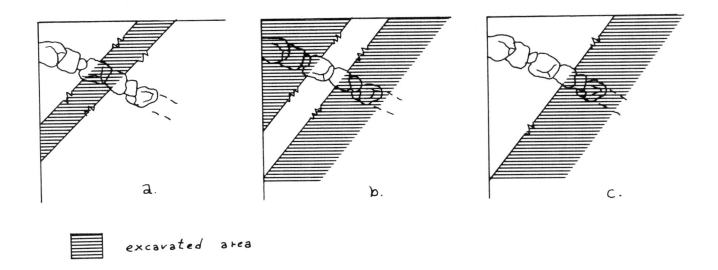

a.   b.   c.

excavated area

Figure 2

In excavating curvilinear walls it may be necessary to cut a wedge-shaped slice in order to get the best angle at the junction of wall and balk.

Mudbrick Walls[3]

So far we have been considering only easy walls constructed of stone. But in the Near East often only the foundation courses of walls are stone-built and the upper courses are mudbrick, while sometimes, particularly in southern Palestine, all the walls are of mudbrick construction only. If the mudbricks are baked, there is little problem; they are as clearly discernible from soil as stones. Unfortunately, much mudbrick construction is unbaked and the excavation of unbaked mudbrick features then poses special problems.

The basic problem is, of course, to know when one has <u>found</u> an un-baked mudbrick wall, as distinct from mudbrick debris, which is treated as a soil layer. Mudbricks were usually made in a mould from field clay with a binder of some sort (often straw), then sun dried. They may have been laid with mud mortar; or sometimes, if mortar was not used, sand may have been used between courses, perhaps as a levelling agent rather than an adhesive. An unbaked mudbrick structure has usu-ally disintegrated in the area open to erosion (which will be the sur-face you will contact first, the top of the bricks). It is quite possible, therefore, that you will not be able to see the articulation of molded bricks at first in exposed outer surfaces; if the background soils are compositionally similar to the unbaked brick wall (and near the wall there will tend to be disaggregated brick debris sloughed off the wall), you may not be able to see a color differentiation between the bricks and the brick debris. A hand lens is helpful in checking suspected brick for straw binder. If the bricks used a straw binder and are still fairly well consolidated then composition will be very revealing. For detecting the presence of still articulated unbaked mudbrick wall, look for the original mortar lines. If you are doing a small probe against suspected mudbrick, you may see in the balks of your probe a network of parallel lines which represent the ghosts of past brick courses. These lines may be a slender clue. Do not be sur-prised if some of the horizontal mortar lines are closer together, or do not extend laterally very far; erosion at the exposed surfaces of a mudbrick wall may have been uneven and bricks may have partly slumped. One caveat: do not be fooled by the tunnels of ant-colonies, which may leave tracks suspiciously like ghost mortar lines!

If you are sure that you are coming down on the eroded top of an unbaked brick wall, it is obviously important to know its extent. The best way to establish the line of the wall is to scrape the area down flat, arbitrarily; then clean it thoroughly and look for variation in color and texture, along a straight edge marking a junction between brick debris and brick <u>in situ</u>. If you wait long enough, differentia-tion in drying between brick and brick debris usually causes a crack to form along the faces of the mudbrick feature. A little water sprinkled on the area will often accelerate cracking (but be extremely cautious; too much water and you get a puddle!). In assessing a crack that has formed a straight edge, keep in mind, however, that many mud-brick walls underwent rebuilding and addition of extra "skins," and the crack may represent separation of one phase of wall from another.

When you have thus determined the approximate dimensions and orien-tation of an unbaked mudbrick wall, from some combination of techniques of compositional analysis and structural analysis, you may drop a probe at right angles on either side to determine the extant height, associ-ated dirt layers, etc. As you move down the face of the wall, however, keep in mind that, unlike most stone walls, it may have been deliber-ately battered out towards the base, or else erosion near the top may have given a false impression of the original dimensions of the wall.

Most mudbrick walls were originally faced with a mud plaster. The chances are that this will have disappeared, but be on the alert for it anyway. Do not be surprised if in many cases, different types of clay seem to be present in one wall; this may reflect several sources of field clay used for brick making. As you approach the face of the wall with a deliberate hand-picking action, the brick and soil debris is generally less compact than the brick itself and will flake away from the wall-face. The best tactic for dealing with a large mudbrick structure might be a kind of rolling probe. Cautiously dig your soils, layer by layer, up to the face of the wall and down to its associated use-surface, then move one side of your probe over a meter and start again.

Unbaked mudbrick structures are probably the most difficult features to dig in the Near East. One of the most helpful things to do is familiarize yourself thoroughly with the appearance and composition of mudbricks at your particular site.

D. Intrusive elements.

This category includes installations dug down. Such installations are perforce intrusive into earlier layers; and, following the principle of removing all deposits in the reverse order of their deposition, must be dug out before the earlier layers. If these installations are not perceived at the phase from which they were dug, they may introduce later material into earlier phases. This kind of feature includes such things as pits, sunken bins and silos, burials, cisterns, wells and foundation trenches. All of these installations are essentially holes in the ground level of the time they were built and were either closed over or filled up near the time of their construction (for instance, foundation trenches and burials) or filled up with debris when they went out of use (pits, cisterns, etc.). Soils in holes are seldom compressed as much as layers which have been walked upon, so these features may first be perceived as areas of loose soil or gravity-sifted soils and rubble, or a regularly contoured depression in a compact layer, where pressure has caused the compacted layer to sink into the less compacted hole beneath. If you suspect an installation of this kind, first try to delimit it. Scraping the soil flat with a trowel will often show up the contours of a pit or other area of disturbed soil nicely. Then section the contents of the feature to its bottom. This will give the stratigraphic history of its filling up, while emptying it out all at once like a dish of jello would not. Bisecting it is a very good idea for all but the largest soil installations (Fig. 3a). Very large holes should be quartered like an orange and excavated so that you get two complete sections bisecting the installation (Fig. 3b). After you have removed the contents of the hole, then section the installation itself.

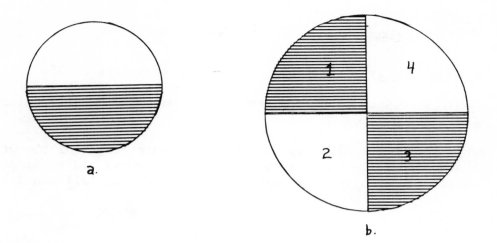

Figure 3

Large tombs filled with debris pose special problems. The best approach might be a combination of a running balk and a quartering balk. The correct tactic would be one which left the skeletons, etc. in situ while relating the remains to the soil layers filling the tomb.

These procedures for probes, soil layers, features-built-up and features-dug-down, while they do not cover all situations, should give one enough guidelines to work out approaches for oneself.

15

NOTES

1. Archaeology from the Earth (London: Penguin Books, 1956).

2. Munsell Soil Color Charts (Baltimore, Md.: The Munsell Color Co.,
    Inc., 1954).

3. This advice was given by Professor Lawrence Stager of the Oriental
    Institute of the University of Chicago, who has had considerable
    experience in digging unbaked mudbrick walls at Tell Hesi, Israel.

Appendix A

ELEMENTARY FIELD CONSERVATION

First Aid in the Field, or What to do Until the Doctor Comes*

If an excavation is sufficiently wealthy, it may be able to afford to include a conservationist on its field staff. Most expeditions are not so lucky and it is the archaeologist who must cope with the lifting, preserving, and conveying of fragile materials to conservation labs.

The basic problem which any material faces in excavations in the Near East is a change in relative humidity. Such a change may involve (a) sudden evaporation of moisture, or (b) an excess of moisture; either of these can have unpleasant consequences.

(a) loss of water

Hygroscopic materials, such as bone, unbaked clay, wood, ivory and textiles, have all absorbed moisture in their buried state and may also have been compressed by the soils surrounding them.

The compression and moisture content have given them a certain dimension. If they are subjected to a sudden loss of compression and lowered humidity, they will lose moisture, tend to develop cracks, shrink and even disintegrate completely.

(b) addition of water

If materials such as terra cottas, metals, lithics, and even the hygroscopic materials have been buried in saline soils, and on excavation are moved from a dry environment to an area of greater humidity (and especially if they are washed), then chemical and physical changes will be produced in the structure of salts within excavated materials. In non-metallic materials, soluble salts recrystallize and can cause disruption and pressures within the material and often massive surface destruction. For metals the reaction is chemical; the unsoluble salt cuprous chloride becomes basic cupric chloride. For the horrified archaeologist, this means that his magnificent metal object disintegrates to a heap of light green powder.

In the face of these dreadful possibilities, the conscientious archaeologist must try to minimize changes in the relative humidity of endangered materials.

---

* This advice on conservation in the field was given to me by Arthur Beale, assistant conservationist at the Fogg Museum, Harvard University.

Before and during excavation, measure the saline content of the soil so you will know whether to expect salt problems.

A Gross Determination for Salinity

Take a pinch of soil and add it to distilled water. Stir vigorously and let the soil sample settle. Then drop several crystals of silver nitrate (A_gNO_3) into the water and watch the results. If the silver nitrate cyrstals turn white or leave small white tracks in the water, then chlorides are present.

Treatment of Hygroscopic Materials

If the material is extremely fragile, infuse both the material and the matrix of soil in which it rests in situ with a 6% solution of polyvinylacetate AYAF (PVA), dissolved in alcohol. Paint on the PVA with a soft brush while the material is still moist. The PVA, as the alcohol evaporates, will give internal cohesion to the object and also cause the surrounding soil to adhere to the material. Thus as the moisture evaporates from the material, the infused plastic remains to strengthen the object structurally and prevent shrinkage. Accretions of soil, etc. can be removed later under lab conditions using alcohol and water as a solvent.

N.B. Really soak the material: don't just paint the surface lightly.

Prevention of Accession of Moisture in Saline Soils

Do not wet or wash metals, terra cottas, or lithics; instead, expose them to open sunshine to dry them off completely. Getting rid of organic material will lessen the chances of moisture on metals, etc. Clayey soils, in particular, hold water. After drying, brush metals, etc. gently with a soft bristle brush to clean. Corrosion will not proceed further unless the humidity is in excess of 60%.

If iron objects or fragments are completely mineralized and too fragile to remove, you may perfuse the corroded material PVA to permit removal.

Packing Materials for Shipment

The best environment for shipping fragile materials is an inert one. Plastic bags are excellent for hygroscopic material and satisfactory for relatively short terms (ship-passage from the Near East to USA) for metals, etc. However, metals, etc. should never be stored for a long time in plastic bags. If they undergo rapid changes of external temperature in shipment, there is danger of condensation of moisture on the inside of the bags. In putting material for shipment in plastic bags, make sure the bag is completely dry, and expel as much air as possible from it in closing. Do not use rubber bands to tie the bags up or attach labels to materials, since the rubber bands contain sulphur. Do not use adhesive tape on metals either, since this contains sulphur too. String or metal ties and paper labels are better.

For insulating fragile material against damage in shipment, expanded polystyrene is an excellent inert packing material. It is marketed in as many shapes as pasta and under many brand names. Flo-pak is one of the best.

A certain amount of care and common sense plus a consciousness of the mechanisms of disintegration (in the Near East, a rapid serious alteration in the environment) will enable the archaeologist to get his fragile materials from the ground to the lab without damage or disaster.

For further reading:

Plenderleith, H. J. and A. E. Werner, The Conservation of Antiquities and Works of Art (2nd ed., Oxford, 1971).

Appendix B

TAKING SAMPLES

Notes on Sampling

This appendix covers only the selection of samples for certain laboratory analysis. The problems of sampling the entire site should be carefully worked out before excavation by the Director. The excavator of an individual Area will collect all pottery, bone, shell, lithics, etc., preferably by coarse-sieving and/or flotation. Selection from among these materials is made not in the field but in the dig-house.

For problems of site-sampling consult the following:

Cowgill, G. L., "The Selection of Samples from Large Sherd Collections," American Antiquity 29 (1964), pp. 467-73.

Cowgill, G. L., "Some Sampling and Reliability Problems in Archaeology," Éditions du Centre National de la Recherche Scientifique (Paris, 1970).

Rootenberg, S., "Archaeological Field Sampling," American Antiquity 30 (1964), pp. 181-88.

C-14 Sampling

Clean thoroughly around the area you wish to sample (an air-puffer is a good tool for this and will disturb your carbon sample least). Take your trowel and clean off any soil on it with water, then wave it in the air to dry it off. Slip the trowel down the outside edge of your sample area and pry up a minimum of 50 grams, more if you can (this minimum amount for carbon sampling will half-fill the average sandwich bag). Bag your sample, seal, and label with basket and locus information, etc. Some people prefer to use aluminum foil for C-14 samples; others favor plastic bags. Contamination of your sample will occur only if your carbon sample comes in contact with other carbon. But avoid sampling from soils full of root-systems, if possible. If the carbon you want is likely to have rootlets in it, be sure and include that information on your data sheet when you send it to be processed. Different C-14 labs require various information on your sample, such as precise geographic location or factors which might alter the groundwater percolation. C-14 work can be done by:

Geo-Chron Laboratory, Inc.
24 Blackstone Street
Cambridge, Mass. 02138

Another excellent (and cheaper) lab is:

> Radiocarbon Laboratory
> Department of Physics
> University of Pennsylvania
> Philadelphia, Penna. 19104.

Sampling for Thermoluminescence

Sherds for thermoluminescence must have been buried for at least two-thirds of their burial time at a minimum depth of 30 cm., and materials with sampled sherds should be homogeneous. Each sample should consist of six or more sherds, minimum dimensions 25 by 25 by 5 mm., plus a handful of the soil surrounding the sherds. Samples should be collected as soon as possible after excavation to avoid evaporation of moisture content. Since you must avoid unnecessary exposure to sunlight, use an opaque black cloth when collecting. Hold it up to make a kind of sun-proof box; bag your sherds-plus-soil in a plastic bag and seal (a sandwich bag-full is adequate). It is a good idea then to wrap the sample bag in an opaque sun-proof cloth and keep it away from sun and high heat. Never expose samples for thermoluminescence to ultra-violet, infra-red, X-rays or beta-rays. If the sherds are sampled from a burial, then you should also include a sample of wall or floor material. If other kinds of materials occur in context with the sherds in major proportions, samples of each type (e.g., shell, bone, building debris) should also be included.

As with C-14, labs require some additional pieces of information. It is a sound idea to find out ahead of time what data they require (e.g., information on seasonal moisture, content of soils at the site, or detailed information about burial conditions). Two of the labs most active in using this technique are:

> Research Laboratory for Archaeology and the History of Art
> 6 Keble Road
> Oxford
> England

and

> Center for Applied Science in Archaeology
> University Museum
> University of Pennsylvania
> 33rd and Spruce Street
> Philadelphia, Penna. 19104.

Reference work for information on the use of C-14, thermoluminescence and other techniques;

21

Michael, Henry N. and Elizabeth K. Ralph (co-eds), <u>Dating Techniques for the Archaeologist</u> (Cambridge, Mass.: MIT Press, 1971).

Flotation

Collection of floral and small faunal data is best done by some system whereby the seeds are floated to the surface of a water-filled tank and skimmed off by small-meshed sieves. Flotation at Gezer was done by a team of environmental specialists from Cambridge University headed by Anthony J. Legge under the general supervision of Professor E. S. Higgs. Their system, designed by Mr. Legge, bubbled the soil and floated the seeds, etc. up with a flocculating agent, then passed them through a series of graded meshed sieves.

In the absence of a Legge machine, you can build an adequate simple flotation tank from an empty oil barrel by cleaning it out, filling the bottom with cement, and inserting a faucet near the base, making a channel in the cement draining towards the faucet. This kind of flotation tank is operated by human armpower. You will also need to make a round wood sieve, smaller than the diameter of the tank with a 2 cm. wire mesh, and a small handled scoop with a carburetor screen mesh. The flotation is done by two people. First sieve the soil to be floated through a coarse dry-sieve (4 cm. mesh) to remove large bones, rocks, etc. Then one person holds the round wet-sieve half in the water and agitates it with a stirring motion while the other pours the soil into the big sieve and skims off (with the scoop) the seeds, etc., which float. Dry the seeds, bag them securely, and label with all pertinent information. You must remember to count the number of buckets of soil removed from any locus from which you wish to obtain a flotation sample so that the analyst knows what ratio of seeds, etc. to soils his sample represents. This is not usually a problem, however, if you are coarse-sieving everything, since you will be keeping a soil-bucket count anyway. See the following for a flotation tank:

Struever, Stuart, "Flotation Techniques for the Recovery of Small Scale Archaeological Remains," <u>American Antiquity</u> 33 (1968), pp. 353-62.

Pollen Sampling

You will need a number of test tubes, cork stoppers and a pen-knife.

Sterilize the pen-knife over an open flame before taking each sample.

A good place to take pollen samples from is one of the main balks.

Insert your pen-knife in each discrete soil layer, so that you get a series of samples, each taken and bottled separately.

Flourine Sampling

This is very simple to do. Bag in plastic a bone sample plus a good sample of the soil matrix in which the bone is sitting.

Chapter II

ARCHAEOLOGICAL TOOLS AND THEIR USE

Dan P. Cole

"The right kind of work calls for the right kind of tools."

Certainly this is true for archaeological digging. Moreover, since almost all of the tools employed in excavation have more familiar uses elsewhere, it is important to stress the proper use of the proper tools. Three imperatives have influenced the selection of tools and the recommendations for their use presented here: controlled separation, clear visibility, efficient use of time and energy.

Controlled separation of diverse materials--from massive wall stones to thin powdery ash layers--is essential in order to determine (a) the character and extent of the different materials deposited by human or natural action, (b) the sequence and relation of adjacent deposits, and (c) the dates of the successive layers as indicated by the pottery and artifacts contained in them.

Clear visibility at the point of digging is essential at all times (a) to help control the separation, (b) to identify the materials and interpret their function, and (c) to record the evidence. A worker's eyes are his most valuable tools. Only through their unobstructed use can he answer such questions as these: "Where exactly are the limits between this rubble layer and that soil deposit?" "Is this merely a rubble heap or a series of metalled street surfaces, and is that soil deposit the water-sorted laminae of silt in a street drain or the loose filling of a later trench?" "Is that cylinder seal on the street surface, in the makeup layer immediately beneath it, or immediately alongside it in the later trench filling?" "Can we see the limits of that trench clearly enough to record it by photograph and drawing in case we decide it was the robber-trench for a wall?"

Efficient use of time and energy is essential, not only for economic reasons but also to maintain effective control. Wasted energy means increased fatigue and lowered morale. The tired or dispirited worker is more likely to be careless, and careless work will destroy evidence instead of preserving it.

The following discussion of tools and their use reflects, of course, the digging problems and conditions characteristic of most Syro-Palestinian excavations. Appropriate modifications would be necessary to contend with specialized problems or conditions in other areas.

Large Pick - used for loosening of soil in potentially large layers of disturbed surface, deep debris, or fill layers.

A railroad-type pick normally will be the largest instrument to be employed in archaeological earth removal. In the hands of a properly trained worker, the large pick can be a surprisingly precise tool. The key lies in the education of the worker, particularly if he has had some experience in construction or road work and <u>thinks</u> he knows how to handle big tools. Before the new worker takes up a large pick in an archaeological area, he must understand the <u>function</u> of his tool in this context and must be taught the <u>technique</u> by which he can achieve that function.

The function of the large pick is not to break up soil as fast as possible, but to loosen it in such a manner as to ensure the least damage to artifacts, surfaces, and architecture which might be hidden in the soil. Even more important, the pick must permit the removal of a soil layer, the limits of which cannot be known in advance, without removing more than necessary of whatever material lies beyond or below those unknown limits. Even where the soil layer to be removed appears to extend for considerable depth, it is impossible to anticipate where surprising changes may emerge immediately beneath the working surface, so the large pick must be employed with restraint and with maximum control over the soil separation.

The following procedures help to convert a large pick from a gross dirt-dislodging tool to a responsible archaeological instrument: (1) The pickman's digging area at any one time should be restricted to approximately one-to-two square meters, using lines strung between nails to mark the limits and to keep the sides of the digging area straight (except where some installation or other discernible locus provides the limit of the operation). (2) The pick should be gripped loosely with the handle in a horizontal position and the chisel-shaped edge of the pick pointing down. The pick head should then be dropped or driven vertically downward with only enough force to dislodge a clod of soil of approximately five-to-ten cubic centimeters (Fig. 1). As the pick strikes the soil, the wrists should be relaxed so that the pick can adjust to changes in the degree of soil compaction. Frequently, this combination of vertical stroke, chisel edge and relaxed grip will allow the pick head to "find" a new surface, since the loosened soil will tend to break away along the differential compaction plane separating the soil layers. With a vertical motion, the pick also will detect the presence of even small cobblestones without accidentally dislodging them. (If stones begin to be noted first in the loosened soil, the pick probably is being used too heavy-handedly.) The pick seldom should be allowed to dislodge more than several centimeters of soil at a time. It therefore need not be swung with force from above head level except when necessary to penetrate very tightly compacted material such as prepared fills of clay or chalk paste. (At such times it may also be necessary to use the pointed end.) The pickman should then pull the pick toward himself before raising it; this will draw the loosened soil forward away from the undug soil, and allow him to see the soil he is uncovering. (3) The pickman should start at one end of

Figure 1. Breaking up the soil with a large pick.

the lined-off area and move forward to the other end, loosening the
soil in five-to-ten-centimeter-deep strips from one side to the other
and cleanly chiseling the faces of the subsidiary balks he is creating
as he goes.

As a worker develops experience with the large pick, he may introduce some personal variations on the technique described above, but he
should keep in mind at all times that the function of any archaeological large-pick operation is not simply to move dirt but to do so in a
manner which will allow the worker to see and feel the limits of the
layer being removed and to prevent damage or premature removal of any
artifacts or installations which may be beneath.

As he begins, the pickman should visually note the color and texture of the soil and the character of its inclusions and should note
the relative compaction of the soil by the degree of resistance it
offers to the pick and the manner in which it crumbles. He should be
alert for any change in the character of the soil as he digs and be

prepared to stop immediately and notify his supervisor when any change
occurs. As a double-check, the supervisor should discuss the character
of the soil with the pickman at the outset of the operation and may
periodically want to take over the pick for a few strokes to test for
any changes. As a supervisor gains experience with his team, he may
feel increasingly confident in allowing at least certain workers to
assume more direct responsibility for determining the appropriate limits of their operations. At the outset, however, and as a general
rule, the supervisor will want to keep a close and continuous eye on
any operation involving the large pick.

After each complete sweep across the lined-out area with the pick
(including the chisel-dressing of the subsidiary balks at the sides and
front of the area), the loosened soil should be removed by hoe or
trowel and brush before continuing. If no change in the character of
the soil is discernible, another cut five-to-ten centimeters deep may
be made across the area with the pick, or the supervisor may decide to
extend the digging area horizontally by moving the string lines. (Normally, a probe would be continued downward for at least one-half meter
in successive sweeps in hopes of locating the next traceable soil
separation. If no change is detected by that depth, even after a careful dressing and examination of the subsidiary balks, the supervisor
might give consideration to extending the operation horizontally by
stages of one-to-two square meters at a time until he reaches the limits of the locus or his main balks before probing deeper.)

At the first evidence of a soil change or the emergence of a possible installation, the large pick may need to be replaced by the
smaller hand pick and trowel. The supervisor must determine whether or
not the nature of the separation is such that it can be followed easily
with the large pick. This decision will depend partly on the character
of the soil and partly on the particular skills of his workers. If the
current operation has disclosed a well-compacted surface from which the
overlying debris breaks away easily, and if the pickman is an experienced and careful worker, the supervisor may be able to proceed with
the large pick without losing control. The general rule should be to
employ the large pick so long as it can loosen the soil without losing
the separations--and only so long as it can do so.

The pointed end of the pick would only be used for clearing soil
immediately around stones or penetrating extremely compacted material.

Handpick - used for most soil layer separation and for cutting
vertical balk sections.

The handpick normally will be the most used and most versatile tool
in the digging area, though for most operations it must be used in conjunction with other tools. Ideas differ as to the ideal shape and size
of this tool. The handpick used at Gezer has a metal shaft and wooden

handle approximately 30 cm. long overall. The head is approximately
15 cm. long, pointed at one end, broadened at the other end to a chisel
blade approximately three centimeters wide. The pick weighs about one
pound. Handpick styles and preferences vary widely. Three things to
avoid are (a) a pick so heavy that it tires the worker's wrist unduly
or so light that its own weight and momentum will not do enough work,
(b) an overly curved head, and (c) a head with a protruding haft.
These latter two features reduce the handpick's efficiency in balk
trimming (see next section).

For soil layer separation, the handpick normally would be held with
a relaxed grip with the shaft horizontal and the chisel blade over the
point of contact. Most often this will mean holding the pick close to
the floor of the digging area; a kneeling position (rather than a sitting or squatting posture) will give greatest control and is least
tiring in the long run (Fig. 2). The supervisor should make certain
that foam rubber kneeling pads are used. The pick should be used in
much the same way as the large pick though with more restricted limits

Figure 2. Using the small handpick.

to the project area and with smaller units of soil loosened by each stroke. It is particularly important to allow the weight of the loosely held handpick to do as much of the work as possible, both to avoid fatigue and to permit the blade to find and follow the differential compaction plane which may separate the soil layer being removed from the different deposit(s) below or adjacent to it. As with the large pick, the pointed end of the handpick should only be used when necessary to clear between stones or to loosen tightly compacted soil.

When using the handpick, the worker normally should keep a trowel in his other hand, pulling the loosened soil toward himself after every two or three strokes of the handpick. This will allow the worker to see fully what each pick-stroke is uncovering without interrupting the pick action. This continuous visual control is important both for detecting soil changes and for observing small objects before they have been removed from their context.

When moving across an area larger than 15-20 cm. square, it may be efficient occasionally to use the handpick to pull accumulated loosened soil away from underneath the worker by laying the pick head horizontally on the freshly uncovered working surface and pulling it through the loosened debris rapidly several times. This action not only has the effect of moving the loosened soil accumulation in the direction of the pulling strokes, it also further breaks up the soil nodules and redistributes them from the bottom of the pile to the surface, giving another opportunity to scan the soil for small objects.

When a stone wall or other installation is encountered, the pointed end of the handpick head should be brought into use to clear the soil between stones which will otherwise obscure the exact contours and relationships of the stones. Care should be taken not to allow the pick head accidentally to function as a lever, dislodging stones prematurely. Care should also be taken to check the character of the soil filling the cracks between stones. Is it uniformly compact and high in clay content, suggesting a mud mortar or facing? Is it loose, relatively uniform, and free from inclusions, suggesting wind-blown dust?

The handpick is the essential tool for cutting vertical sections, or balks. These will be discussed at length in the next chapter, but some general remarks are in order here. Each digging project, however modest in scope, should create and maintain vertical balk faces at its limits wherever these are not constituted by a soil change or installation. A probe through an earthen surface adjacent to a stone wall, for instance, will have the wall itself as one limit of the probe area. Its other three sides, the two perpendicular to the wall and the one opposite, may all be arbitrary limits within the surface and its makeup. When cut cleanly to provide vertical faces, these sides of the digging area will constitute at least temporary balks, important controls for detecting soil layer separations which may not be evident in the digging. (One side of the digging operation may actually be a main balk for the area; other sides will be subsidiary balks.) The handpick wielder should consider it part of his task after each sweep across his digging area to dress the sides of his area so that they can be "read" as balk sections. To do this, he will move from one end to the other of each side, using firm strokes with the chisel blade of the pick along a vertical plane. The strokes may range from downward to oblique, but should not be sideways lest the chisel lines obscure a faint but important line in the section. (Some lines will be inclined to the vertical, of course, such as the sides of a pit or of a mudbrick wall or of high-standing debris. In such cases, however, there is normally a more discernible contrast between the adjacent materials than may be the case with sequential horizontal deposits.) In dressing a balk section, the pointed end of the pick is useful for cutting around a protruding stone or sherd. For careful dressing, usually the handpick must then be supplemented by a shaving action with the trowel and perhaps a light dusting with an air sprayer. (The technique for dressing the main balk sections will be further discussed in the next chapter.)

An experienced worker will keep the sides of his area relatively vertical and straight as he goes and will sometimes only need to trowel-scrape them to bring them to readable quality.

Trowel - used for moving loosened soil, for fine-dressing sections, and for tracing some kinds of surfaces.

A bricklayer's pointing trowel is second in degree of use and versatility only to the handpick, and these two tools will frequently be used in conjunction. Unanimity is lacking as to the ideal size, thickness (rigidity), and pointedness of a trowel for field use. Preferences among the Gezer staff have ranged from a blade length of about 14 cm. to about 18 cm., from the relative rigidity of the Marshalltown brand to the flexibility of a thinner Austrian model, and from a sharp point (useful for accenting balk lines) to a rounded point (useful for avoiding the etching of extraneous lines!). Definitely to be avoided are the Japanese and local models which have completely inflexible blades. These will not be sensitive enough either for tracing surfaces or for trimming balks (Fig. 3).

For moving loosened soil during a normal handpick operation, the trowel is held in the left hand (of a right-handed worker) so that the blade is parallel to the face of the soil being dug. After every few cutting strokes of the handpick, the trowel should be placed with the edge of its blade as close as possible to the point of cutting and pulled toward the worker with the blade kept perpendicular and in contact with the newly created stopping-surface beneath the loosened soil. By this bulldozer-like action the loose soil is pulled away from the point of digging so that the newly exposed soil can be seen without obstruction. (Note: some workers will try to convert this soil-moving action of the trowel into an excavating action by digging the blade

Figure 3.   The small trowel, shown here being
used to "peel off" an earthen surface.

into the unexcavated soil and scraping the blade through it in search
of the next surface. This is inefficient and usually ineffectual and
should be discouraged. Use the pick to loosen soil, the trowel to move
it.)

If digging proceeds over an extended area, the worker may find it
convenient occasionally to make some extra-long bulldozer strokes with
the trowel in order to move accumulated loose soil behind himself.
This will allow a teammate to remove pottery and load the loose soil
for removal while the cutting operation proceeds.

The teammate who loads the loose soil into rubber "guffahs" (see
below) may also find a trowel useful, first for breaking up and spreading the soil to look through it for pottery and small objects, then to
lift or pull the soil into the guffah. For this last function, some
prefer a large plasterer's tetragonal trowel because of its greater
surface area. (Some would argue that the trowel is too slow a tool for
loading soil into guffahs and that this job should be reserved for the

hoe, discussed below. If the _guffah_ is laid on its side, however, so that the worker can pull the soil into the _guffah_ instead of lifting it, the trowel can load soil almost as fast as the hoe and has the advantage of bringing the worker's eyes and hands much closer to the pottery and small objects for which he must be alert.)

When a soil layer of only a few centimeters' depth is being removed from a well-compacted surface, it frequently will be possible to retire the handpick altogether and use only the trowel, sliding the blade forward along the surface and lifting the overlying layer away along the differential compaction plane. In slightly harder or thicker soil, the handpick can be used to break up the overlying soil somewhat, with the trowel then being used to trace the surface proper in the manner just described (Fig. 3).

The trowel is essential for fine dressing of most balk faces (except in rubble) and is used with an obliquely-angled scraping action, being careful to avoid etching extraneous lines with the trowel point. Balk-trimming technique will be more fully discussed in the next chapter.

Hoe - used for soil removal.

A hoe with a broad flat blade has been the common tool for loading pick-loosened soil into _guffahs_ for removal. The most efficient stance is for the worker to face the soil pile and to place the _guffah_ between his feet on its side so that its flexible rim is flattened against the ground. The worker then pulls the soil toward the _guffah_ with the hoe, turning it over once or twice as he rakes it into the _guffah_, taking care to look for pottery and small objects (Fig. 4).

The disadvantage of the hoe is twofold. It necessitates a standing position, keeping the worker's eyes at least one meter away from the soil (in contrast to a half-meter or less when using a trowel or hand-scoop), and it permits the movement of so much soil with each stroke there is danger of overlooking pottery and small objects. Except when removing massive fills or inconsequential tell surface layers, it is perhaps archaeologically more efficient to replace the hoe with the trowel or hand scoop. It must be remembered, on the other hand, that archaeological efficiency also depends on workers' morale and interest, and this will suffer if the work pace lags. Better to lose a few sherds and even a scarab or two by employing the hoe _if_ the use of the somewhat slower trowel would lead to loss of general control and efficiency through lowered morale.

Figure 4. Filling the rubber basket or <u>guffah</u> with a large hoe.

<u>Sledge</u> - used for breaking up boulders such as large wall stones to facilitate their removal from the area.

If possible, it is preferable not to break up a rock <u>in situ</u>, since the resulting debris can obscure the soil layers beneath and the pounding can compromise their fabric and configuration or dislodge nearby stones. After a rock's position has been sufficiently recorded, its relation to adjacent loci noted and its possible function investigated, and only after the supervisor has authorized its removal, it should be lifted or rolled away from the immediate area, with care taken to check its underside for possible evidence of tooling or carving. The person wielding the sledge should be careful (1) to don work gloves, (2) to warn other workers in the area to avert their eyes from flying stone chips, (3) to let the weight and momentum of the sledge do the work rather than to risk breaking the sledge handle by leaning on it at the end of his swing, and (4) to try to find the natural fracture plane of the rock. This last will take some practice or instruction from someone with experience, but can avoid many a backache and broken handle.

Sledges should be left to soak in water each night to prevent the wood helve from drying out and becoming loose. The tightness of the head on its helve should be checked regularly during use.

Brooms and Brushes - used for cleaning during digging operations, balk dressing, and prior to photography.

One of the hardest things for new workers to learn is the concept of digging in dirt cleanly. Consistent stress on proper cleaning during each of the initial days' operations, however, should soon develop working habits which will allow continuous visual control and will minimize the risk of contamination from one locus to another.

Brooms and broad-handled stiff-bristled brushes will be helpful only in preliminary cleaning over an extensive area. And, of course, everyone knows how to use a broom...or do they? Powder-dry loose dust must be dragged by the broom or stiff brush, never propelled. If the bristles are brought past the vertical, they will spring forward, tossing the dust up into the air, where it will simply resettle and have to be swept again.

Soft-hair brushes are necessary for the completion of any cleaning operation, since stiff brushes or brooms will leave a film of dust which will obscure the surface beneath.

A broad brush, approximately 20-30 cm. long with soft hair bristles will be most efficient for most cleaning (Fig. 5), although smaller paintbrushes will be needed in very restricted areas and among stones.

In pick operations a broad, soft-haired brush should be employed for cleaning after every use of the hoe or trowel to remove loosened soil. This will provide an unobstructed view of the newly exposed soil, sometimes revealing a change in color or texture which had not been detected during the preceding picking and which may signal the limits of the locus being removed.

There always should be a thorough soft-haired brush for cleaning at the end of a digging operation so that no loose dirt remains to obstruct the view or contaminate adjacent or subsequent operations. At the end of each working day, there should be a general cleaning of the entire area to which workers will be returning, and the area supervisor will need to allow sufficient time at the close of the day to ensure that this can be done. At the beginning of each day a visual check should be made of the area to see if any pockets of dirt have been missed or have been deposited since the area was left. This check should not overlook the balks adjacent to the area. Traffic along these balks will loosen the surface soil (and pottery in that soil) which can too easily be kicked into the working area, contaminating the operations in progress. In cleaning the tops of balks, it will be most

Figure 5. Using the large brush for cleaning an earthen surface.

efficient to employ a soft brush and to use short strokes, pushing the
dust and loose pottery and pebbles back from the balk edges approximately one meter. On a balk between two areas it will be necessary to
brush back from both edges to the center of the balk and collect the
sweepings.

In cleaning before photography, it is important to avoid duplica-
tion of effort by (1) brushing the highest surfaces first, working down
to the lowest surfaces, and (2) brushing outward from the center or
from one side to the other according to a pre-arranged plan. If the
photograph may incorporate one or more of the adjacent balks, these
must be brushed first, of course, as the highest relevant surfaces.
(In brushing for photography, balk surfaces and "non-surfaces" in the
area--i.e., intermediate stopping surfaces--need not be cleared of all
dust. They should be "cosmeticized" by brushing away the sherds, pebbles, and larger clods of soil, leaving the finer dust particles. The
brush can then be tapped over the surface to produce a stippled effect
which will contrast visually with the cleanly swept true surfaces.)

Much of this discussion of brushing may seem commonsense, but volunteer workers frequently tend to devalue cleaning as a housekeeping chore unrelated to the exotic "archaeology" they came to do. Some stress at the outset on the importance and technique of proper cleaning can avoid the inattention which leads to carelessness which then leads to inefficiency and frustration.

Small Digging Tools - used for delicate work.

Exposure of fragile artifacts, charred wood, skeletal remains, etc., will call for appropriately delicate tools. Dental picks, pocket knife blades, syringes, small paint brushes, and toothbrushes all have proved useful in turn; but there is still more art and ingenuity than science in the determination of which tools and techniques are best suited for different kinds of delicate operations. Perhaps the one essential tool to be cited here is patience.

Water and Air - used for delineating distinctions in balks and surfaces.

It may seem odd to list natural elements as tools, but they are. A water-filled plastic spray bottle (of the kind used to dampen clothes for ironing) is very useful in detecting differences in degrees of compaction in soil layers of the same color. A pit, for instance, may be filled with soil of exactly the same color as the soil layers through which the pit was dug. The pit fill, however, will be less compact and will absorb and release moisture at a different rate from that of the surrounding soil. Conversely, a foundation trench for a wall may be filled with soil more tightly compacted than surrounding layers, though similar in color. Whether in the floor of an area or in the balk, the presence of a suspected pit or foundation trench frequently can be substantiated by spraying water across the general area and noting the outline which emerges as the water evaporates.

Air is an extremely useful tool for articulating the lines in a balk or section. In small doses, air is conveniently dispensed from an enema syringe. For articulating a major balk, a more efficient dispenser is a back-pack pressure tank, such as is used in fighting brush fires, spraying trees, etc.

Dustpans, Flour Scoops, and Tablespoons - used for getting rid of dirt.

Over the seasons of the Gezer excavations, staff and volunteers have introduced several new tools to the archaeological repertoire which have proved to be highly successful additions. Notable among these have been (1) the dustpan: surprisingly efficient when used with a trowel or brush for--would you believe it?--collecting loose dirt off a flat surface (Fig. 4); (2) the flour scoop: more efficient than the trowel for loading loose dirt into <u>guffahs</u> quickly yet in controllably small amounts from small probes, pits and other depressed areas; and (3) the tablespoon: so well adapted for clearing the dirt from ancient rat burrows that Gezerites have affectionately dubbed it the "rat-o-rooter."

<u>Buckets, Boxes, and Baskets</u> - used for collecting and removing pottery, small objects, and soil respectively.

(1) Plastic water buckets have proved to be far superior to the traditional woven straw basket for the collection and transportation of pottery. They have so many advantages it would seem foolish not to use them wherever they are obtainable. They are light yet durable; when empty they stack together compactly for storage or carrying; they will not permit the "leaking" of pottery in or out through the sides that could produce contamination; even when partially filled with pottery, several can be stacked together without danger of contamination. Since they hold water, pottery brought from the fields in them can be put to soak without being removed. Finally, since they usually are available in several different colors, they could be dispensed in such a way as to minimize confusion among different operations (although this would require proportionately more buckets per area than we usually have had available at Gezer).

(2) Most small objects require special handling from the moment they first are discovered for three important reasons. First, because of their size, objects such as scarabs, cylinder seals, coins, beads, etc., must be protected against loss. Second, small finds frequently are in a fragile state and must be protected against breakage while being handled. After a careful worker has laboriously exposed a highly corroded, wire-thin bronze toggle pin on a surface and has successfully extricated it from the soil in one piece, it is embarrassing to have it break into three pieces in the Area Supervisor's hand. Finally, non-ceramic objects from a locus necessarily will be separated from their associated pottery and will travel different individual routes through the steps of cleaning, preservation, recording, analysis and publication or display. It is vital that before each object is removed from its locus operation--let alone from the digging area--it must be able to take with it the same information which will accompany the pottery on the pottery bucket tag.

To meet all three of these needs, supervisors should have in the area a ready supply of boxes, cotton padding and strong rubber bands. The boxes should be in graded sizes, but not smaller than approximately 5 x 10 x 2 cm. They should be of sturdy cardboard or plastic, to provide a rigid protective shield around the object. They should have a light surface finish for visibility and one which will hold writing.

(Some excavators prefer to use gummed labels for object boxes. This has the advantage of allowing the box to be re-used indefinitely and avoids the risk of forgetting to cross out obsolete information. If the label adhesive is such that there is no danger of the label separating from the box, this would seem to be an improvement over the equipment and procedure employed at Gezer.)

A suggestion for further refinement in the small object box, if it is not prohibitively expensive, would be to use clear plastic box lids. A fragile object could then be transferred immediately from the soil to its cotton cushion in a protective box, the box lidded and labeled and the lid secured with a rubber band. In this condition the object could be transported safely to the object cleaner and Registrar in camp without being removed from its box while not denying the curiosity of all those persons along the way who will want to look at what you have found--from the workers in the area across the balk to the Director.

(3) Few things might seem less worthy of discussion than the containers in which dirt and debris are carried away. They are rather essential pieces of equipment on any digging operation, however, and if poorly designed or constructed they can be a source of frustration and problems. The ubiquitous container for dirt in Near Eastern countries is a basket made from strips of rubber bolted together, with two rubber handle strips bolted to opposite sides of the rim (Fig. 4). Since there is no equivalent in the western world, the Arabic name, guffah, has become a part of our archaeological vocabulary.

We probably cannot excape from the guffah for some time to come, so it is important to know what distinguishes a good one from a bad one. The criteria are derived from the two functions the guffah must fulfill: it must be loaded and it must be carried across and out of the area with its load. For the first of these functions, the guffah ideally should have a wide, flexible rim so that when it is laid on its side the rim will flatten out along the surface, allowing soil to be pushed instead of lifted into the guffah. For the latter function the seams of the guffah should be tight, avoiding the messy and potentially contaminating dribble of dirt which marks the trail of the leaky guffah. In addition, the rubber around the bolt holes must be strong enough and the bolts tight enough so the handle straps will not pull off.

At present writing, the guffahs made in the West Bank communities --e.g. Nablus, Hebron--are of better quality on both of the above counts than are the ones generally available in Israel. Someday, it is to be hoped that a flexible plastic guffah may be produced which would reduce the present problems of leakage and breakage.

Meanwhile, there are three measures which can make life with the guffah more endurable. (1) Do not allow the guffah to be filled to the brim; two-thirds full is about right. Overloading increases the strain

on the handle straps and seams (not to mention the strain on workers'
backs) and increases the risk of spilling dirt over the rim. (2) Do
not allow empty guffahs to be thrown back into the area; have them
handed back down. Throwing loosens the fastening nuts, aside from
raising unnecessary dust and endangering balks and workers. (3) Have
all guffahs checked regularly by the crew in charge of tool care. Pre-
ventive care in the form of tightening loose nuts is much less costly
in time than cleaning up after guffahs which leak or lose their straps.

Ladders and Hoists

One of the unavoidable problems of archaeology--as with some other
professions--is how most gracefully to climb out of the hole you have
dug. In archaeology, of course, the more successful you are, the
harder the problem becomes. Special situations will require their own
solutions; but for the typical square surrounded by four balks, the
answer definitely seems to be a ladder. This may not sound like more
than a truism, but there are those of us still alive who can remember
cutting steps into balks or leaving earthen stairways inside our areas
to permit access. The fact that we are still alive is no testimony to
the sturdiness of those steps, and we can remember hours of valuable
time spent recutting steps, cleaning up the contaminating debris from
their constant erosion, and cursing the fact that we could not move our
steps from one side of the area to another. Do not begin digging without a sufficient supply of sturdy ladders of graduated lengths, starting from one meter. And be sure you know where you can find a longer
ladder to replace one which no longer reaches above the balk rim.

Even with sturdy ladders of the right length, two problems arise.
Ladders' feet wear holes in sometimes significant surfaces, and the
ladder tops tend to wear away the rim of the balk. Both of these problems have been dealt with by refinements introduced recently at the
Tell Jemmah Excavations. Foam rubber pads placed beneath the ladder
feet cushion the feet and also inhibit slipping. And sections of corrugated asbestos roofing placed against the edge of the balk, help to
preserve the balk edge (Fig. 6a). An alternative to the corrugated
roofing section has been suggested by John S. Holladay: two boards
1.5 m. in length nailed together to form a movable "cap" for the balk
edge with two small slats nailed just outboard of where the ladder
would rest in order to prevent slippage of the ladder to the side
(Fig. 6b).

The problem of how to move guffahs of dirt out of an ever-deepening
area used to be a simple one to solve: hire five, or fifteen, or fifty
local boys at a few paistres per day to form sometimes seemingly end-
less meandering lines to pass guffahs from the digging area to the
dump. When R. A. S. Macalister dug at Gezer seventy years ago, he
hired dozens of women and boys from the nearby villages to do the job.
On most modern excavations manpower is not readily enough available to

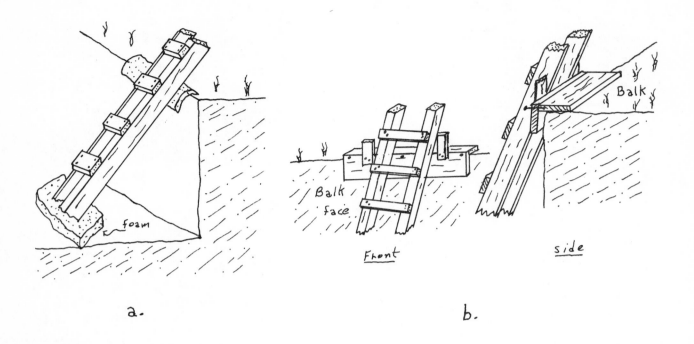

Figure 6. Ladders for access to Areas.

squander in that fashion. On the other hand, motor-driven equipment such as a conveyor belt, if not too bulky to move adjacent to each digging area, is too expensive to use for moving dirt at the modest rate it normally is generated in an area under controlled excavation.

A partial solution has been provided in the hand-operated hoist (Fig. 7). At least adjacent to the outside areas of a grid, a frame can be erected to suspend a pulley and rope above the area. One laborer at the hoist can raise the loaded guffahs from an area and normally have sufficient time to empty them into a wheelbarrow and run the loaded wheelbarrow to a nearby dump. Without the hoist, an increasing number of workers will be tied down to the guffah line as the area deepens, first one and then more having to take positions on the ladder as well as on the balk in order to move dirt out.

The hoist design used at Gezer is not the final answer. It was too bulky, for instance, to be installed on a one-meter-wide balk, and its use was therefore limited to outside areas of the multi-area grid in Field VI. Here again, the staff at Tell Jemmah have made improvements on design, but experimentation needs to continue. Perhaps someone will devise a metal hoist frame, for instance, light and compact enough to install at the juncture of four one-meter-wide balks, with an arm which

Figure 7. A simply constructed wooden hoist,
counterweighted with stones.

can swivel to service all four adjacent areas and an inexpensive motor-driven winch. Then cheers would rise from thousands of liberated workers.

Sieve - used for screening soil for small objects.

Several types of fine-mesh sieves have been employed at Gezer, and the perfect sieve probably has yet to be designed. Milton Wolfe, a 1971 volunteer, introduced us to a model he had worked with in excavations in Florida and which has proved more efficient than others previously employed. The sieve frame is mounted to pivot at waist height on an inverted U-shaped steel pipe support, which in turn is set into concrete foundations. A removable brace or spring holds the frame in a horizontal alignment (Fig. 8). A screen with approximately one-half square centimeter mesh will hold all pottery and bone fragments and all artifacts except the tiniest beads. With a wheelbarrow beneath the sieve to catch the soil, the siever dumps a basket of soil at a time onto the sieve. Then with one hand he is able to rock the sieve on its flexible mounting, both backwards/forwards and up/down, while his other hand is free to move over the sieve screen with a trowel, breaking up clods of soil. (Some sievers have claimed to increase their efficiency further by employing their abdominal muscles to rock the sieve, thus freeing both hands! Their example is not likely to be widely adopted.) After most of the soil has passed through the screen, the siever is then able to use both hands to sort through the remaining debris. The sorting procedure should normally begin by tilting up the near side of the screen to move the debris to the far side. Then, with the screen returned to the horizontal or with the far side slightly higher, the side of the trowel is used to pull a portion of the debris at a time across the screen to the near side. This action allows most of the remaining soil to fall through and spreads out for view the residue. With his other hand, the siever then removes any pottery and small objects (and bones, if they are to be saved) and deposits them in properly labeled containers.

Work Gloves and Kneeling Pads - used for keeping workers efficient.

These hardly qualify as tools, but the alert supervisor will see that his supplies include enough gloves and pads to protect workers who have not yet developed callouses, and will see to it that they are used just as he will want to see to it that new workers protect themselves against overexposure to the sun. This is not to be disdained as a matter of compassion on the supervisor's part nor of self-indulgence on the workers' part. Discomfort lowers morale, which lowers efficiency.

Figure 8. Pipe-mounted pivoting sieve.

An Area Tool Kit

The following tool list for a typical six-man area team could be trimmed at one point or another, but it should be emphasized that a few hand tools are cheaper than the man-hours wasted in constant borrowing across the balks when teams are under-supplied.

    2 large picks
    2 hoes
    5 handpicks
    5 pointing trowels
    3 plasterer's trowels and/or sugar scoops
    3 brooms and/or stiff brushes
    5 soft brushes
    2 paint brushes (one 2" and one 4"?)
    3 dust pans
   12 pottery buckets (to be supplemented during day as needed)
   12 guffahs (to be supplemented where long guffah lines are necessary)
    4 pairs work gloves
    4 kneeling pads
    2 pick handles or equivalents (for hanging plumb bobs)
    1 sledge (per four areas)

In addition, the Area Supervisor's basket should include, along with measuring and recording equipment:

    1 syringe (for air dusting)
    1 spray bottle (for water)
    1 pocket knife or equivalent
    1 small paint brush
    1 tablespoon
    2 plumb bobs (for balk trimming)
    1 spirit level (for balk trimming)
   10 small object boxes (several sizes) with cotton and rubber bands

Tool Care

One or more workers experienced with tools should be assigned to the job of tool maintenance and repairs from the beginning of the excavation for as much of their working time as is needed. There will always be pick handles to replace and guffahs to mend, but much repair time can be avoided by proper regular maintenance. Picks and sledges should be stored overnight heads down in water; guffahs should be checked for loosening nuts; wheelbarrow wheels should be oiled, etc.

As part of his duties, the tool caretaker should see that an adequate inventory is maintained of replacement parts such as pick handles and nuts and bolts. He may also be the logical person to construct some of the equipment needed as the excavation proceeds, such as additional ladders and hoists.

Once tools are assigned to areas, disputes in the field over missing or "borrowed" tools can be reduced--if never completely eliminated --by color-coding the tool handles with splashes of paint of different colors. Tools which are then loaned out of an area during the work-day to meet some short-term need elsewhere can be easily identified for proper re-assignment. Color-coding was used with some success at Gezer, but it should be emphasized that to be fully effective there must be an adequate initial supply of tools so that the need for borrowing can be kept to a minimum.

Chapter III

BALKS: THEIR CARE AND READING

John S. Holladay, Jr.

"A well cut and scraped balk is not only a treat for the eyes, it is a vital necessity in both the interpretive and recording processes which characterize modern archaeological research."

Three major functions of an excavation are aided by balks. In the order of increasing importance these are: (a) the housekeeping and logistic functions; (b) the architectural planning function; and (c) the stratigraphic-interpretive function.

(a) The logistical function of primary balks (i.e., those bounding the four sides of an Area or "square") plays an increasingly greater role as the excavation increases in total exposure and depth of excavation. If the sides of the Area are not kept rigidly perpendicular but are allowed to slant inward into the area of excavation ("overcutting" the balk), the area available for excavation will shrink correspondingly. At a depth of a couple of meters this might not be particularly serious; but at greater depths, this restriction of the digging area can become a serious matter. And redressing a balk face higher than one-and-a-half meters from the current surface is a ladder job--difficult, potentially hazardous and needlessly time-consuming. Moreover, overcut balks soon develop gulleys from winter rains; and little gulleys have a distressing habit of growing into major gulleys, eroding balks and covering excavation areas with layers of winter wash.

Undercutting a balk is even more serious, since dirt once removed can never be replaced. Quite apart from the chaos introduced into the recording process, undercutting weakens the very structure of the balk itself, making the balk progressively less capable of sustaining its own weight or of serving as a traffic-way for earth removal or inter-area communications, a vital balk function in any excavation more than two squares wide. Given the cohesion present in most soils commonly encountered in Palestine, a vertically cut and well trimmed balk-face will stand for a surprisingly long time, resisting the ravages of winter rain and summer drought for years on end. As undercut balks dry out, however, they soon develop cracks and scale off, with potentially lethal effect to those below. And the already narrow access way along the top of the balk grows narrower and more dangerous.

Even on a day-to-day basis, vertical balks minimize contamination of the area under excavation. A pebble falling out of a vertical balk seldom disturbs other delicately affixed items, but one rolling down the face of an overcut balk may well take other things with it. And an undercut balk can be counted on to produce a slow shower of unwanted debris as the drying summer winds reduce the binding force of water in the soil. Some "fall-out" is probably inevitable unless synthetic stabilizers can be developed for balk preservation, but a well cut balk is a valuable ally in keeping the amount of contamination in an area to a minimum.

(b) Plotting the grid of an excavation and planning architecture are greatly facilitated by good balks. A word on the method of planning architecture generally employed at Gezer will make this more clear. (For the detailed discussion of this aspect of the Gezer Excavations, see Chapter VI.)

Due to the size of many of the excavation areas, depth of excavation, and discontinuities produced by standing balks and differential rates of excavation in adjacent squares, it was seldom feasible to employ triangulation or plane-table planning at Gezer. Indeed, elaborate planning of this sort is far less useful for Palestinian excavations in general than the simple stone-for-stone recording of structures and their associated features. These plans, drawn by measurement from fixed lines and known points, seldom cover more than a single square, due to the scale (1:50) employed. Since many plans must be consolidated to produce the finished plan of any given stratum in a particular field, it is _essential_ that all measurements be based upon fixed points; otherwise the plans will not fit together. At this point, again, care with one's balks pays handsome dividends, since the grid of the field as a whole constitutes a matrix of fixed points. Thus it becomes possible to use meticulously maintained balks and their intersections as fixed measuring points; and the entire procedure for establishing a setup for drawing, say, a particular stretch of wall, is immensely simplified. It need hardly be pointed out that time saved by the architect translates directly into more time for active excavation. Even in the case of three-dimensional recording of small finds and the production of top plans for the Area Supervisor's notebook, it is far easier to measure from well-maintained corners and sides of the square than constantly having to refer to cross-balk stakes and stretched surface-level balk lines meters overhead. But, to take proper advantage of his balks, the Area Supervisor must at all times be aware of just how trustworthy a particular balk face or corner is. This sort of double-checking very soon becomes a part of the daily routine of the supervisor and his technical man, and presents no particular problems.

(c) By far the most important function served by a balk is its role as the arbiter of stratification. In the first place, the balk face or "section" provides the excavator with his single best chance of actually _seeing_ tangible evidence of the various activities which have resulted in the disposition of the various earth layers which he is uncovering. Wind-blown soil is very different in appearance in the section than is water-laid material. Courtyard accumulation differs in turn from the rough accumulation of stones, pebbles, sherds, and refuse which characterize the typical street build-up. Imported fill brought in to level up local irregularities carries its own peculiar signature. How much you can see in the balk section, however, is very closely tied to the quality of preparation of the balk face itself. No interpretation can get past the limitations imposed upon it by the quality of the data upon which judgment must be made. Working with a poorly cut and inadequately trimmed balk is like trying to read fine print through a gauze curtain, or like reading Braille wearing gloves. You might get a few clues as to the drift of the story, and then again, you might not. And in any case, you would never be sure.

On a more functional level, however, the balk is an excavator's only means of proving to himself that he has indeed kept his total exposure within the square at one stratigraphic level. Many are the times a frustrated excavator has carefully traced a line in his balk only to find it plunging beneath his supposedly horizontal living-surface. Only slightly fewer are the times when he has carefully traced a surface entirely around his four main balks only to find himself one layer above the one he started with. Until an excavator can satisfactorily explain his balks to another person—and then successfully draw what he has seen and explained—it must not be assumed that he has fully grasped the significance of what he has excavated. Similarly, when the cross-balks between squares are taken down and lines of stratification can be traced from one square to another, the final word is said regarding what levels in Square A correlate with those of Square B, and the stratigraphy for an entire Field becomes something more than mere equation of relative levels or similarity of building techniques or ceramic finds.

Finally, the section itself can be preserved and relayed to future investigators through photographic recording and measured drawings. Here the archaeologist offers the same kind of proof for his stratigraphic assertions that he does for his architectural assertions when he publishes his conventional series of plans and photographs of building remains. (The entire process of careful balk recording is treated at length in Chapter VI.)

These last three points form, in fact, the sole justification for the use of balks. In most other respects, balks are an out-and-out nuisance. Balks regularly hide vital walls, dramatic drop-offs, important doorways and a host of other closely guarded secrets. They hinder communication between closely related areas, get in the way of earth-moving operations, make architectural planning more difficult, photography less self-explanatory, and take a lot of effort to get rid of when they have finally served their intended purpose. One of the truest and most basic unwritten laws of archaeology states that "If a balk can possibly obscure any vital feature, it probably will!"

Yet, despite all these and many other drawbacks, the lowly balk remains indispensible for the order it brings out of stratigraphic chaos and for the means it gives—via the section-drawing—of relating the actual stratigraphic sequence, as it was understood by the excavator, to the student of the final publication of the excavations. Since we cannot do without it, we make necessity a virtue by using our balks as aids to recording, highways for earth removal or tourist travel, somewhat inconveniently placed and precarious photographic platforms, and a simple means of dividing large Fields into smaller Areas. But nobody in his right mind should deliberately go out of his way to make trouble for himself by including balks in his digging strategy unless he really intends to make use of them. And that means a great deal more than merely having earthen walls between adjacent squares.

I

BETTER BALKS AND HOW TO MAKE THEM

The primary responsibility for establishing the archaeological grid falls to the surveyor. The maintenance of that grid is the excavator's responsibility. Permanent iron stakes embedded in concrete and sited at mid-balk lines and intersections are a great help in maintaining a permanent grid--if they can be kept in place. At some excavations it has been a race between the boys of the village to see who could remove bench marks the quickest. Sometimes they have not even waited until the excavators have broken camp. At Gezer, kibbutz tractors driven by weekend sight-seers took their toll, but some survived. (At other sites, a few have been saved through the simple stratagem of burying them.) These stakes should be established with great care, locating them exactly at the cross-point of intersecting mid-balk (or grid) lines and either 50 cm. or (better) one meter outside the excavation area for the outer balk lines. Elevations taken from the tops of the stakes (kept short in the interests of safety and to reduce their chances of being bent over) may be written in the well-troweled wet concrete. These measurements will also be particularly helpful in pre-venting confusion about beginning levels the following year. Stakes driven directly in the corners of excavation areas quickly drop out, generally taking some earth with them and leaving you with an imaginary point in empty space for your corner. For this reason, all corners should be marked by the intersection of strings tied to stakes located far enough beyond the balk edge so as not to loosen the earth at the corners. The use of heavy, brightly colored string pegged down with a large nail at mid-balk will reduce the chances of tripping and string-breakage. (See further Chapter VI below.)

The normal width of most permanent balks is one meter. This pro-vides sufficient strength and stability to withstand heavy traffic under most soil conditions, and allows a margin of safety for the inevitable accidents and minor cave-ins. For temporary balks which need not bear traffic the width may be reduced to 50 cm. or so. This thinner balk has the advantage of obscuring fewer features, but may be unstable in the vicinity of wall remains or loosely-filled pits. Nor will it survive a winter well. For particularly sandy soil, or as a permanent centrally located balk in a large field where the depth of excavation may exceed three or four meters, it may be advisable to plan on a slightly wider balk, say one-and-a-half meters or even two meters. Wooden gang-ways or even concrete toppings could be laid down along such heavily-traveled balks, although to date this remains in the cate-gory of "things somebody really ought to try."

Once the grid has been established and the balk lines (defining the actual areas of excavation) have been laid out, it is a good idea to clear the area of stones and brush to about three meters beyond the

outside balk lines. Once you have begun your excavations, it is far
more difficult to trim unsightly weeds near the balk without loosening
dirt at the edge of the balk. The problem of maintaining good balks
begins immediately with the first picking of a new square. It is very
easy to undermine or overloosen soil at the balk line. Pickmen should
always leave a few centimeters of dirt along each balk line. The
technical man then will be able to devote his skill and attention to
the problem of maintaining the balk with the proper sort of hand tools.
This topsoil, which is generally disturbed agricultural soil full of
tough roots (which may be trimmed with nippers or a sharp knife), is
less compact than the more intact layers beneath and provides, through
its troublesomeness, an excellent training-ground for technical men.
Initially, balks may best be trimmed with the aid of a carpenter's
level in conjunction with the usual technical man's tool-kit of
Marshalltown (or the equivalent) pointing trowel, hand-pick, and well
sharpened clasp- or sheath-knife. Later, plumb-bobs will supplement
the use of the carpenter's level. A worker never should trust his eye
to find the vertical. The eye is easily deceived.

The technique for cutting straight balks is more easily explained
in the field than in print, and each good technical man will develop
some techniques of his own. In general, the steps run as follows:

(1) Check to see that the balk-line across the face of the balk is
taut and correctly positioned at each end. Failure to check the latter
has produced a number of unintended trapezoidal "squares."

(2) Starting somewhere in the middle of the roughly cut balk-face,
cut two vertical and carefully plumbed channels, about a meter or a
meter-and-a-half apart, back to the balk line. These can be somewhere
in the area of 10 or 15 cm. wide at their vertical balk-face.

(3) Then, with diagonal strokes of the pointed end of the handpick (this loosens fewer rocks and potsherds) trim off the standing
column of earth between the two channels to within a centimeter or so
of the balk line, taking care not to strike, dislodge, or loosen rocks
or other objects protruding from the balk face. These are as much a
part of the balk section as is the dirt itself. During the trimming-
back operations, frequent recourse should be made to the spirit level
and balk line to ensure against either undercutting or overcutting.

(4) Finally, the balk-face should be shaved as nearly smooth as
the soil will permit. This is a real spit-and-polish job, and if
properly executed, will pay handsome dividends in readability of the
completed balk. Start at the top and work down, so that falling dirt
will not stick to damp finished surfaces below and obscure the lines
of stratification, which are often obscure enough anyway. Strokes
parallel to the lines of stratification seem less inclined to blur
them. Many workers prefer to use a sheath-knife for some portions of
this final scraping operation. Others have returned for their second

year with special tool-kits of miniature pointing trowels, offset knives, and even dental tools! In the long run, however, a small Marshalltown pointing trowel (ca. 5" blade) and a good sheath-knife seem to be about as good as anything for 99% of the work. With the first panel finished as close to excavation level as possible, a third vertical channel may be cut to one side or the other, and the whole process repeated.

One cautionary note should be entered here. Balk tags, liberally sprinkled over the balk face, are an essential step in the recording process and ensure that you will be able to locate "Floor 1001" or the two sides of "Pit 1002" at a glance. As the technical man trims back the balk, it is a common mistake for him to remove the tag, trim the balk, and then "restore" the tag. This must never be allowed, since the whole point of the exercise is to mark with your tag exactly what you excavated as "Floor 1001" at that point, and if you later are proved wrong in this judgment (by tracing "Floor 1001" from some other balk to a layer above or below your tag) this is information you have to know in order to keep your notes accurate. Usually the worker can trim around the nail and then punch it in further. But since it is difficult to trim back substantial quantities of balk without relocating tags, not to mention the fact that the very character of the balk itself can change drastically in 10 cm., this is a most powerful reason for insisting on keeping balks trimmed as close to current levels as possible. Scraping can be left more easily till later than can the actual trimming. If a balk tag must be moved for any reason, it should only be moved by or under the direction of the Area Supervisor himself.

Special care should be taken to ensure that the corners, which generally become favorite measuring-points, are cut true and square. Since these areas often suffer the most near the surface of the tell, it is necessary constantly to be certain that the re-tightened balk lines, and not the upper walls of the balk itself, are used as reference points.

As the area deepens, some means must be found for relating the (string) balk lines, which are always necessary reference points, to the face of the balk. Fortunately, one means of doing this also affords a means of speedier channel-cutting and trimming-back of the standing column. It works like this: Suspend a plumb-bob from the balk by wrapping the line several times around a pick-or hoe-handle which is then held in place on the tip of the balk by a couple of flat stones. Adjust the line height, so that the bob is just above the level of the current surface and exactly 10 cms. out from the taut balk line. This latter figure is for convenience only, and could be any figure, even the length of the technical man's trowel handle. The important thing is to have some consistent and easily remembered distance between the balk line and the line of the plumb-bob. Then, with the plumb-bob lying against the untrimmed balk face, rapidly cut a vertical channel behind it until the bob can hang free. Measuring from the plumb-line with a tape measure, trim the entire channel back to within "shaving distance" of the balk line. Cut the other channel the same way, and reposition the plumb-line in the center of the standing column to serve as a guide for cutting it back. In time, a good technical man can become very proficient with this technique, so that what initially seems like a long and almost impossible task actually becomes for some a most enjoyable specialization. A tip: carpenters, farmers, and sculptors often make the best technical men. If someone admits he can't drive a nail straight, find some other job for him.

A few suggestions follow. The first two, which can hardly be improved on, are quoted directly from the original Gezer Manual (H. Darrell Lance, Excavation Manual for Area Supervisors (New York and Jerusalem: HUCBAS, 1967), p. 4):

(1) Keep the balks cut as close to the level of where you are excavating in the center of the area as possible. There are a couple of reasons for this. In the first place it is impossible to read an uncut balk, and your balks can be no guide to you in your digging unless you can read them. Secondly, balk trimming is a constant source of contaminating pottery, and the higher up the side of the balk the source of the trimmings, the greater will be the confusion resulting from any contamination. (The higher the layer, the later the pottery.) Balk cutting should never go on in a part of the area where there is danger that its debris will mix with the debris being dug from a controlled locus. (A word to the wise: It is far easier to trim a fresh balk than one that has been drying out for several days.)

(2) Never pull anything out of the balk. If things fall out of the balk while dirt is being trimmed away, no damage is done; but if stones that are firmly embedded in the balk are pulled out, they may pull a large chunk of the balk down at the same time. The most difficult time to observe this principle is when a tempting piece of pottery or some other object is halfway in the balk. But yield not to temptation! If a loose stone in the balk appears to be a safety hazard, consult with your field supervisor. (Cut roots, never pull on them. There are always more roots inside!)

(3) Often it is necessary to cut a balk so that some large stone or line of stones is left hanging half or even eight-tenths of the way out of the balk. In most cases it is impossible to tell just how much of the stone actually is still embedded, and stones can hang on to a balk face seemingly by suction alone. This is partly a matter of cohesion caused by moisture in the soil. When balks dry out and ominous cracks develop above the stone you have no ready alternative to removing it. There is no easy solution to this problem. Large stones can jut out of balks for decades, as at Megiddo, but one can never be sure. A small

consolation lies in the fact that a stone generally comes out of a balk more cleanly and with less damage after the drying process has had its effect than if you try to get it out at the first. Sometimes it seems best to leave a small tapered stub of earth under the stone to support it. If this is cleanly done, with well trimmed sides and the stub bevelled back into the balk line in a reasonable way some 40 or 50 cm. below, the effect is usually quite satisfactory.

It is most important to insist, as a general rule, that as many stones and sherds as possible be preserved in the balk until the drawing is completed. It is easier to trim a balk which has had all the rocks knocked out of it, but often the only trace of a cobbled surface in the section is a scrappy line of fist-sized stones set in loose earth--ready to fall out at the first blow from a handpick. If they do fall out or if they are removed in the interests of more attractive balks, the resulting blur of earth is often very difficult or impossible to interpret correctly. So coax those little ones into hanging on, and don't discourage them with rough handling. After drawing, of course, awkward stones may be removed with little loss.

(4) Often the difference between a readable balk and one that defies interpretation is simply the difference between a roughly scraped (or unscraped) balk and one that has been carefully shaved, trimmed, and knife-shaved around protruding rocks and sherds. Lumps of soil attached to protruding stones and sherds have to be trimmed before drawing and an otherwise "good-looking" balk may have a lot of these fuzzy edged protrusions. Don't skimp on quality here. In every stage of the balk-trimming process it is necessary to avoid etching artificial lines in the balk face with your knife or trowel. The eye tends to follow any continuous feature of the balk face, even accidental scratchings. When you are reasonably sure of your balk readings (see below), it is reasonable and proper to emphasize various features of the section by means of etched lines, but random or accidental etchings will only prove potentially misleading and have no place in a properly prepared balk.

(5) Dust from foot traffic around an excavated area sometimes blows down on damp balks, obscuring detail. No fully satisfactory solution presently exists; but spraying the surface of nearby paths with a mixture of used motor oil and some lighter oil, such as diesel oil, helps somewhat. Proportions are not critical: 1:4 or 1:6 seems adequate. Care should be taken not to spray the balk face itself. (Petroleum products, of course, will quickly ruin the normal rubber gaskets of a sprayer, so replacements should be available.) At one excavation the entire surface of some heavily travelled sections of the tell was sprayed down with water every day. It was said to have been successful in holding down blowing dust, but not many sites are blessed with that much running water. Polyvinyl acetate ("PVA" or synthetic white glue), well diluted with water and soaked into the ground may help to keep crumbling edges or sloping banks intact. It does not, however, seem to

stand up well to traffic, nor can you apply it after you have used oil.
When sprayed on balk faces, it tends to form a skin which then may
accumulate dust or peel off. It must be admitted, however, that our
experiments in the use of PVA in the field were not exhaustive, and
further experimentation with this or similar substances may well produce superior results.

An obvious point, but worth mentioning nevertheless: no one--
supervisor or volunteer--should rub against, lean against, lean tools
against, throw baskets or buckets against, or otherwise mutilate un-
drawn balks. A balk face will not take rough handling and stay readable.

II

THE INTELLIGENT ARCHAEOLOGIST'S GUIDE
TO THE USE AND CARE OF SUBSIDIARY BALKS

Once you discover what your balks can tell you, you will find
yourself constantly studying and referring to them. One
problem, however, will soon be obvious to you: The main
balks are around the sides of your area. How do they help
you stratify a locus which occurs only in the middle of your
area and does not touch the main balks at any point? This
difficulty can usually be overcome by making sure that there
always remains some stratigraphic link between the locus in
the center and the main balks. Small temporary balks running
the length or breadth of the area can often give the needed
connection. But this necessity to maintain some link with the
main balks gives rise to an _exceedingly_ important point to
remember: Never trench around a locus (or an _in situ_ vessel
or object) or along the face of a wall; to do so destroys all
stratigraphic connections between it and the main balk, and
there are few archaeological sins more heinous. When you
probe in the layers beneath a locus, always make your probe
trench perpendicular to the wall or whatever--_never_ along its
face.

H. Darrell Lance,
Excavation Manual for
Area Supervisors, pp. 4-5

Temporary or subsidiary balks can be used in a number of ways.
The balks created in the sides of a probe trench constitute the most
obvious case of temporary balks. By its very nature, a probe trench
is designed to penetrate deeply enough into the mysteries of hidden
strata below so as to allow the excavator to make the most economical

and intelligent attack possible. Since you had had to sacrifice this material, make the most of it. Shave, minutely examine, and tag the balks of the probe before you make your next major move. Often this may mean putting off the decision about how to proceed until the next day since it is very difficult to read a balk in the midday sun. For this reason probe trenches should be planned and executed, if possible, before all the final clean-up work on the previous stratum has been completed. Sometimes, even usually, this will be impossible, due to the necessity of obtaining final photographs. But an afternoon's detailed examination of your probe's carefully shaved balks will pay dividends in the end.

As you begin stripping off a new layer, it is often a good idea to set up a temporary balk line running either completely across the area at about the half-way mark, or at some point where it is possible to run a subsidiary balk between a wall line and one of the permanent balks. Check the connection between surface and wall, then check the balk for signs of missed surfaces or indications of intrusive activity between the wall and the main balk (or from main balk to main balk). A tag in the balk(s) marking your new surface at this point is then much surer than one spotted at random.

Perhaps the most common use of subsidiary balks, however, is in the excavation of layers which are either unclear or unusually complex, or in situations where you have fears of losing control of the square as a whole. Once you are out of control it is very hard to regain it short of a really spectacular change in stratification, but placing a subsidiary balk-line about 2.25 m. into the square and excavating the smaller half of the square in a fairly rapid fashion as something of an oversized probe-trench often will yield enough information or develop enough balk indications so that the situation will clarify itself. It is best to do this in a part of the square that does not involve digging all along the face of your principal balk, i.e., that balk continuing a main line through several areas which promises to be the likely candidate for publication. Often this use of a temporary balk occurs when you encounter a situation involving fills or deserted areas in which extensive pitting and/or rubbish disposal have taken place. Once understood, the remaining half of the square can be peeled off layer by layer from the indications in the temporary balk. If, however, by the time you have gotten down 50 or 75 cm. the situation still seems hopeless, then a 50-cm.-wide temporary balk can be left and the other half of the square excavated. Sometimes a small balk at right angles to the 50-cm.-wide balk will be of assistance, although this does chop up the square overmuch and is of most help only in very mixed stratigraphic situations. By the time you have eight or ten balk-faces to examine-- the subsidiary balk(s) giving data on the slant of surfaces which would otherwise be hard to visualize from the four main balks--the situation should become much clearer.

A similar use of subsidiary balks is in the excavation of large pits. Here, half or a quarter of the pit (if it is large enough) may be excavated in the manner of the probe trench. The balk then is developed across the face of the unexcavated material, and--following a determination of how the pit filling was accomplished (e.g., massive refill, gradual debris accumulation and collapse of put walls over a long time span or relatively rapid accumulation of midden)--the remaining material may be removed in a manner commensurate with its character.

Other uses for subsidiary balks will arise from time to time, in fact, any time you are not particularly sure that you understand the stratigraphic sequence in which you are involved, and any time that it appears that a feature is turning up in some portion of the square which is likely to lack a clear stratigraphic link with the main balks. Where to position these balks and when you really need one are not questions that can be answered in advance of the concrete situation. A good rule of thumb for the latter point is: if in doubt, establish a small balk and take it out if it proves to be redundant (i.e., if the needed evidence can be developed in some other way). A general principle governing the question of placement is: put it some place where you think you can get the needed evidence and where it will interfere least with your exposure. Note that the main balk you connect with should be sufficiently clear and continuous in its stratification to serve as a good tie-point. In passing, we could note that not all subsidiary balks need to run to a main balk. Sometimes a connection between two adjacent walls or similar features--each individually stratified through connection with surfaces which run to main balks-- needs to be examined. If both reach the same balk or adjacent balks, there is no need for yet another balk. But if one or both end in mid- square, then a balk between the two will serve well to determine their stratigraphic relationship to each other. I.e., if the walls all share the same surfaces or have foundation trenches cut from the same surface, they are contemporary. If they share some surfaces but not others, they may be partially contemporary. If they are built on or founded in trenches dug from different surfaces, they are non- contemporaneous. In all cases, you need constantly to keep in mind the basic stratigraphic question: "What is the relationship of this fea- ture to the rest of the features in the square and what sort of evi- dence do I need to include in my notes to prove this when I have destroyed the physical evidence?"

Usually it is not necessary actually to make a formal drawing of temporary balks. But it is wise to remember that if you were having trouble with the stratigraphy in the field, you or someone else will probably have trouble trying to put it all together in the "Field Report." And what seems crystal-clear today may be less than that in a week and totally forgotten in a month. If you took the trouble to make a subsidiary balk, take the trouble to record what it showed, either verbally or (preferably) by means of a scale sketch, taking care to see that it is properly labeled with all the pertinent locus numbers.

Remember that the drawings of the main balks will show the stratigraphic sequence of the square as a whole, but localized areas, not reaching the balk, can only be stratified in so far as they can be related to stratification which does reach the balk, and the only way of recording that particular information is through drawings or descriptions of subsidiary balks.

In addition, a record photograph of a well-scratched and tagged balk, with tag numbers large enough to be easily legible in the photograph, is a valuable asset for later interpretation of the field notes.

Subsidiary balks are temporary. Keep them only wide enough to ensure that they will stand as long as you may need them, remembering that you may have to re-dress them once or twice. They should not have to carry traffic. They should be well-dressed on the face, but need not be made as straight or plumb as the main balks. Tag them as carefully as your main balks unless it is clear after the initial dressing and reading that they have served their purpose and may be removed immediately. Tags will make it easier to trace a given line right around all the adjoining balks.

Do not let a subsidiary balk overstay its usefulness. A five meter square is small enough as it is, and subsidiary balks and probe trenches make it still smaller. When you take them out (and this holds true for all balk removal), be sure to check on the actual identity of striations previously identified on the opposite faces of a balk.

In conclusion, a slight homily on the improper use of secondary balks and probe trenches might not be out of place. Valuable as these tools are, there is no question but that some supervisors tend to use them as a substitute for more purposeful and intelligent activity. Chopping a square into little cubicles with unnecessary subsidiary balks or poking an unnecessary probe into tomorrow's stratigraphy is like cutting a map into small pieces or cutting plugs out of a book. The plug might give you some idea of how many pages you have to go and where the plates are located, but it is going to give you headaches when you turn the page. Probes are sometimes necessary, but they are by no means a cure-all to stratigraphical befuddlement. Nine times out of ten, the person who habitually turns to probes as a way out of his perplexity has not been maintaining his balks down to current excavation levels or has not studied them carefully enough. It is easier to understand a whole map, a complete picture, a larger area as an architectural unit than it is to figure out how each little piece of the puzzle fits together. Yesterday's probe is tomorrow's gap. All too often you may find that a badly-pitted surface has only one stratigraphic connection with a main balk. It would be a shame to have yourself needlessly created the trench that makes that connection a leap of faith or matter of conjecture.

III

BALK READING AND BETTER BALK READING

Explaining the interpretation of balk sections to someone who has never participated in an excavation is rather like attempting to reveal the finer points of oenology to a teetotaler. Short of reproducing actual color plates of characteristic features--and even these would fail to provide the full range of data necessary (consistency, hardness, composition under a hand-lens, cohesiveness, and the like)--there is little one can do about formal book-training in this vital discipline. Nor can everyone become equally proficient in it. In this respect it is much like literary criticism, art criticism, or tea-tasting. Ability, long exposure, and disciplined habits of observation all play their role.

But some things can be said which may make it easier for the beginner to catch hold in what is admittedly a difficult subject. These will be treated under three headings: "Pre-Field Preparation," "Conditions and Technique of Field Observation," and "What's in a Balk? A Primer of Palestinian Balk Interpretation."

A. Pre-Field Preparation.

The ideal grounding in this discipline is a good university degree in the geology of sediments (see Reuben Bullard's introduction to the topic in The Biblical Archaeologist, XXXIII (1970), pp. 98-132, reprinted as Chapter VIII below). Short of this ideal, the beginner should thoroughly ground himself in Edward Pyddoke's Stratification for the Archaeologist (London, 1961), and in some good basic introduction of principles of sedimentological analysis such as W. C. Krumbein and L. L. Sloss, Stratigraphy and Sedimentation (San Francisco and London, 1951). I. W. Cornwall's Soils for the Archaeologist (London: Phoenix House, 1958) is helpful, though Palestinian soils are not very complicated. G. A. Reisner, C. S. Fisher, and David G. Lyon, Harvard Excavations at Samaria, 1908-1910 (Cambridge, Mass.: Harvard U. P., 1924) also includes many valuable stratigraphical observations, despite its early date.

Keep your eyes open when you take walks, particularly in rural or neglected areas. Note such things as the appearance of dirt paths, graded road banks, or roadways in the wet seasons (often covered with stones, gravel, etc., some of which originate in the soil itself, being exposed as the finer soils are eroded from the hard-packed surface.) Note the dusty character of heavily traveled paths such as cattle-paths in dry seasons. Think how this material would appear slightly compressed in an earthen section: mostly fine particles, but with a number of larger particles, and some organic matter mixed in. Undisturbed

windblown soil, on the other hand, exhibits a uniform mix of relatively
fine particle sizes throughout, while water-borne sediment shows graded
sorting--first the larger particles, then finer and finer particles.
To see this at first hand, shake up a quart jar of water and garden
soil. Put it in a spot where it may settle undisturbed. Examine the
layering of the sediment two or three days later. The section of an
ancient mud puddle will be much the same. Note how the sands and
gravels in road-side ditches grade according to the velocity of the
flowing water, itself a function of the size and slope of the drainage
areas as well as the slope of the ditch itself. Find a dried mud puddle and break a chunk out of it, noting as in the quart-jar experiment
the succession of coarse sand, finer sand, and banded silts in the section. Look at the character of soil through which water has repeatedly
washed. Squeeze some of it in your hand and note the high proportion
of sand and gravel and the lack of clay or silt binders. Squeeze some
ponded mud in your hand and note how the high percentage of clays and
silts give it plasticity and cohesiveness. Watch an earthen dump grow,
noting the angle of repose of the growing pile and the graded sorting
of the larger particles. Rocks roll down the slope and out in front of
the pile. As the pile grows, it overrides these rocks and more rocks
roll down. Result: lines of stratification tipping down at about a
45-degree angle with the largest stones forming a basal layer upon the
original ground level. What would happen if the dump ended against a
vertical wall? (The section would show the level of larger stones
continuing up the face of the wall.) Examine some horticultural manure
under a hand-lens. Note the small size and consistency of the vegetable fiber, a result of the mastication and digestive processes involved.
Think of the different character of ashes from a wood or brush fire and
that produced by dung. What would the section of a burned-out campfire look like? (Powdery white, oxidized ash on top, compressed and
perhaps discolored by the soil above it; darker, smothered ash beneath
still containing some fragments of the original fuel.) What would
happen if wind attacked the campfire ashes? What would happen if it
rained heavily first?

In present-day Near Eastern countries and in many other countries
practicing a similar economy and with similar seasons (e.g., some parts
of Mexico) village life is not that much different than life in ancient
Syria-Palestine. Use your eyes to see signs of rebuilding of walls.
Notice where adobe walls decay and where the decayed brick goes. Note
especially the washing and replastering near ground level of mudplas-
tered or mudbrick walls and the erosion of surfaces under eaves. Try
to form a mental image of types of road and courtyard surfaces in different seasons, utilization of available natural resources (e.g., dried
dung for cooking), intimate association of newly-built structures with
decaying abandoned ones, general unevenness of the land, piles of lit-
ter in corners of courtyards, how excess water is channeled from habi-
tation areas. Notice the dead animals and rubbish thrown into pits and
ditches outside of the settled area, etc., etc. Any observation you
can make is grist for your interpretive mill; and the more you observe

and interpret the effect of human activity upon the character of the soils, older structures, etc., in a settled community, the better interpreter you will be of the earth layers you encounter in the field.

A small but important point: try to visualize all those phenomena both as horizontally exposed and as they would appear in section. This will prepare you both for the stratigraphic separation and identification of your materials during excavation and for the way they will appear in the balk section. Remember also that learning these things takes both time and experience, and until you actually get involved in an excavation, you will have little idea of what the various possibilities commonly encountered are.

Finally, spend a few hours going over published sections in books such as Kathleen Kenyon's Beginning in Archaeology (New York: Praeger, 1962), Sir Mortimer Wheeler's Archaeology from the Earth (London: Penguin Books, 1956) and especially such recent archaeological reports as G. Ernest Wright's Shechem: Biography of a Biblical City (New York: McGraw-Hill, 1965) and William G. Dever, H. Darrell Lance, and G. Ernest Wright, Gezer I: Preliminary Report of the 1964-66 Seasons ("Annual of the Hebrew Union College Biblical and Archaeological School in Jerusalem," Vol. 1, Jerusalem: HUCBAS, 1970), noting the relationships between surfaces and walls, walls and foundation trenches, surfaces and pits, etc. Notice the relatively large amount of imported fill utilized at Gezer and Shechem to level up areas for building purposes, the depth of some major destruction layers and the relative thinness of others, and the depth of accumulation representing decayed mudbrick walls. Try to think architecturally about the relationships between various features, the activities which produced each feature you can see, and the arguments for establishing the probable sequence of events which would serve to bring about the various configurations of elements involved. The more analysis of this sort you do, the less foreign you will find your first actual balk.

B. Conditions and Technique of Field Observation.

It is very hard indeed to see much in a balk after about 9:00 or 10:00 in the morning. The bright sunlight washes out detail, even of balks in the shade. Before 9:00 the light can be very good, but it steadily degrades as the day matures, just when you are beginning to get somewhere. Perhaps the very best light for balk reading occurs just before dusk. At this time color differentiations can be made that simply cannot be seen at other times of the day. The use of artificial light sources to extend the period of readability remains yet untested. In general, from the time balks first come into the shade after 4:00 o'clock in the afternoon until dusk may be considered productive balk interpretation time. It is also a good time for balk trimming and scraping and delicate technical work, since the regular work force usually is not in the field; and the more pleasant afternoon temperature

conditions are conducive to more careful workmanship. The Area and
Field Supervisors should plan on spending most of this time in the
field, analyzing the developing stratigraphical indications of the main
and subsidiary balks both in the light of preparing for the following
day's excavations and preparing for or executing the final balk drawings. You will find you can think much clearly in the cool afternoon
quiet than in the hectic hot mid-morning. Usually it is a good idea to
go over your balks with another supervisor or an intelligent workman,
explaining your interpretation to him and getting his reaction to it,
as well as his independent observations. Being forced to explain a
balk to another person is second only to drawing a balk in forcing you
to face all the problems head-on and find a solution which makes sense
of them all.

Often a number of days of staring at the balks, scraping delicately
to bring out faint lines, tracing faintly preserved surfaces, relating
one thing to another, trying to decide just how each layer came to be
and what it signifies, precedes any certain understanding of the
stratigraphic situation of the area as a whole. Often, too, the examination of a continuation of your balk or its reverse face in the adjacent area will bring to light factors which will make the interpretation of your own balk much easier. Always remember that ancient man
did not live in five-meter squares!

All major surfaces should be traced completely around the four
balks of the square, the limits of pits or other intrusions established
(note that the bulging side of a rounded pit caught in section is a
most confusing rounded, amorphous blob cutting off lines of stratification to either side, but often possessing no true character of its
own), and the genetic origin of each layer established (e.g., fill,
courtyard or street accumulation, destruction debris, wall collapse,
wash layer, eroded mudbrick debris, midden heap, agricultural refuse
layer near threshing floors, dung pile, ash heap from bread ovens,
cooking fires, or pottery kilns, etc.). Compositional description and
genetic interpretation can often best be done in conjunction with an
archaeologically trained geologist, but it is a question which must be
put to each individual earth layer. The days of "sticky green layer"
balk descriptions should be past.

During this process, more balk tags can be added to clarify the
interpretation; but it should be obvious that at no time should a properly affixed balk tag be moved until you are sure of your final interpretation and have made any necessary corrections and warnings in your
notebook. If you went well beneath Surface 2041 at one end of the
square while thinking that you were still above it, this is information
which must be recorded on the locus sheets and the intrusive baskets
identified. Even then it is best to leave the old tag, suitably modified, in place and insert a new tag (Surface 2041!) in the right place.

As you become relatively certain of some features in the balks, it is a good idea to accentuate the divisions between key strata and associated features by scratching the balk. This can be done best by running the point of a sharp trowel or sheath-knife along the junctures of layers or the margins of pits, debris heaps, individual bricks, and the like. This should not be done until you are fairly confident of the divisions nor should it be done where it will obscure delicate features. Some excavators prefer to identify the various strata by means of a line of small nails with colored heads before they commit themselves to scratched lines. Others scratch such features only lightly or intermittently. In any case, it is a good idea to firm up the evidence before the balk dries out too much, leaving you with a uniform grey dusty surface distinguished more by texture than by color changes. Additionally, scratching a balk lets you stand back and evaluate the balk as a whole, and makes the execution of the final balk-drawing much easier. There is some danger that in scribing your balks you will tend to fix a premature or incorrect interpretation, since the eye follows the lines more readily than the actual earth layers. This problem is minimized if you continually force yourself to check out all the relationships between things in your section; which came before which and how did this layer get cut by this pit, etc. Added assurance is given the interpretation when scribing is done in consultation with another supervisor or a sharp-eyed worker, and it should be taken as normal operating procedure that balks should be scribed only in consultation with another critical interpreter. In the event that your first interpretation or a trial interpretation requires revision, however, there is little harm done. Lines scrape out easily and new ones may be added. By far the greater danger is that your balk will dry out and dust over so badly that you will no longer be able to read them accurately, and un-scribed features of which you once were quite certain will fade into the uniformly grey mass.

All this is sufficient reason to show that you must begin early (and will undoubtedly work late) to sort out the mysteries of your balks. This is also another argument for keeping your balks trimmed to current excavation levels. Tomorrow's problems would be much smaller if you got today's problems out of the way. At times, however, it is quite true that you simply cannot understand some features in your balks until you get down to the next layer or two, and it is a dangerous fallacy to insist that balks be drawn down to the limit of the excavation each day. Either you will wind up with very messy balk drawings and a stubby eraser or your drawings will be so premature as to be worthless. But if you do not put in your time every day staring at the balks, making trial scratchings and generally trying to understand them and if you do not draw the balks as they become clear, you will rue the loss of this time when the final reckoning comes and the balks must be drawn willy-nilly. If your balks are completely understood, properly tagged at both ends of all lines, pit edges and bottoms, etc. and clearly scratched, the actual drawings may well wait for some time, for they will not take long. But bear in mind that there is little time for thinking during the last week, and balk drawings well in hand make life sweet! Remember also that drawing reduces a set of balks to a more easily comprehended scale with the result that errors of interpretation show up more glaringly. And trying to get a fresh <u>correct</u> interpretation out of a dried-out six-week-old balk at 10:00 AM on the last day in camp is a nightmare.

Dried-out balks are a considerable pain, but they are not absolute disasters. With a little care and a lot of hard work, they can be restored to rosy life. Before <u>anything</u> can be done, the accumulated dust must be blown off. This can be done the hard way (with a rubber syringe) or the hardest way (by mouth), but an easier way is to blow the dust off using dry pressurized air from an ordinary pump-type gar- den sprayer. Start at the top and work your way down. This often etches the balk in a most informative way and occasionally reveals details you had missed before. An ordinary fire bellows might come into its own in this situation, possibly utilizing a modified nozzle. Once the dust has been blown off, and not before, it is safe to spray the balk with a fine mist of water; spraying a dusty surface bonds the dust in place and often yields nothing but a textured uniformly brown surface. Again, while a hand-sprayer will do good temporary service in dampening a small area for detailed investigation, a pump-type garden sprayer is much more efficient; and enough moisture can gradually be worked into an entire balk to enable detailed study of the balk for quite a while with only occasional light respraying to maintain the color. The spray should be kept fine to avoid eroding the surface or causing drips to trickle down the face of the balk, obscuring detail. At Gezer we have successfully used this technique more than once on particularly difficult balks, with only slight degradation of the balk surface due to new dust-deposit each time. Eventually it might be necessary to scrape, re-shave the balk surface, re-dust and start all over, but even year-old balks yielded new secrets through the use of this technique which should be more generally used than it seems to be. Future expeditions might well investigate the use of small portable compressors with paint-sprayer type hoses and guns with a variety of nozzles. The hand pump garden sprayer, however, has the advantage of availability practically everywhere; and it requires only a good deal of elbow grease to make it work quite satisfactorily. One hint may be useful: For one reason or another, the sprayer seems to go through seals and gaskets rather rapidly. It is a good idea to keep a supply of spare parts on hand.

C. <u>What's in a Balk? A Primer of Palestinian Balk Interpretation.</u>

We have already alluded to many of the features which characterize certain layers or constructions when seen in section. Here it may be helpful to summarize certain features which may be encountered in the typical Palestinian archaeological site. Regional idiosyncrasies, of course, will create differences between various sites. Cities located in the alluvial plains utilized stone to a much lesser extent than those in the hill-country, for example. Nevertheless, certain features are common at most Palestinian tell-sites. These sort themselves conveniently into five main categories: (1) Man-made structures (or deposits) and occupational accumulations; (2) water-carved or water-laid structures or sediments; (3) wind-associated phenomena; (4) animal disturbances; and (5) effects caused by vegetation.

1. Man-made structures and occupational accumulations

a. Robber trenches: One of the chief characteristics of a site utilizing stone for building material is the high degree of re-utilization of stones from earlier structures. If these earlier buildings had "freestanding" walls built in foundation trenches (walls with wide foundation trenches) or "trench-built" walls (walls placed in a trench only as wide as the foundation) or "surface-built" walls buried under piles of collapsed mudbrick, stones could only be removed by robber-trenches unless the whole area was scraped away to provide fill for some adjacent area. In other cases, however, stones were simply lifted from the surface and transferred elsewhere. In this second instance, the only sign of the original line of the wall might be a narrow strip of unevenly compacted earth showing depressions of individual stones, perhaps continuing the line of a nearby wall-remnant with packed earth surfaces to either side of it--much easier to see by means of surface clearance than in the section. A robber-trench in cross-section looks very much like a U-shaped pit, but it is usually back-filled with ordinary earth containing little midden deposit.

b. Pits: These come in many sizes and shapes, all with differing functions. Grain storage pits are often unlined, but they can be lined with stones, field clay, or plaster. Fumigating fires often were built in wheat storage pits, while barley was mixed with ashes (verbal communications from Lawrence Stager). Often a very thin, white layer composed of the silica skeletons of chaff--a white, fluffy, very delicate material--lines the bottoms and lower sides of such pits. Other pits may be garbage or midden pits distinguished by tipped-in filling, large quantities of bone fragments, broken pottery and other organically rich material yielding a dark trashy humus, often with a peculiar musty smell. Latrines would appear much the same but often have a peculiar greenish cast to them and regularly show distinct signs of worm-holes in freshly broken clods. Other pits were cut to extract brick-making materials, for treasure-hunting, or for reasons which are now obscure. The Iron I and early Iron II periods were especially active times for the digging of pits. Larger pits often have under-cut rims and are not always totally regular in shape. The hoes used in their excavation were short and operated in a stooping position, creating walls rounded in vertical section. Pits regularly bottom out when they encounter harder layers, indicating little change in human nature over millenia. And it is not at all unusual to find one pit cutting into another. In section, pits may chiefly be distinguished by the fact that they interrupt the

normal horizontal lines of typical occupational accumulation. When you
suddenly find that you can no longer trace a line, it is time to start
looking for the vertical side of a pit or even a series of pits. On
the other hand, some pits have stratified fillings; and the ending of
lines of stratification may indicate that you are out of the pit and
into something else--maybe a massive fill. Often pits have large
stones over part of the bottom and up much of one side from the back-
filling operation. As we have already observed, when you catch only
the side of a pit in a balk, lacking rim or bottom, it is usually very
confusing. Suspect that any irregular blotch of amorphous nature may
be part of a pit, particularly if it has largish stones toward the bottom and/or an unusual number of bone fragments in the upper portions.
Following the drawing of the balk and just prior to balk removal, you
can easily test your evaluation by clearing the offending section back
into the balk until the normal stratification commences. A similarly
amorphous condition often occurs when the balk face immediately paral-
lels the face of a heavy wall hidden in the balk. Sometimes probing
with a steel rod or long ice-pick will save you a good deal of eyestrain
and confusion. Specialized instances of pits would include foundation
trenches (embracing either side of a foundation wall, or, in rare cases,
cut into earth banks on one side with a floor coming up to the base of
the wall on the other side), robber trenches, drains (characterized by
their shape: vaguely square or trapezoidal in section, often with flat
stone bases, upright stone sides and flat cover stones--and their filling: water washed soil), post and stake-holes, and cisterns or well-
shafts, the latter two usually stone-lined. Stone-lined pits, cisterns,
and silos are often trench-built, i.e., with stones jammed right against
the side of the cutting, so that the cutting itself may be hard or impossible to detect. Often the top courses of a silo, vat, or cistern
shaft are secondary, added later in conjunction with a general raising
of level in the area.

    c. Walls: Stone house walls may be one, two, or more rows wide
depending on the site and period. In general two-row stone walls are
only a few courses high, forming a socle for a mud-brick or packed-earth
wall. You should always look for a foundation trench--either quite wide
or barely wide enough to accommodate the wall--in conjunction with a
wall, although walls may be surface-built as well. Always look for
evidence of a standing stub of mud brick above a one- or two-course two-
row wall or single-row wall about 30 cm. wide or wider, and for evi-
dences of mudplaster on the face of any wall. This will often be easier
to do in the section than in the excavation area. Bricks could, of
course, be made to suit narrower walls, but the chances diminish with
the width of the wall since such a wall would lack strength and stability. Look above the floor and exterior surfaces of the house for
traces of brick or stone fall, signs of destruction, burned roof members, rolled mud-and-straw roofing material with horizontal striations,
etc. Bear in mind that a seven- or eight-foot wall has to go somewhere
when it collapses. If that wall was built of mudbrick, there would have
been no building materials worth salvaging from it, so the evidence of

its destruction ought to be present unless the whole mess was dug out and dumped elsewhere. Slumped mudbrick may be distinguished by homogeneity of texture--small pebbles and occasional small sherds mixed all through the matrix--and a generally well-mixed amorphous appearance. Straw moulds may show in relatively intact lumps (break them open), and rain washing over the mass of fallen brick will yield ponded clay-like sediment in low-lying spots, often with a banded appearance (see below). Burned brick will usually be colored yellow to yellow-brown to reddish-brown and will usually have straw casts well preserved. It often has a peculiar crumbly character. Intact mudbrick <u>in situ</u> can usually be recognized by its straw casts and regular shape. Not all bricks utilized straw, but most did. Upon drying, joints in the mudbrick tend to open up and become more distinct. Heavy walls regularly compress layers running under them.

    d. <u>Terrace walls</u> are often missed in excavation reports. Generally they have a slight batter towards the uphill side. They may look like house walls, or they may not. Usually they are completely stone-built. Often they were built (or repaired) in sections, resulting in a structure of uneven quality. Very frequently they will be nothing more than a sloping one-row revetment of an earthen bank. The balk section is the logical place to identify the various use-surfaces associated with a wall and should yield the necessary data to determine the nature of any such wall. But remember that one year's house-wall could become the next year's terrace-wall.

    e. <u>Benches and Platforms</u> occur regularly in rooms and occasionally may appear in your sections. Usually the top surfaces are of stone, brick or plaster with plastered or stone sides and earthen fill. In modern villages water jars, lying tipped on their sides for easy dipper access, are often kept on such platforms in courtyards.

    f. <u>Vats, Basins, and "Bins"</u>: Often vats and basins are lined either with chalk or marl paste or (more frequently) with red field clay. In section they will generally appear as broadly U-shaped stone constructions with waterproofing in the joints. Often your first clue to a waterproof construction is the discovery of bits of chunky red or brown field clay in the section or debris of excavation. "Bins" are generally one-course semi-circles of large stones placed beside house walls. In most cases they were roughly plastered with mud paste which rarely can be identified. In section they may appear only as a large stone lying on a surface at an indeterminate distance from a house-wall, usually 1.5 m. or less. By analogy with modern village houses, these would appear frequently to have been mangers for domestic animals. In this case, one might expect to find evidence for a tethering-stake and trampled earth in the immediate vicinity. Dung will probably have been removed daily to a storage area or to a preparation area where it was pulverized to serve as fuel (raw dung does not burn readily).

g. <u>Cobbled Floors</u>: Characteristically these are laid on a soft
ashy substratum, probably designed to keep moisture from seeping up
through the floor, and are not particularly strong, coming up all too
readily in excavation and falling out of the balk all too easily during
balk-trimming. Nor do they often appear solidly stone-to-stone in the
balk section. Prompt and careful tagging of such features in the balk
is a real desideratum.

h. <u>Plastered and Packed-earth Floors</u>: These tend to wear through
in the center of a room. Look for a sagging floor line and signs of
more than one flooring near the walls. Layers of ash often were used
as an underlayer for interior floors. One of the basic laws of balk-
reading is that very few good prepared packed-chalk floors show up as
more than just a string of minute spread-out chunks of chalk in the
balk section. Often the floor is just as well defined by the flat-
lying sherds and odd pebbles above it or by the destruction debris
immediately overlying it as it is by its own character. Packed-earth
floors are even harder to identify in some sections, and, again, should
be very carefully traced to the balk, the balk carefully trimmed to
floor level, and the floor level immediately marked with colored nails
and tagged at frequent intervals along the balk. Unless this is made a
rigorous rule, you are going to spend many afternoons tracing floors in
the balk that were perfectly obvious during excavation. An interesting
phenomenon regarding floors is that frequently they cannot be traced
any nearer to a wall than three or four centimeters. Whether this is
because the mud wall-plaster was laid down first, occupying that particular space, or because traffic close to a wall was impossible, or
because the wall served as a "dry well," leaching fine clays out of
soils buried next to the wall, or because small animals tended to burrow along buried walls, is impossible to say. Probably all factors
enter in in differing combinations. At any rate, do not give up in
despair if a floor does just this. Softness next to a wall need not be
a sign of a foundation trench. If it <u>were</u> a foundation trench--and you
obviously have to check the balk with <u>this</u> possibility in mind--it
would mean that the trench cut the pre-existing floor and you are dealing with a <u>later</u> trench-built wall. The floor belonging to a wall will
either be intact or demonstrate the minor kind of weakness discussed
above. Note, however, that if a floor <u>does</u> run up to a wall, it probably will tip up slightly against the wall.

i. <u>Exterior Surfaces</u>: In general exterior surfaces accumulate
much more rapidly than interior floors which, as noted above, tend to
wear out through traffic and sweeping. The rate of build-up varies
with the situation, being influenced by patterns of traffic, patterns
of erosion/wash accumulation, etc. Exposed hill-top streets might tend
to remain constant or even waste away somewhat. Protected inside
streets can easily rise as much as a meter and a half to two meters in
a century. Occasionally streets may have been drastically lowered in
repair programs. For example, in the Iron Age gate at Gezer, used continuously from <u>ca</u>. 950 to <u>ca</u>. 733 or 700 B.C., late eighth century

destruction debris lay directly on a surface which covered a series of late 10th/early 9th century surfaces. In section, most streets show an irregular series of stony layers, often with thin layers of summer dust or fill separating them. Sherds in streets are very characteristic: broken to minimal size and usually badly worn. Bits of bone and other rubbish occur. Chuck-holes and small gullies often cut the surface of a street, and patches and local repairs complicate both the tracing and the street's appearance in the balk. Exterior surfaces on a slope often may be identified by a coherent surface layer of washed gravel and sand. Scour-and-fill wash gullies--irregular U-shaped trenches filled with water-washed coarse sand and gravel--commonly occur. Note that broad areas of sheet-washing connote a downward-sloping exterior surface and that gullies, unless obstructed, tend to follow the easiest down-hill course and indicate a somewhat steeper slope draining a greater runoff area. Take factors like these into account when relating layers in one balk to another, particularly when relating to balks from an adjacent square. Exterior surfaces will seldom be neatly horizontal and may often be quite irregular, reflecting sloping terraces, the contours of ruined buildings beneath the surface, or random earth removal for local building purposes.

j. <u>Courtyards and Animal Enclosures</u>: Large courtyards in modern primitive villages are often quite untidy except near the door of the house, whereas small walled entrance-courtyards tend to be kept meticulously clean by sweeping and sprinkling with water. Courtyards are characterized by a general uniformity of soil texture. That is, they are usually fine-textured with a few rocks or stones and a good deal of very fine charcoal distributed throughout. Crush a small amount and examine it closely with a hand lens, looking for fine charcoal from animal dung, another major component of the soil. Small sherds and pebbles tend to be randomly scattered throughout the section with flat-lying sherds often lying rounded-side-up on or embedded in faint horizontal striations which mark the courtyard surface at one particular time. Near a baking installation or a cooking fire area this surface will be covered with dark, partially oxidized ash. Usually this is fine-textured dung ash with a small admixture of charcoal from twigs and brush used to start the fire. Beside the oven itself you will usually encounter a large ash-heap. Often courtyard surfaces are separated by layers of fill, basketfulls of locally obtained earth evenly scattered about and levelled off for the succeeding surface. Here, pot-sherds appearing in the balk will frequently be found lying on a diagonal slant or vertically wedged between clumps of dirt--an impossible stance if they had fallen on an area of active traffic. In shallow raked-out fills of this kind no coherence or clearly demarcated tip-lines should be expected. Courtyard surfaces often have broad undulations in the section or slope from one side to another. Where a high portion meets a worn spot in the succeeding surface, it is quite easy to jump from one surface to another in surface-tracing or balk analysis.

Animal enclosures differ from courtyards mainly in the fact that they contain much more. dung, which often colors the soil a light reddish-brown color. Ash, bone, and charcoal will probably be missing or in minor proportions. Under a hand lens the fibrous make-up of the organic material is generally discernible. In wet weather, the ground will be churned up by the hooves of the animals, particularly if they are not tethered; and in dry weather the ground will be pulverized into a thick dust layer. In either case the typical banded courtyard striations will be missing, and the layer will show a very mixed appearance in section. Surfaces like these are very difficult indeed to identify in the balk or trace horizontally in excavation, and it must be admitted that we do not, as a result, know very much about exactly where animals of various types were quartered in ancient Palestinian towns.

k. Imported fills: Imported fills are characterized by sloping tip lines, gravity sorting of rock and soil particles, slanting sherds and--in more massive operations--by a run-out of stones along the original ground level or against the sides of pits or walls. Robber trenches were usually backfilled; pits less frequently so, depending on their intended function. Faint earthen surfaces of limited extent and scrappy wall fragments often appear in more massive fills, representing stages in the filling operation (see Dever, Lance, et al., "Further Excavations at Gezer, 1967-71" in The Biblical Archaeologist, XXXIV [1971], pp. 97-99). Minor fills may not show all these characteristics, but the presence of potsherds of varying orientation is often sufficient indication of a fill, as in the presence of a mixture of differing kinds of soil, rocks, pottery, etc. in no discernible order or arrangement. (For more on fills and their archaeological significance, see G. Ernest Wright, "Archaeological Fills and Strata," The Biblical Archaeologist XXV [1962], pp. 34-40.)

2. Water-sorted or water-laid sediments

These have already been discussed somewhat in connection with "pits" and "exterior surfaces." Characteristic of water-laid material is graded bedding. Materials washing down from a ruined mudbrick building (or a slope of similar earth) into a depression show regular banding and a preponderance of very fine sediments. Near the bottom of the depression, silt may be deposited in a broad clay-like band which will develop vertical cracks as it dries. Layers like this indicate undrained low points in the immediate topography. Under hand-lens examination of a freshly broken or carefully shaved vertical section this layer should show regular banding (coarser materials succeeded by finer sediments). During the summer months, dust may have settled in the same depression. A hint: if you shave a chunk of the vertical section on a bevel with a sharp knife to something like a 30° or 45° slant, the individual bands will appear more spread out and more easily identifiable. This technique may also be used on a larger scale for minor subsidiary balks involving courtyard surfaces and the like. A simple test for the presence or absence of silts is to squeeze a small handful of the damp soil in question and note the degree of cohesion. Silts sedimenting in an environment lacking drainage will have a high degree of clay present. Water washing through drains or gulleys will remove fine silts, leaving the soil sandy and crumbly in texture. Mud-puddles, having a high silt content, regularly develop vertical cracks upon drying. A chunk of the puddle should show a regular series of graded bedding lines unless it has been trampled by passers-by or cattle.

Sub-surface water courses or streams may develop where softer layers overlie less permeable layers. To tell whether a cut-and-fill channel really was an open drain or an underground stream is occasionally difficult, but an open gulley should show some relationship to the surface from which it initially started. The section of a closed water channel often shows the shape of a pointed arch, i.e., an isosceles triangle with point up. An open system is wide-topped unless there is a steep slope, in which case it develops vertically-cut sides.

3. Wind associated phenomena

Wind-sorted material tends toward a uniform mix of fine particle sizes, that is, from a certain maximal size down to the very finest particles, all mixed evenly together. Frequently it will fill shallow trenches or hollows, especially in the vicinity of walls; and it will deposit on the lee side of rocks, or in the corners of rooms. Soft, fine soils with few or no pebbles or pottery and no sign of graded bedding in these contexts usually are wind-deposited. Contours of such deposits may be very irregular on the bottom but should be smooth or rounded on top unless secondary disturbance has taken place. In the Sinai and Negev these wind-deposited materials account for most of the soil and are responsible for the remarkable preservation of remains at places like Arad and Beer-sheba. Exposed areas may be largely denuded of finer soils by wind activity, unless there is sufficient vegetation to break the force of the wind. Vegetation serves further to cause deposition and to fix wind-borne dust in place.

4. Animal disturbances

To some extent these have already been discussed. Animal burrows, however, are a frequently-encountered problem. These may range in size from ant colonies and worm-workings in mud, dung, and moist earth through mouse, owl, and lizard burrows to porcupine and fox dens. Characteristically, these are filled (if relatively old) with soft loose earth. Since small animals would rather tunnel through soft earth than harder layers or rocks, these burrows often run along the face of walls or between harder-packed surfaces. Rarely are they a problem although there are occasions when they obscure or obliterate

lines in your balk. Before you make any conclusions regarding post-
holes in beaten floors and the like, check carefully to see that you do
not have a "rathole" instead. Pottery occasionally could drift down a
large burrow, and the possibility should always be borne in mind.
Large burrows and dens should be treated like pits in excavation.

5. Effects of vegetation

Ancient humus layers and the like are seldom encountered in Palestinian excavations. If present, they should show up as a dark band
with indistinct lower margin, possibly showing some traces of root
structure under hand-lens observation. The dark band, if there are no
charcoal flecks present, should give reasonable evidence by itself.
Tree roots (and planting pits) are occasionally met with, though probably much less frequently than they should be if we knew how to interpret the signs properly. We know from Assyrian reliefs and writings
that some ancient cities had ornamental gardens and trees within the
city walls. Egyptians also loved their gardens. Whether or not this
was true of ancient Palestine is something we cannot answer from the
archaeological evidence until someone can determine how to identify the
evidence for such plantings. But it would be very strange, in light of
the frequent biblical reference to sitting under one's own vine and
fig-tree, if vines, trees, and small plants were not a regular feature
of the larger Palestinian house complex. Perhaps the reference is only
to smaller unwalled villages. If not, however, the evidence is there
somewhere, still unrecognized. Little attention has been paid to date
in the Levant concerning the evidence for fixation of windborne soils
by plant life in the vicinity of ruined buildings, but this must have
been a normal feature.

SUMMARY

Most of the evidence we will ever have for the daily life of
ancient man depends upon careful excavation and even more careful questioning of the traces developed by this process of excavation. The
balk section gives one vital dimension of present-day excavation procedure and is capable under intelligent questioning of yielding more
information than we presently are getting from it. The brute questions
of seriation of walls and surfaces--although they are the basic questions to be answered in any serious archaeological endeavor--are only
the beginnings of wisdom, and the intelligent student of balks will in
time be able to provide us with far more interesting and valuable data
than we are yet extracting. If there is one theme in the immediately
preceding section on balk-reading, it is: "You are not going to find
an answer unless you pose the question." Common sense, close observation, and a questioning mind, here as elsewhere in archaeology, can
make the critical difference between exhilarating success and baffled
bewilderment.

Chapter IV

THE FIELD RECORDING SYSTEM

H. Darrell Lance

"To excavate is to destroy."

The archaeologist who has not pondered the implications of this sober but true statement is not a scholar but a treasure hunter. When an excavation is finished in the field, nothing remains but shelves of artifacts and samples, the records of the excavator, and a hole in the ground. The records--the plans, sections, photographs, and field notes --constitute the only link to the archaeological context which has been forever obliterated.

An archaeological recording system must be designed to perform three functions: (1) It must provide a complete and accurate description of all features which disappear during excavation or which cannot be removed--largely earth layers and architectural features. (2) It must provide a way to identify and organize the materials removed from the field for study and preservation--pottery, small objects, and samples. (3) It must provide the information which will make possible a correct reconstruction of the stratigraphic relationships among everything discovered. It is this third purpose which is often neglected, and yet any subsequent use of the material for historical or cultural synthesis depends upon it. The recording system must permit the excavator after the season and anyone else who wishes to check the conclusions of the excavator to answer this question: What was the original stratigraphic situation of this particular locus or artifact? If the recording system and the subsequent publications do not provide the answer to this question, they are seriously inadequate.

Some major aspects of the total process of recording--architectural planning, photography, and the interpretation and drawing of sections-- are treated thoroughly in other parts of this manual; and we shall be concerned here only with the notebook recording system used by the excavator in the field. The field notebook, however, is the heart of the matter; for it is only the information in the field notebook which permits all the other aspects of recording to be brought together to produce a coherent synthesis.

I

SOME BASIC CONCEPTS

The Syro-Palestinian tell is a human artifact of enormous complexity. It is the result of centuries, often millennia, of human activity --building, razing, leveling, pitting, plowing, tunneling, and terracing--and of natural forces--blowing, eroding, quaking, collapsing, undermining, gullying, and silting. The end result--what the excavator confronts--is often an unholy mess. Theoretically, the task of the excavator is to take this mound apart in the exact reverse order from that in which it was built, starting with the latest features, proceeding to the next oldest, and so on. This theoretical ideal might be achieved if the excavator had something like X-ray vision plus the ability to make the layers of different ages glow in contrasting colors so that every phase and sub-phase could be infallibly disentangled. But until and unless science presents us with such improbably capabilities, we must accept the unhappy truth that the stratigraphic history of any site as reconstructed by the archaeologist will only approximate the actual history of the mound. The conscientious excavator can only seek continually to devise new methods and approaches that will cut down his margin of error and misinterpretation and to increase his measure of control.

Digging in squares or rectangles of a standard size is one such technique for increasing control. The carefully scraped sides of the square show in section the vertical relationship of strata. No one is under the illusion that the ancients lived in squares five meters on a side or even that the archaeological picture might not change dramatically ten centimeters outside any of the sides of the square; but at least for what is excavated, the use of squares and sections greatly increases the control of the excavation process and reduces the margin of error. The five-meter square, therefore, is a kind of theoretical "tool," unreal in respect to the actual situation of antiquity, but a device which permits a more exact analysis than would a romantic attempt to try to follow one particular stratum across the surface of a mound wherever it might wander.

There are two other theoretical "tools" which are central to the excavation and recording system employed at Gezer; and to understand the system, one must first understand these concepts. They are (1) the pottery basket (or bucket--the words are interchangeable), and (2) the locus.

A. The pottery basket.

The term "pottery bucket" or "pottery basket" as used at Gezer has two distinct though related meanings. The first is the actual plastic bucket, tagged and containing sherds recovered from an excavated area. The second and equally important meaning of the phrase is that three-dimensional bit of the tell which produced that particular bucket of pottery. The double meaning arose from the fact that in Palestine, pottery is the primary means of dating; the pottery fragments recovered from a unit of tell debris give the excavator information about the date of any structures or artifacts associated with that unit of debris. The pottery bucket, in this second sense, therefore, refers to a three-dimensional bit of the mound which once excavated is atomic; it is never subdivided. It remains forever a unit defined by its description in the field notebook. Any small object discovered during the digging of a particular pottery basket is also permanently associated with that basket. The pottery basket, therefore, is the smallest practical unit of excavation; and the sequential numbering of pottery baskets is the basic framework of the field notebook.

B. The locus.

If the pottery basket is the smallest unit of excavation, the locus is the smallest coherent unit of stratigraphy. In practice, the locus is any stratigraphic unit which can be meaningfully isolated from those adjacent to it--e.g., a layer of earth with a uniform character, a surface, the destruction debris or fill resting on the surface, the makeup under the surface, a single-phase wall, each phase of a multiphase wall, the stone lining of a pit, the contents of the pit, etc. The phrase "meaningfully isolated" is important since this concept of locus, taken to an extreme, might declare each striation or lens in a fill or each thin resurfacing of a beaten surface to be a locus, breaking the stratification into thousands of fragments which could not be meaningfully re-assembled. Thus a locus as the term was used at Gezer is not entirely empirical--some subjective judgment was usually called for. The best practical rule of thumb to determine whether something should be designated a locus is the following: call anything a locus if it becomes necessary to distinguish it or to refer to it apart from another feature. Suppose, for example, that in clearing a surface which has already been designated Locus 15041, the excavator finds in one corner of the area a patch of cobblestones which obviously form part of the surface. Rather than referring to "the cobblestone part of Surface 15041," the excavator will give the cobblestones a new number, Locus 15042. Or suppose that a plaster floor has been located in one corner of the area and soon in another corner at the same depth a similar plaster floor appears. Unless there is a clear connection visible in a section or unless the excavation is proceeding in such a way that the possibility of a connection will be tested immediately, each patch of surface will get its own locus number. If later on they prove to be the same surface, it is simple to cancel one of the numbers.

Everything excavated belongs to one locus or another. There is no such thing as "the earth between Locus X and Locus Y" or "the debris over Locus X." If that "earth" or "debris" occupies space and can be distinguished from its surroundings, then by our definition it belongs to some locus. Conversely, nothing can belong to more than one locus. If the excavator is unclear of the boundary between loci--and such situations are inevitable, then he is losing control of the excavation and must pause to re-evaluate his situation. Mention of his uncertainty in the notebook will serve as a caveat to anyone using the material later. But at the moment of excavation, after he has re-examined the immediate problem, the excavator must make a decision; he must assign a pottery basket to one locus or another; he cannot equivocate. Since the excavator must always be digging one specific locus or another, he is forced to come to terms with the stratifica-

tion, to theorize about it, to look for relationships among the elements, even if those ideas change. If he makes a mistake about the
boundaries of a locus, the pottery, as we shall see, provides an avenue
of correction. But in the meantime, it is impossible for him to wander
indecisively among walls and through layers until his stratigraphic
ideas become hopelessly confused.

The definition of locus used at Gezer has the advantage that everything excavated is immediately locked into a coherent three-dimensional
framework which is easily described and recorded; nothing is left
"floating" to be subsequently lost or ignored. Hence it becomes possible to demonstrate at the time of publication the exact stratigraphic
situation of everything excavated from architectural complex to individual artifact. Those who read the publications can use this information to test the synthetic conclusions of the excavators. Moreover,
the system has flexibility; no decision about a locus made in the field
is immutable. Mistakes can be corrected and loci redefined without
misplacing material and without disrupting the processing of material
which has already left the field under an old locus number, for pottery
and objects are tied permanently only to the pottery basket, not to the
locus. This important corrective relationship between the pottery basket and the locus will be developed in the next section, Section C.

A word should be said about the numbering system for loci used at
Gezer although the concept of locus proposed above is not tied to any
particular system of enumeration. The major sites around the mound at
Gezer were called "Fields" and were designated by Roman numerals. The
individual squares within each Field were called "Areas" and were numbered consecutively in Arabic numerals. The locus numbers within a
particular Area were formed by taking the number of the Area and multiplying by 1000. Thus the first locus number in Area 6 would be 6000,
the second would be 6001, etc. For Area 15, the first locus would be
15000, etc. If it should be necessary to discuss a locus from Area 3
of Field I in the same context as a locus from Area 3 of Field IV, the
Roman numeral of the Field can be prefixed for precision, e.g., Loc.
I.3056 and Loc. IV.3124. The same series of numbers was used for all
types of loci within an area, i.e., we did not have separate series of
numbers for walls as is the case in some recording systems. The next
locus to be identified was simply given the next available number.
Only one series of locus numbers was used for the complete excavation
of an Area, i.e., the locus numbers at the beginning of a new season
picked up exactly where the last season left off.

In order to encode some helpful information into the locus numbers,
we developed three numbering conventions. If, for example, a L.1054
was found to have more than one phase, the second phase was not given
the next available number but rather the same number as the first plus
the letter "A", i.e., 1054A. A third phase would be called 1054B.
Sometimes the addition of letters after a locus number signified that
the locus in question had in retrospect been subdivided into two. In

short, the addition of letters after locus numbers was a means of
gaining "space" between numbers wherever that seemed desirable; and the
individual letters A, B, C, etc. in and of themselves carried no consistent meaning. A second convention which we used added the letter
"P" which did carry a consistent meaning: if a whole or nearly whole
pottery vessel were found smashed on a surface, that pottery was
treated as a discrete locus in itself and was given a locus number
formed by adding "P" to the number of the surface on which the pottery
was found. Thus in studying the pottery later, one would know that a
vessel from L.5036P was found broken on Surface 5036. The third convention involved the addition of "point one" (.1) after a locus number,
e.g., L.5036.1. A number of this type was always assigned when a surface was being removed to designate the material in and 10 cm. under
the surface. This locus would contain therefore the material trampled
into an earthen surface or mixed with the plaster which made up the
surface plus the material in the make-up directly beneath the surface.
Again the purpose of this convention is to point the ceramicist to
those loci which can be expected to contain pottery important for fix-
ing the date of a phase or stratum. In short, three locus numbers of
the form 4032, 4032P, and 4032.1 would indicate a surface, the pottery
found smashed on that surface, and the material in and 10 cm. underneath that surface.

C. The relationship between pottery baskets and loci.

The pottery basket, once excavated, remains forever a unit. At the
time it is excavated it must be attributed to some locus although hind-
sight may decree that a bucket with its associated pottery and small
finds be shifted from one locus to another. Let us assume, for example, that an excavator does not detect a pit of late material in his
Area and mixes the pottery of the pit with that of an earlier layer.
At the daily reading of the pottery from his Area he will be alerted to
the fact that there is unexplained later pottery present. If the excavator returns to the field and discovers the pit, then the pottery basket dug in the area of the pit, containing the later sherds, will be
shifted into the locus of the pit after the season when the field
report for the season is being written. (A word to the wise: one
should never try to intercept a basket of pottery once it has left the
field and has entered the stream of processing for the purpose of correcting the locus number. The attempt will almost certainly result in
contradictory records for that basket. The basket should be processed
in its wrong locus and the correction made after the season when all
the records can be changed consistently. A simple note of the problem
in the field notebook will suffice for the moment.)

It has been noted that each pottery basket can belong to one and
only one locus and that even if the excavator is not clear about the
division between two layers, for example, he must nevertheless make a
decision and attribute the basket to one locus or the other. As a

general rule it is better in such cases of uncertainty to attribute the basket to what is stratigraphically the later locus since some earlier pottery mixed with a later locus will not seriously distort the dating, seeing that the locus will be dated by the latest pottery in it. Later pottery introduced mistakenly into an earlier locus, however, will throw the dating process off the track.

Although no pottery basket may belong to more than one locus, not every locus will produce a pottery basket, e.g., a dry-laid wall or sterile fill. Another group of loci, namely surfaces, produce no pottery by definition. If sherds are found on a surface, they belong to the locus which overlies the surface. If broken pots are found on a surface, they will go into a "P" locus. If sherds are found embedded in a surface, they will belong to the ".1" locus. The surface itself, in effect, is two-dimensional and never produces pottery. Although this is obviously an arbitrary definition, it worked well in practice.

There are several possibilities of correcting the relationship of baskets and loci after the season. Since the daily reading of the pottery of each pottery basket serves in the Gezer system as a check upon the stratigraphy, a bucket of pottery which was dug as part of one locus may have to be shifted to another. The example given in the third paragraph above is a case in point. This is not an arbitrary manhandling of the evidence as long as the stratigraphy is given equal weight with the pottery readings. This can be illustrated by developing the example just referred to a bit further. Let us suppose that in reading the pottery from what is assumed to be a consistent layer, some baskets begin to appear with unexplained later pottery. There are two possibilities: (1) There may be an undetected pit as presupposed in the example given above. If re-examination of the excavation area and careful analysis of the sections should confirm this hypothesis, then the baskets containing the intrusive late pottery will rightly be shifted from the layer locus to the pit locus. (2) The second possibility is that after re-examining the area of excavation, the possibility of a pit or later disturbance is ruled out. In that case, it becomes necessary to rethink the nature of the locus which produced the late pottery--it may be for example, a fill containing mostly early pottery but put in place at the time indicated by the later sherds. In this case the problem of the late pottery would not be solved by creating a new locus (the pit) since such a locus does not in fact exist. Rather the locus would remain intact as originally excavated, but the nature of the locus itself and its history of deposition would have to be rethought.

Loci can also be joined and simplified after the season. The most obvious case would be a wall or a surface which appeared at different places in the square without any clear connection but which later proved to be one and the same. In this case one of the locus numbers should be canceled and the pottery baskets shifted into the surviving locus. Sometimes in a situation where the stratification is unclear, the excavator will create loci which later are seen to be part of a larger whole when the situation is finally clarified. In this case, the original loci becomes meaningless since they do not represent the smallest unit of stratigraphic coherence, and they should be collapsed into a single larger locus and the pottery baskets reassigned accordingly.

II

THE FIELD NOTEBOOK

Field records at Gezer were kept in a three-hole looseleaf notebook using 8-1/2 x 11-inch paper. Each notebook contained the records of a single square or "Area" and the same notebook continued in use in that square as long as the square was excavated. The looseleaf arrangement permitted the addition of extra pages when required and the removal for safe keeping of unneeded portions as the seasons progressed. The obvious danger of a looseleaf notebook is that rough handling in the field can rip out pages. We found, however, that the danger was minimal if we took proper precautions. For note paper we used the heavyweight lined paper available in large stationery stores in which the holes are reinforced by a strip of plastic tape. For the top plans and the locus sheets we used German-made plastic hole reinforcers. The front and end sheets which take the worst beating can be further protected by a few blank sheets inside the covers.

The notebooks comprise three sections: (1) the daily note page, (2) the daily top plan, and (3) the locus sheets. The note page and the top plan are arranged facing each other in daily order at the front of the notebook, the note page or pages on the right and the top plan on the left (see Sample Pages 2 and 3 in Appendix). The locus sheets are ordered in numerical sequence at the end of the notebook (see Sample Pages 4 and 5).

The system was designed so that the same information is recorded in at least two places--usually in the notes and top plan or in the notes and locus sheets. If excavators were infallible and if archaeological work proceeded at a leisurely pace, this redundance would be unnecessary. But the forgetfulness and illegibility that inevitably result from a typically hectic day can play havoc with the recording process. The "double-entry" aspect of the Gezer system helps to assure that the information is correctly recorded in at least one place.

A. <u>The note page.</u>

The note page is a verbal description of the excavation of a single day arranged in simple chronological sequence (see Sample Page 3 below).

It is the first line of the recording process, the place where everything that is of archaeological importance should be recorded. It is
organized by the sequence of pottery baskets dug that day from that
square. It should contain the verbal description of the provenance of
each pottery basket; running comments and observations about exposed
loci; notation and description of any small object along with a verbal
description of its find-spot; the number and orientation of any photographs taken; a note of any features drawn by the architect on that
day; sketches of subsidiary balks, architectural details, or stratigraphic relationships; and comments, questions, and observations about
the on-going process, for example, the results of discussions with the
Director or Field Supervisor on matters of over-all stratigraphic
interpretation or phasing. In short, it is a diary of the day's excavation, the raw data which must be recorded as it occurs or which will
be forgotten. It should not attempt to be a final synthesis or a
finished statement; it should concentrate on accurate recording of
information from which a reliable synthesis can later be constructed.

B.   The top plan.

     The top plan is a schematic diagram of the area under excavation
viewed from above, drawn to scale on graph paper (see Sample Pages 1
and 2). The drawing scale can be determined by individual circumstances; at Gezer we tried to maintain the scale of 1:25 at which most of
our plans and sections were drawn in order to facilitate comparisons.
A new top plan is prepared for each day. It shows whatever architecture or other loci are visible in the area and any changes or removals
of those loci during the day. It shows the exact provenance of each
pottery basket dug that day, the find spots of any small objects,
restorable vessels, or other notable finds. It shows the reduced elevations of loci and especially of the tops of each basket of pottery,
particularly along the main sections. In addition it can be used to
illustrate any other information which lends itself to graphic repre-
sentation--the direction from which photographs were taken, stones
which must be removed before their possible architectural significance
can be determined, etc. It might appear that such a diagram would
become too confused by the end of the day to be of much value, but any
problem can be resolved by reference to the verbal description in the
note page if the note page is accurately maintained. Also since a
fresh top plan is begun each day, confusion rarely arises.

C.   The locus sheet.

     The locus sheet is a summary of information about each locus (see
Sample Pages 4 and 5). A supply of pre-printed sheets is kept at the
end of each field notebook; and as soon as a new locus is detected in
the excavation, the excavator gives it the next available number and
begins to fill out a blank locus sheet. As excavation of the locus

proceeds, the other sections of the sheet are filled in so that by the time the locus has been completely excavated, the locus sheets contain all the information necessary for a complete description of the locus. The following commentary on the numbered items of Sample Page 4 will clarify the function of the locus sheet.

1. <u>Locus No.</u> - This item and at least some brief notes in Item 2 are filled out immediately as soon as a new locus is detected. This prevents the assignment of the same number to two different features. As previously explained, each locus is numbered in the order in which it is discovered; there are no separate series for different kinds of loci. The only exceptions are those locus numbers which are followed by letters or by ".1". In those cases the locus sheets are inserted later as needed and grouped together following the main locus number. As previously explained, the series of locus numbers is different for each Area and at Gezer was formed by taking the number of the Area and multiplying by 1000 for the first number. Thus for an Area 8, the locus numbers would be 8000, 8001, 8002, etc.

2. <u>Initial description</u> - This will usually be a brief first impression, a verbal description to remind the excavator of the referent of the locus number.

3. <u>Top and bottom levels</u> - These are the reduced elevations of the top and bottom of the locus along with a reference to the daily top plan which shows where those levels are recorded. Since layers, surfaces, and walls tend to be uneven, there should be a double entry for both "top level" and "bottom level" i.e., the highest and lowest levels on the top of the locus (separated by a slash mark) and the same for the bottom. See Items 3a and 3b on Sample Page 4.

4. <u>Drawn by architect</u> - Here is written the date the locus was placed on the master architectural plans. This information will also be found in the notes, but it is important to have it on the locus sheet so that the excavator can see at a glance whether the locus has been recorded so that it may safely be removed.

5. <u>Photograph No.</u> - All black-and-white photographs taken by the staff photographer are numbered for identification. The number of each photograph in which the locus appears is recorded here along with the date (right hand blank). Again this information is critical when it comes time to decide whether the locus may be removed.

6. <u>Best sketch (top plan)</u> - The date of the top plan which bears the most accurate sketch by the excavator is filled in here. Not all loci can be drawn by the draftsman, and occasionally a locus which should have been drawn is removed prematurely. In these cases it is most useful to know which of the sketches in the top plans the Area Supervisor deems to be the most accurate one.

7. _Final summary description_ - The initial description is simply the first impression, useful for quick reference. The information in Item 7 is the final judgment as to the nature and description of the locus.

a. _General identification_ - Wall, surface, pit, fill, layer, destruction layer, _tabûn_, bin, burial, etc., etc.

b.1 and b.2. - The purpose of these items is apparent--to fix the locus in its proper stratigraphic relationship. In many cases, of course, it will take more than one locus number to fill the blanks.

b.3. _Its specific horizontal extent is_ - There is a natural tendency for excavators to concentrate on a locus at those points where it is clear and unambiguous and to avoid the question of its boundaries. For example, a beaten earth surface will be described in great detail as to its appearance, color, make-up, etc., but the question of the precise limits of that surface--and hence the problem of why the surface is found here but not there--will be slighted or ignored altogether. Getting Area Supervisors to struggle with this particular item of the locus sheet was difficult because the situation was often ambiguous. However, if some attempt is not made to decide these questions in the course of excavation when the locus can still be physically examined, the problem certainly will not be solved when all that remains is a written description.

b.4. _Its tip, slope, or lean is_ - This is a call for information about the horizontal or vertical orientation of a locus. "Tip" would apply to the direction from which a fill was put in place; "slope" would refer to differences in elevation of a surface, layer, drain, etc. and "lean" would refer to walls or other vertical structures. If a sufficient number of reduced elevations is recorded on the top plan, this information can be reconstructed from them; but the judgment of the excavator as he surveys the actual locus is also necessary.

c.1. _Composition, texture, etc._ - Of what is the locus made? If it is a layer, is it composed of destruction debris, field soil, tell debris, etc.? If it is a wall, is it stone or mudbrick? Are the stones undressed, hammer-dressed, ashlar? The manual which we provided to our Area Supervisors contained check lists (see below) to help the excavator ask the right kind of questions to fill in this and other parts of the locus sheet.

c.2. _Color_ - This applied mostly to surfaces and layers. Wherever possible we used the readings from the Munsell scale (_Munsell Soil Color Charts_ [Baltimore, Md.: Munsell Color Co., Inc., 1954]).

d. _Relationships_ - Excavators who have never had to write a synthesis of excavated material, putting it together into consistent strata and phases, tend to think atomistically in terms of individual loci. They often do a superb job of description of the individual locus but then fail to provide the crucial information necessary to put that locus into a proper stratigraphic relationship with its neighbors. If the locus impinges on a main section (Item 7.D.1), the vertical relationships are provided automatically. But if not, then there must be some verbal description or a sketch of a subsidiary balk in the notes. For an example of the problem, it is not unusual to find in the notes or locus sheets a detailed analysis of the color, texture, and contents of a pit, but no clear indication of the surface from which the pit was cut or mention of what subsequent layers or structures were disrupted by the pit. Two intersecting walls will be individually described in great detail, but the notes will not indicate whether they are bonded. A wall and a surface will be described, but one searches in vain to learn whether the surface lapped up against the bottom stones of the wall or ran under the stones. This problem can be avoided only if the excavator is thinking holistically. Since most Area Supervisors do not have responsibility for synthesis of the material, it will probably be necessary for those who do to keep a constant check on the notebooks to make sure that this information is being recorded.

    e. <u>Comments and interpretations</u> - This item is self evident.

There is one further problem in conjunction with Items 2-7 that needs consideration, but first let us quickly finish commenting on the remaining items of the locus sheet.

8-11. Since the daily reading of the pottery serves as a constant check on the excavation and stratigraphic analysis, it is necessary to keep an up-to-date list of all pottery baskets from a particular locus along with the field readings. This information is provided by Items 8-10 of the locus sheet with the necessary information arranged in vertical columns. The date on which a particular pottery basket is dug is listed in Column 8, the number of the basket in Column 9, and when the pottery is read, the field reading is listed in Column 10. If no pottery is dug from the locus on a certain day but the locus is mentioned in the notes, then that date is added to Column 8. Column 8 thus provides a complete index to all the pages of the notebook where information bearing on the locus can be located. If any small objects are found during the digging of a particular basket, that object with its number (obtained later from the object registry) is listed in Column 11.

Since some loci produce many baskets of pottery, the locus sheets were ruled on the back as well as the front, and the basket list if necessary was continued on the back.

For the locus sheet to fulfill its purpose, it must provide complete information about the locus. But in the heat and confusion of the typical day in the field the excavator can easily forget to ask all the questions pertinent to each type of locus, the answers to which are necessary for a complete description. In his excavation manual for the second phase of the work at Gezer Seger used the locus sheet described above as a "working description" but designed in addition five "final" locus description sheets covering the five most commonly encountered types of loci. The sheets provided blanks to be filled in to answer all the questions pertinent to that particular type of locus (J. D. Seger, Handbook for Field Operations [Jerusalem, HUCBAS, 1972], p. 27 and Appendix Items #3-8). In the first phase of the Gezer dig, we provided the Area Supervisors with check lists to help them remember what information to provide. They are repeated here with some slight adaptations:

I. Earth and debris layers.

    A. Levels marking top and bottom, in particular near the balks and in the center of the area.

    B. Physical description.

        1. Color -- the Munsel reading or as precise a verbal description as possible--light chocolate, light gray-tan, etc.

        2. Contents -- sand, wood ash, dung ash, charcoal chunks, burnt brick, chalk, clay, stones, etc. In describing the size of stones, some Area Supervisors used the terms "pebble, cobble, and boulder" as defined in the Wentworth scale (cf. F. H. Lahee, Field Geology [New York: McGraw Hill, 1961], pp. 38-39; reference courtesy of J. D. Seger). Others used terms such as grape-sized, fist-size, head-size, etc., which were probably sufficiently precise for our purposes.

    C. Amount of pottery in the dirt, especially if unusually small or great.

    D. State of sherds -- small bits, badly worn, normal size, very large pieces, etc.

    E. Extent -- Does it cover the entire area or does it lens out in one direction or the other? Does it occur only in the middle of the area without touching any of the balks?

    F. Relationships to other loci -- Under what and on top of what loci does it lie; what loci cut through it; does it run up against certain loci, etc.? Since layers are three-dimensional, the connections of the layers with adjacent loci must be recorded for all sides, not just top and bottom.

II. Walls.

A. Material -- stone, brick. Average size of bricks or stones.

B. Levels of top (several should be taken if the wall has any length or abrupt irregularities).

C. Founding levels -- levels underneath the lowest course of stones at two or three places along the length.

D. Number of courses high.

E. Dressing of stones -- unhewn, hammer-dressed, ashlar, etc.

F. Manner of laying -- mud mortar, dry-laid.

G. Additional features -- plaster facing, construction patterns, etc.

H. Any evidence of phases.

I. Relationships.

1. With what walls does it join?

2. Is it bonded to these walls or not? If not, is there evidence for which wall is later?

3. What surfaces were in use with the wall?

4. Does the wall stand on or cut through surfaces contemporary with it?

5. Does the wall have a foundation trench?

6. Are there noticeable differences in the founding level of the wall and other structures of the same phase?

7. Is it disturbed by other loci, pits, etc.?

III. Floors, surfaces.

A. Description of type -- beaten earth, plaster, flagstone, cobblestone, mixed.

B. Appearance -- uneven, sloping (in what direction?), broken, etc.

C. General description of residue found on the surface -- ashy places, bones, smashed pottery ("P" loci), objects, etc.

    D.   Levels at several places, in particular near the balks and in the center of the Area.

    E.   Extent of area where it is clearly discernible, shown either on a top plan or on a special sketch inserted after the locus sheet.

    F.   Phases, resurfacings, etc.

    G.   Relationships.

        1.   Up to what walls does it run?

        2.   By what pits, bins, walls, etc. is it cut?

        3.   Covered by what debris layers?

IV.   Pits.

    A.   Extent -- diameter and depth.

    B.   Description of contents -- loose earth, bones, ash, pottery, etc.

    C.   Nature of lining, if any.

    D.   Shape -- cylindrical, flask, rounded, etc. Illustrated by a sketch in section if necessary.

    E.   Relationships.

        1.   Dug from what level?

        2.   Sealed by what floor or layer?

        3.   Cuts through what loci?

V.   Foundation trenches.

Since a foundation trench is a specialized form of pit, the pit check list can be used for most of its features. It will always be related to a wall unless the wall has been robbed out.

VI.   Burials.

    A.   Dug from what surface?

    B.   Sealed by what locus?

C. Type of burial container -- stone-lined, sarcophagus, store-jar, etc.

D. Measurements of burial container.

E. Orientation of skeleton to points of compass.

F. Description of skeleton.

   1. Articulated or disarticulated.

   2. If disarticulated, what is arrangement of bones? Any bones missing?

   3. If articulated

     i. Is skeleton complete?

     ii. Position of skeleton -- on back, on side, flexed, etc.

     iii. Position of hands and feet.

G. Relation of grave goods (if any) to body _in situ_.

H. Complete description of grave goods.

VII. Other.

From the above check list one can infer what information would be necessary for the other types of loci common in Palestinian tells--hearths, _tabûns_, vats, bins, sumps, drains, etc. Any adequate description will include in addition to drawings and photographs:

A. A complete description of the physical appearance.
B. All relevant measurements.
C. Levels.
D. Relationships to other loci.

III

A TYPICAL DAY

In using the Gezer recording system, one should keep in mind that the purpose of the system is to ensure a clear, consistent, coherent, and logical description of the excavation process and results. The system is but a means to that end, and one should not become so fascinated by the details of the system that one loses sight of the goal of clear and logical recording. Since consistency results in clarity, the system should be followed wherever possible. But in ambiguous situations or where the system does not provide an easy way to handle a problem, the excavator must be prepared to exercise independent judgment and devise a solution that is compatible with the system as a whole and which results in clear and complete records.

The first step in any day's recording is the preparation of the top plan for the day. This must be done the night before so that time is not lost at the beginning of the day. The most efficient way to prepare the top plan is to take the former day's plan and trace the proper lines over a light box. Care must be exercised however, that repeated tracing, day after day, does not introduce a cummulative error.

It is not necessary that every stone in a top plan be accurate to the centimeter; that is the responsibility of the draftsman who draws the features for the master plans. However, the features should be placed with reasonable accuracy in the square in relation to the balks and to each other. A stone wall which is five stones long should show five stones on the top plan, and the drawings of the stones should bear enough resemblance to the original so that elevations taken on a particular stone will be accurately recorded on that stone and not mistakenly on its neighbor. Reasonable care should be taken in drawing a stone feature, a <u>tabûn</u>, etc. on at least one of the top plans on which it appears; thereafter this best drawing can be traced for subsequent plans.

Some of the most common drawing conventions used on top plans are the following: a reduced level taken by line level is located on the plan by an X: a reduced level taken by transit is marked by a circled X. An arrow with a curved tail points to the place on a wall where a founding level was taken (e.g., at the southwest end of Wall 5054 on Sample Page 1). If a pit was cut from the surface shown, the edge of the pit is shown by a solid line; if the pit was cut from a higher level and thus cuts through the surface shown, the edge of the pit is dotted (e.g., Pit 5031 at lower center of Sample Page 1). A plaster surface is represented by stippling (e.g., Surfaces 5070 and 5072 on Page 2). Locus numbers are enclosed in rectangles. The area excavated in each pottery basket is normally marked out by solid lines. If, however, the areas dug in subsequent baskets on the same day overlap in a confusing way on the top plan, other conventions can be used as outlines, e.g., small x's--xxxxxxxxxxx; small o's--ooooooooooo; alternate x's and o's--xoxoxoxoxox; dots and dashes--.-.-.-.-.-.-.-; etc.

On the day of our example, the top plan looked like Sample Page 1 at the beginning of the day. A complete phase had just been cleared, most of the architecture had been planned, the surveyor had taken transit levels throughout, and the area had been prepared for photography in the early morning when the light conditions are optimum. By the end of the day the top plan appeared as in Sample Page 2 which faces the note page for that day to which we now turn our attention (Sample Page 3).

The note page, as already mentioned, is simply a running commentary on the archaeological activity of the day, organized in chronological order. Since simple sequence of events determines the order of comments on the page, the excavator is freed from any concern to synthesize material or to find "the proper place" to make a comment. If all comments had to be made on locus sheets, for example, the supervisor would often be furiously thumbing from one sheet to another, probably misplacing or losing information in the process. The note page provides a place where any comment is appropriate; if need be, the comment can also be recorded on the proper locus sheet when opportunity presents itself.

The following commentary on the note page is organized in the form of footnotes to Sample Page 3:

[1] The top plan and the note page are dated at the top.

[2] As explained in the chapter on photography in this manual, the black-and-white negatives at Gezer were ordered in simple numerical sequence. In each photograph was placed a call board which bore this number and the number of the major locus shown in the photo. The Area Supervisor would be given the photo number by the photographer. The number of this photo should also be recorded on line 5 of the proper locus sheets. Not all photos were repeated in color (for slides); hence the notice.

In the case of critical photographs, the negatives were developed immediately to make sure that the picture was satisfactory before excavation resumed in the field. Normally, however, the photos would be printed during the day, mounted on stiff paper-board, and returned to the supervisor in the evening. The supervisor wrote any appropriate comment on the sheet and then added it to his notebook after that day's note page.

Photographs at Gezer were classified either as "publishable" or "record." (1) Publishable photographs were ordered in cases where the subject was certainly or possibly important for the final synthesis—coherent architectural horizons, important finds in situ, etc. Also in this category were items difficult or impossible to represent in other ways—details of construction, hard-to-describe structures, or installations, important relationships between loci, etc. Publishable shots were always carefully prepared for—the area cleaned, the best light conditions sought, etc.—and often repeated in color. (2) Record photographs were taken, for example, when something probably unimportant had to be removed before it was fully understood. In these cases the photograph would be taken quickly without special preparation or set-up.

How many photographs should one take? This is always a difficult problem if cameras and photographers--and money!--are limited. One develops a sense through experience about what will and will not be important to photograph, and there is probably no other way to learn it. It is difficult, however, to have too many photographs; and some Field Supervisors at Gezer carried their own black-and-white camera to supplement the work of the photographer.

[3]The draftsman had not finished drawing all of the architecture in the area and returned today to complete the job. The supervisor had recorded in the previous day's notes those loci which were drawn then. This information will be transferred to Line 4 of the appropriate locus sheets so that when the time comes to dismantle the loci in question, it can be seen at a glance whether they have been properly recorded. Care should be taken that the draftsman records not only the major architectural features of a phase but also the exact extent of surfaces, the perimeters of pits, etc.

[4]This is a basket number. The Roman numeral is the number of the Field, the middle number is the number of the Area within the Field, and the last number is the basket number within the Area. Together they form a unique combination that will not be duplicated anywhere else in the excavation in any season. All objects and pottery are tied to one and only one pottery number; hence, if the provenance of the pottery basket is accurately described, the provenance of the associated material is certain. Each pottery bucket bears a tag which carries this number along with other information in the following form: "G71, 7/25 (or 7/25/71), I.5.91, L.5063.1" which means "Gezer 1971, July 25, (1971), Basket I.5.91 taken from Locus 5063.1." (See the chapter on pottery for a sample pottery tag.) The tag is written with a felt pen (for legibility), always using the same color (for recognizability in the pottery washing and reading process). Pottery should never be collected in an untagged bucket, or even worse, in a random heap somewhere; the possibilities of confusion and contamination are too great. One practical hint: The first few minutes in the morning are always the most hectic of the day. Some time can be saved at that point by making up several pottery tags the night before. All that need be added in the field is the locus number.

The note page is organized by pottery baskets which are listed along the left side of the page with the body of notes and comments indented. A line or two is skipped between baskets. This layout makes for easy reference.

Each pottery basket must be listed on the appropriate locus sheet. When the basket number has been registered on the locus sheet, it is underlined e.g., Baskets I.5.91-95. The lack of underlining for

Baskets I.5.96-100 will remind the supervisor that he has not yet
recorded these baskets on the proper locus sheet.

[5]The first part of the entry for each pottery basket is an exact
verbal description of the provenance of the basket. First, or as soon
as practicable, is given the number of the locus being excavated. In
this case since a surface is being removed, it is a ".1" locus; 5063
is the number of the surface. To avoid ambiguity, features in the area
are referred to by their number e.g., Wall 5054, not just simply "the
wall."

The provenance of the basket is also represented diagramatically on
the top plan (at right on Sample Page 2). The basket number with locus
number underneath is written somewhere where excavation will not go on
that day--outside the diagram is best--with an arrow or arrows drawn to
the excavated area. Sometimes when the excavated area is irregular in
shape, only the top plan can give a clear idea of the provenance of the
basket.

Since this basket begins a new locus, the excavator must fill in
Items 1 and 2 on a new locus sheet. In this case, since the new locus
is a ".1" locus, the new locus sheet will be inserted following the
sheet for the surface, i.e., following L.5063 (see Sample Page 5). The
same, _mutatis mutandis_, will be done for L.5064.1. See Sample Page 4
for an example of a completed locus sheet.

One thing missing from this basket description that one would
normally expect whenever a new locus is begun is the levels for the top
of the new locus. But these were taken by transit on the previous day
and are already recorded on the top plan. See Item 3a on Sample Page
5.

[6]The supervisor notes that he has marked the line of Surface 5063
in the main balks with balk tags. The tags should be written with a
felt pen and placed before excavation begins. To wait until later is
to risk losing the line; some surfaces which are unmistakably clear out
in the Area have a curious way of vanishing utterly when viewed in section. Moreover, it is possible that what was called the surface was in
fact not the true surface which subsequent examination of the section
will prove to be higher or lower. In this case it will be necessary to
be able to identify those baskets which were dug as part of the wrong
locus. The supervisor also notes that he has "nailed" the balk. This
is a technique used by some excavators of driving small nails, the
heads of which have been painted some bright color, into the balk along
the line of demarcation between loci. This preserves the line without
taking the more permanent step of scratching the (supposed) line into
the balk. Once the line has been agreed upon and scratched, the nails
are pulled and reused.

[7]The letter "A" after 5012A indicates that there is also a L.5012
which may or may not be related to L.5012A. Usually, however, locus

numbers of this type indicate either that a feature has more than one phase or else that a locus has been subdivided for some reason. Perhaps Wall 5012A had an upper phase which has since been removed.

[8]Much excavation is probing, testing, or tracing with some theory or possibility in mind. Whenever this is the case, the purpose of digging here or there should be clearly stated and a report given later in the notes about what was found. Incidentally, the reason that the excavator approaches Wall 5012A allowing for the possibility of a foundation trench but digs right up to Wall 5054 is that Pit 5031 acts as a probe and gives him a look at the foundations of Wall 5054 which Pit 5031 has cut off. The excavator is able to see that Wall 5054 has no foundation trench and is laid directly on the surface.

[9]As just mentioned, a pit like Pit 5031 functions in the same way as an intentional probe, and examining the sides of a pit can give much information about what to expect in the next layer. We must assume that on some earlier note page the excavator has reported an examination of the sides of Pit 5031 in which he detected a horizontal separation about 25 cm. below the level of Surface 5063. However, he was not able to trace the line all the way around Pit 5031, and so he decides to cut a quick probe at the junction of Pit 5031 and the south balk all the way down to the level of the bottom of the pit to try to clarify the situation.

Note that this probe, even though it is to go down through all the debris between Surface 5064 and the bottom of Pit 5031 is attributed to L.5064.1. Some excavators would be inclined to create a special locus in this situation, a probe locus with its own number. There are several problems with the concept of the probe locus. (1) In the first place, the locus by definition should reflect some stratigraphic reality; it should not be an arbitrary creation. It is true that Basket I.5.93 will have pottery in it from much deeper than directly under the surface of L.5064. But since a locus is always dated by the latest pottery in it, it will not hurt the dating of L.5064.1 to have some earlier material thrown in. (2) A second objection to the probe locus is that it provides a too easy escape from stratigraphic difficulties. When the stratification is unclear, there is the temptation to create many such probe loci with the result that the evidence is broken into fragments which are stratigraphically unrelated, making overall synthesis all the more difficult. (3) Thirdly, since the probe locus is a man-made locus, it is difficult to relate to the genuine loci which surround it. A probe locus cannot be described in terms of the actual stratification but only in terms of the measurements, for example, "an area 1 meter by 50 cm., 75 cm. from the west balk and 60 cm. from the east balk." Such a description is stratigraphically meaningless in terms of the occupational history of the tell which must be told in terms of walls, surfaces, fills, destructions, etc. Or put another way, probe loci punch holes into the genuine loci which are difficult if not impossible to fill. Granted that there is always some loss in any probe, that loss can be minimized by combining the probe with the latest locus through which it cuts; to create a special probe locus is to aggravate the situation.

10
Small objects are placed in the small boxes provided in the supervisor's basket and labeled with the same information that was put on the tag of the pottery basket associated with it, i.e., in this case "G71, 7/25/71, I.5.92, L.5064.1." In addition some identifying phrase is added, e.g., "Astarte plaque." Since the plaque was found loose in the dirt, the original context was already disturbed. Hence no attempt was made to plot the find spot three-dimensionally. The pottery basket itself already provides a three-dimensional framework.

11
Having completed the removal of Surface 5064 and the make-up beneath it in Basket I.5.92, the excavator now begins a new locus, taking the next available number, 5068, and filling in at least Items 1 and 2 on a new locus sheet. In starting a new locus he must also start a new pottery basket since no basket can contain pottery belonging to more than one locus. Within a single locus, usually the only factor which controls the change of buckets is a practical one, viz., the need not to fill pottery buckets too full. Sometimes, however, if there is uncertainty about the boundaries of a locus, the pottery basket can be changed arbitrarily as a way of minimizing the mixing of loci.

Since one of the functions of the locus sheet is to act as an index to all the information about that locus, the date a locus is mentioned in the note page must be listed on the locus sheet even if no pottery baskets are dug from that locus that day. One way to make sure that the index of references is complete is to enclose the locus number on the note page in a box after the date of the note has been entered on the locus sheet. It will be important, for example, in drawing final conclusions about Wall 5054 to have the information which will be gleaned during this particular day's excavation. Note that the supervisor has thus far indexed his loci only through Basket I.5.93.

12
Another task that must always be performed when beginning a new locus is to take levels. If the transit is not available, quite accurate levels can be taken using a line level. In the corners of the Areas at regular meter or half-meter intervals are placed datum nails or pegs used as the horizontal base lines for the drawing of the sections. Tie a thin nylon cord to two or three of these datum nails where it can be rolled up and hung when not in use. When a level is needed, the line is stretched from the datum nail and a carpenter's line level is hung near one end or the other--not in the middle lest the bubble indicate the line is level when actually it is sagging symmetrically. Swing the leveled line over the spot to be measured, and using a retractable three-meter metal tape, measure the distance from the spot to the line (needless to say, this operation requires more than two hands). Care must be taken in this last step that the metal tape is absolutely vertical. In measuring down from the line, one can

let the metal tape-holder act as a plumb bob. In measuring up from the spot, the horizontal lines on the metal tape can be aligned with the leveled line. Sometimes the use of a plumb bob may be called for. Once the distance from the spot to the line is known, it is simply subtracted from the known value of the datum point; the result is the level of the spot. Let us use the levels taken at the beginning of Basket I.5.94 as examples. The datum nail in the corner of the area has been set at 225.00 m. above sea level. The measured distance down from the leveled line in the first case was 90 cm., in the other 88 cm. These two figures subtracted from 225.00 give 224.10 and 224.12, respectively. If a dig crew is well trained in the necessary steps, several line levels can be taken quickly with very little interruption of the digging.

The levels which result from the measurements should be marked on the top plan at the points where they were taken and recorded in the note page with some indication of the order--from south to north, from east to west, etc. Some supervisors simply numbered the levels throughout the day, keying a small circled number near the X to the same number in the notes. Without some such system, a written indication must be made on the top plan to indicate at what stage in the excavation those particular levels were taken, resulting in unnecessary clutter on the top plan.

[13]This comment illustrates the way that pottery baskets can be shifted from locus to locus. If the bucket has already left the square, no attempt should be made at this stage to effect the change. If an attempt is made now the supervisor will likely change the basket tag, be distracted, and forget to change the notebook. Or vice versa. It is much better to leave the situation alone and let the Field Supervisor make the changes systematically at the end of the season.

It is desirable, insofar as possible, to excavate one stratum completely before proceeding to the next. This is particularly important in the case of pits in order to prevent late pottery from the pit from being mixed with earlier strata. Pit 5031, therefore, had been removed as completely as possible when the stratum from which it was dug was cleared.

[14]As always in starting a new locus, the next available number is assigned, Items 1 and 2 are filled in on the next locus sheet, a new pottery basket is started, and levels are taken. Even though L.5068 and 5069 look alike and are probably stratigraphically the same, they are treated differently for the time being since the connection is not certain. If a sure connection is established later, it will be easy in writing the field report to collapse the two loci into one.

[15]As soon as it becomes necessary to make reference to the new locus, in this case the new-found plaster floor, it is assigned a locus number and a locus sheet is prepared.

[16]Here we see illustrated not points in recording but in organization and methodology. In the typical Area there are often two digging operations going on simultaneously, and the supervisor must oversee the work, do his recording, and keep the work under control and flowing smoothly. It is a sign of poor organization if, for example, a supervisor lets the work in his Area grind to a halt while he labors over his notebook. In this instance the supervisor has important information to record as a result of the excavation of Basket I.5.94. However, before he takes the time to note his observations, he sets up a new excavation project for his workers (Basket I.5.96); only then does he take time out to do his recording.

Secondly a point in excavation method: A plaster surface, L.5070, has been detected at the level of the separation previously seen in the east side of Pit 5031. This separation has now been confirmed to the northwest of Pit 5031. However, since the probe of Basket I.5.93 was inconclusive, the existence of this separation is not clear to the west and southwest of the pit. The supervisor notes: "Therefore we shall have to work out [on some future day of excavation] from our new surface 5070 toward the SW, trying to trace it." This illustrates a cardinal rule of excavation; whenever possible, move from the known to the unknown, from where something is clear to where it is unclear. This maximizes the chances of locating the cause of the anomaly and minimizes the chance of mixing loci, i.e., it increases control of the excavation process.

[17]Note that to indicate the area being excavated on the top plan by this new basket, all the supervisor has to do is to add the number 98 after I.5.93 since both the boundary of the area being excavated and the locus remain the same.

[18]This is the next available locus number.

[19]A good example of the value of subsidiary balks. In digging pits and trenches, the ancients, being no more energetic than we, would often dig down to the first hard surface and quit. In this case, they dug their foundation trench down to the level of Surface 5070 which discouraged them from going any deeper and founded their wall on Surface 5070. Without the subsidiary section A-B, it would appear that Wall 5012A was surface-built on Surface 5070 and that the two loci belong to the same phase. The section proves that Wall 5012A is in fact later and belongs with Surface 5064 and Wall 5054.

[20]The placement of section A-B is indicated on the top plan.

[21]The new surface will receive the next available number, 5072, so the restorable pottery found on the surface is L.5072P. The supervisor will write "Restore" on the pottery tag so that no sherds will be discarded until the <u>formatore</u> has gone over them.

[22]As in the case of L.5068 and 5069 (above, note 14), no conclusion is drawn about the equation of Surfaces 5070 and 5072. If they prove later to be one and the same, one locus or the other will be canceled.

[23]Unlike the Astarte plaque which was found loose in the dirt, the scarab was found in situ. Therefore the find-spot is plotted three-dimensionally.

[24]Conscientious supervisors often agonize in cases like this over whether this basket should--in this case--be assigned to L.5063.1, 5064.1 or to a new locus. It really makes little difference so long as the provenance is clearly described.

The stone removed is marked with cross-hatching on the top plan, thus avoiding any possible ambiguity.

[25]One can only sympathize with the exuberance of the excavator, for in the "real" archaeological world, too often surfaces that "ought" to connect refuse perversely to do so. Whether to retain two separate locus numbers for the surface or simply to cancel one of them at this point will be determined by common sense and the situation at hand. Any reasonable solution is permissible--here as elsewhere--so long as it is clear, logical, and fully explained.

ADDITIONAL NOTES: During the course of the day's work, the supervisor would have provided for the collection of samples of "material culture"--bones, flints, plaster samples, etc. In the case of bones, precise stratification is unnecessary, and a single bucket would have been used for each stratum for the entire day represented above. Other kinds of samples were collected in the same manner as small objects except that they were labeled "Material Culture."

In preparing the top plan for the next day, none of the basket information will be carried over. The area will be drawn as it appears at the end of this day with all exposed loci identified and their levels indicated. The beginning of the day is a good time to check to see that all needed levels have been taken before excavation continues.

If this day had been the last day in the season, the first basket of the next season would simply have the next number--I.5.101. And the locus list would likewise resume uninterrupted. One practical hint for "recording" the stopping place at the end of a season: Take two or three small squares of plastic, 15 by 15 cm. or so, and place them in the lowest levels in the area--the points where water will collect during the winter rains--and cover them with a layer of clean earth. The depth of silt that can sometimes accumulate at the bottom of an area over a single rainy season has to be seen to be believed, and this simple marker will save much uncertain searching for the first undisturbed locus at the beginning of the following season.

Appendix

SAMPLE NOTEBOOK PAGES

NOTES

Sample Page 1

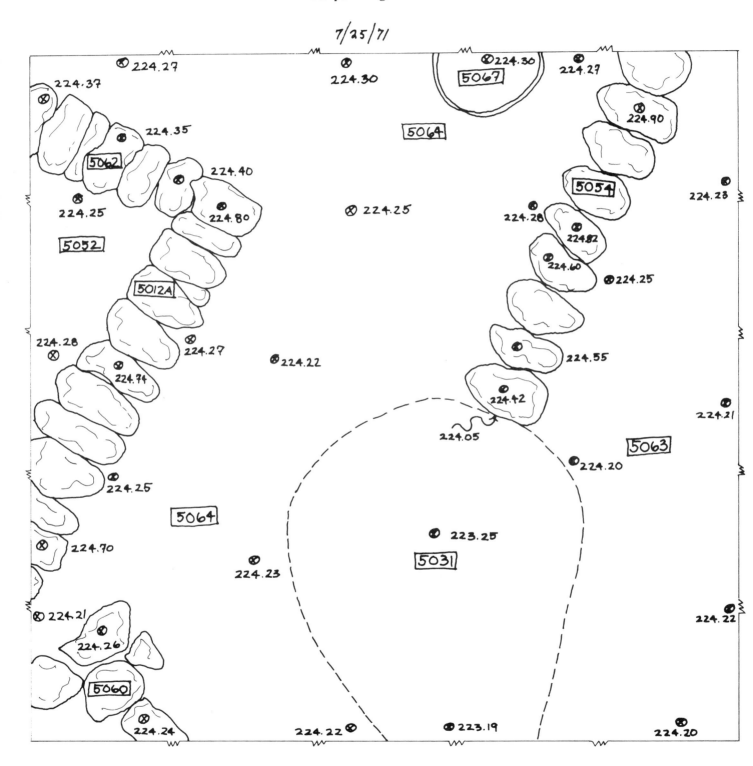

NOTES

Sample Page 2

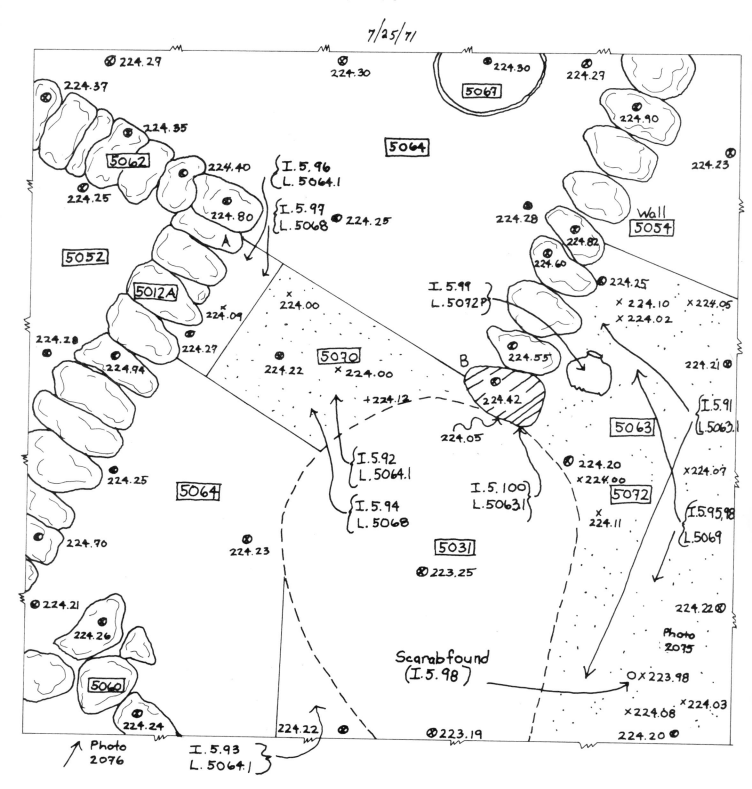

Sample Page 3

(See pp. 90-97 above for footnotes to the following)

7/25/71 [1]

Last - minute cleaning for photography

Photos taken:

No. 2075 -- View from S.E. corner toward N.W. Main locus is 5021A. (Also color shots.) [2]

No. 2076 -- View from S.W. toward N.E. Main locus is 5067 (Also color). Draftsman is finishing Walls 5012A & 5062. [3]

I. 5. 91 [4] -- L. 5063.1. Removing Surface 5063 in area bounded by Pit 5031, S. and E. balks, and line perpendicular to Wall 5054, from 1.5 m. N. of Pit 5031, running to E. balk. Down 10 cm. [5] Nailed and tagged L. 5063 in S. & E. balks. [6]

I. 5. 92 -- L. 5064.1. Removing Surface 5064 in a probe between Walls 5054 and 5012A, up to a line 25 cm. from Wall 5012A to allow for a possible foundation trench along Wall 5012A [7]; probe runs N.W. from Pit 5031, is 1 m. wide; down 10 cm. Purpose is to determine stratigraphic relationship between the two walls. [8] Material in both L. 5063.1 and 5064.1 is very dark, reddish-brown field clay, mixed with lime ash.

I. 5. 93 -- L. 5064.1. Cutting fast probe from Surface 5064 down to level of

(Sample Page 3, cont'd.)

bottom of Pit 5031 in area bounded by Pit 5031, S. balk, and a line 1.8 m. E. of W. balk. Nailed and tagged L. 5064 and 5031 in S. balk. Purpose of probe is to see if separation visible in E. side of Pit 5031 can be traced on W. side as well.[9] Top half of an Astarte plaque in I.5.92, in excellent condition.[10]

I.5.94 -- L. 5068.[11] Below L. 5064.1 in same area as I.5.92. Top levels at start of basket, from N. to S. = 224.10 and 224.12.[12] In digging I.5.93 we have found what looks like more pit material, so this basket may belong to L. 5031.[13]

I.5.95 -- L. 5069. Below L. 5063.1 in same area as I.5.91. Top levels at start of basket, taken from N. to S. = 224.10, 224.11, and 224.08. This material is very similar to L. 5068 -- bits of charcoal, soft crumbly light tan material, and bits of burned brick; looks like destruction debris. Probably L. 5068 and 5069 are the same.[14]

I.5.96 -- L. 5064.1. Removing skin left against Wall 5021A as precaution against possible foundation trench. This basket extends trench begun in I.5.92 up to Wall 5021A. Down 10 cm.

(Sample Page 3, cont'd.)

Under L. 5068 in area dug in I.5.94 we have found a substantial plaster surface, L. 5070, at 234.00. [15] There are signs of burning on the surface. This surface appears to be the separation line previously noticed on the E. side of Pit 5031 which we tried to trace around to the S. balk in probe cut in I.5.93. Along W. balk of this probe and in S. balk of Pit 5031 this separation is not clear. Therefore we shall have to work out from our new surface 5070 toward the S.W, trying to trace it. [16]

I.5.97 -- L. 5068. Below L. 5064.1 in same area as I.5.96. Level at beginning of basket = 234.09.

I.5.98 -- L. 5069. Continues I.5.95. [17] Beginning levels = 234.05, 234.07, and 234.03, N. to S. Now that the probe between Walls 5054 and 5012A has been completed and the balks scraped, it is clear that Wall 5012A is set into a foundation trench. The trench (L. 5071) [18] was back-filled with a dark earth mixed with white flecks, easily distinguishable from the lighter tan destruction debris of L. 5068. Thus baskets 96 and 97 certainly should be switched to L. 5071. The N.E. section (A-B on top plan) clearly shows that although Wall 5054 was laid on the surface and Wall 5012A was trench-built, both of them were in use with Surface 5064 and thus are contemporary. The subsurface course of stones of

(Sample Page 3, cont'd.)

Wall [5012A] rests on Surface [5070], but this is clearly coincidental.[19] Here is a sketch of section A-B:[20]

I.5.99 -- L. [5072P].[21] In area of I.5.98 we have found a plaster surface (L.[5072]) which covers the entire area exposed and appears to be the same as [5070].[22] L. [5072] is at the level of the previously-noted separation in the E. side of Pit [5031], i.e., 224.02, 224.00, and 223.98 from N. to S. in the area thus far exposed. On this plaster surface between Wall [5054] and the E. balk we found the top half of a broken storejar which we are removing in this basket. In cleaning the new surface, L. [5072], in I.5.98, we found a scarab right on the surface at a level of 223.98, 50 cm. from the S. balk and 73. cm. from the E. balk.[23]

I.5.100 -- L. [5063.1]. As a quick end-of-day project we are removing the end stone of Wall [5054] (cross-hatched) and going down to level of Surface [5072] in a probe to see if we can connect Surfaces [5070] and [5072].[24]

They connect. Hooray![25]

Sample Page 4

1. Locus No. _5031_

Initial Description:
(Of function and/or genesis)

Pit in S. central part of Area at juncture of walls [5024] *and* [5026]

Dates

3a. Top levels _225.01/224.98_ (Top-Plan) — _6/26/71_

3b. Bottom levels _223.25/223.19_ (Top-Plan) — _7/3/71_

4. Drawn by architect — _7/12/71_

5. Photograph No. _1982, 1983_ — _7/13/71_

6. Best Sketch (Top Plan) — _6/26/71_

---

7. **Final Summary Description:**

General Identification: *pit*

Dimensions
1. This locus is <u>below</u> Loc. _5011, 5017_
2. This locus is <u>above</u> Loc. _____
3. Its specific horizontal extent is:
   See top plan on 6/26/71
4. Its tip, slope, or lean is:
   The section dug through the pit on 6/27/71 showed that it had been filled all at once from the southeast.

C. Physical Properties:
1. Composition, Texture, *Destruction debris, partly-fired mudbrick, much pottery*
2. Color *Light tan to orange*

D. Relationships:
1. Touches Balk(s): *South*
2. Relationships to other loci: *Cuts from Surface 5030. Cuts through 5038, 5044, 5054, 5063, 5064, 5068, 5069*

E. Comments and Interpretations

Appears to have been filled in the clean-up after the destruction of Str. 5B. Similar pits found in Areas 15, 16.

Date of basket or mention in notes:	9. Basket:	10. Field reading:	11. Objects:
6/26/71			
6/27/71	I.5.35	LB II, 12th cent.	
6/27/71	I.5.37	12th cent. homog.	Zoomorphic Head No. 10.23
6/27/71	I.5.38	12th cent., few earlier	
6/30/71	I.5.42	12th cent. homog.	
6/30/71	I.5.44	1 LB IIB, mostly 12th cent.	
7/3/71			

Sample Page 5

1. Locus No. **5063.1**

2. Initial Description:
   (Of function and/or genesis)

Makeup in and 10 cm. under surface 5063

Dates

3a. Top levels **224.25 /224.20** (Top-Plan)   **7/24/71**

3b. Bottom
    levels _____ (Top-Plan)   _____

4. Drawn by architect   _____

5. Photograph No. _____   _____

6. Best Sketch (Top Plan)   _____

7. Final Summary Description:

A. General Identification:

    Pit

B. Dimensions
   1. This locus is <u>below</u> Loc. **5063**
   2. This locus is <u>above</u> Loc. **5069**

   3. Its specific horizontal extent is:

   4. Its tip, slope, or lean is:

C. Physical Properties:
   1. Composition, Texture,

   2. Color

D. Relationships:
   1. Touches Balk(s):
      S. and E.
   2. Relationships to other
      loci:

E. Comments and Interpretations

Date of basket 8. or mention in notes:	9. Basket:	10. Field reading:	11. Objects:
7/25/71	I.5.91		
7/25/71	I.5.100		

Chapter V

THE POTTERY RECORDING SYSTEM

Joe D. Seger

"All serious students of archaeology, anthropology, and related fields appreciate the necessity of giving extravagant attention to the humble potsherd."

Despite a growing number of scientific advances in methods of chronological determination, ceramic analysis continues to provide the only reliable backbone for historical reconstruction in a wide sphere. Accordingly, almost all organized excavations give close attention to the means of handling and controlling the ceramic materials that are recovered. Given this situation, it may seem redundant to say that processes of pottery handling and treatment hold a place of special importance at Gezer. The point needs emphasis, however, because these processes do play an unusually significant role in shaping Gezer field techniques. It is no overstatement to say that it is impossible to have any clear understanding of Gezer methodology or to be able to appreciate the detail of its digging and recording system apart from the rationale provided by the serious respect for cultural and chronological data pottery affords.

Growing out of the American traditions of ceramic study and analysis established by W. F. Albright, G. E. Wright, and Nelson Glueck, it was only natural that pottery was given a special emphasis in the development of the methods used at Gezer. From the start of the project, this emphasis was shaped by two basic interests. The first of these involved the desire to continue the processes of refining and elaborating the chronological index of reliable ceramic types pioneered by Albright and his followers.[1] The second was the intention to utilize this developing index as a practical guide within the process of excavation itself.[2] The effectiveness of the Gezer methodology in achieving these objectives can of course be proven only by the published reports of the materials excavated. It is not our purpose here to do any special pleading, but rather to describe the actual processes employed at Gezer in the handling and recording of ceramic materials and to trace procedures through from excavation to publication. Thus, both the advantages and the limitations of this aspect of our work will be documented.

I

POTTERY HANDLING IN THE EXCAVATION PROCESS

A. Collecting Pottery in the Field.

Care in controlling ceramic materials must begin with the excavation process. Within the digging and recording system used at Gezer, the basic control unit is the "pottery basket." This term refers to more than simply a collection of pot sherds. It represents an

archaeological unit or dirt section discretely excavated and specifically located in three-dimensional terms within the recording grid. In
this sense it is a "mini-locus." However, unlike the locus proper,
which under review may be added to or combined with other loci, the
pottery basket unit remains unchanged. From the moment its excavation
is completed, its dimensions and character are fixed. It is the least
common denominator within the recording system; and accordingly, it is
with reference to the pottery basket that all pottery and small finds
are registered.

The basic numbering system used for Gezer work is tripartite in
nature. It includes a Field reference in Roman numerals, and Area and
basket notations in Arabic numbers: for example, VII.14.34 (Field VII,
Area 14, Basket 34). Basket numbers are assigned in sequence within
each Area. Together, the three numbers provide a discrete notation
which will not be repeated or used again within the recording system.
When completed, the identifying pottery tag also includes notations
indicating the date on which the excavation of the basket took place,
as well as the number of the larger locus unit to which it was initially assigned.[3] Thus, notations such as G72 (Gezer 1972), 7/18/72
(July 18, 1972), and Loc. 14003 also always appear on the tags (Fig.
1).[4]

As is perhaps obvious, this system requires that great care be
taken to protect the integrity of the basket unit. Techniques employed
to effect basket (and locus) control in the digging process have been
discussed in a previous chapter (see Chapter I above).[5] In the collection of the pottery itself, control is facilitated by the use of plastic buckets or pails. Into these receptacles only the sherds and
vessels from the specified sections are placed, each bucket being
tagged according to the system already described. To guard the buckets
against contamination or mixing, some simple rules have been found
effective. For example, a bucket is never used untagged.[6] It must
always be marked before sherds are collected in it. Nor are sherds to
be collected in miscellaneous piles around the digging area. Obser-
vance of these simple conventions helps to prevent possible confusion
with respect to the original provenance of materials, i.e., they are
always moved from the section being excavated directly to the basket
tagged for that section. Sherds for which the specific provenance is
not known beyond question are discarded. Moreover, no bucket is ever
filled more than half full. This helps avert possible spilling and
provides a more manageable unit for further processing. Finally, a
finished bucket is always placed well away from the area of digging so
that "foreign" sherds cannot be added to it inadvertently.

In special circumstances, some modifications and additions to this
otherwise routine process are required. There are a number of instances where pottery recovered may need special treatment. These include:

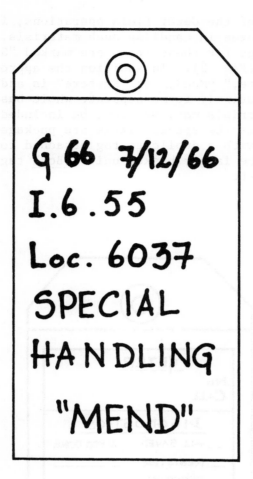

Figure 1.   Sample pottery tag.

1.   Instances where delicate or fragile materials are involved, as
     e.g., pointed ware, pottery not fully baked, etc.   In this
     case the word "Delicate" can be added to the tag.

2.   Instances where sherds from individual mendable vessels are
     involved, the pieces of which should be kept together.   Add
     "Mend" to the tag.

3.   Instances where sherds from whole basket or locus units are
     involved, all of which should be checked for large scale res-
     toration.   Add "Restore."

During Phase II of the Gezer field operations, it was found useful to regularize procedures in handling such materials.[7] To accommodate this, the pottery tags for these items are marked "SPECIAL HANDLING" in large block letters (Fig. 2). In addition the appropriate notation, i.e., either "Delicate," "Mend," or "Restore" is added to the tag. "Restore" pottery routinely forms separate whole basket units. "Delicate" and "Mend" materials may, however, be included within a normal basket. In such cases the special items are packaged separately (in a plastic bag or box) with a duplicate tag attached to identify them clearly as part of the larger basket unit. Both tags are marked "SPECIAL HANDLING," etc.

Figure 2. Field-reading tag.

B. Handling Pottery in the Camp.

1. Pottery Washing

Completed baskets (buckets) of pottery are subsequently removed
from the field and delivered to the custody of the Pottery Registrar in
camp. The received buckets are grouped according to Fields and Areas.
"SPECIAL HANDLING" materials are separated to receive required special
treatment. At Gezer, the nature of the mound's tenacious soil requires
that all materials be "pre-soaked" before washing and further handling.
The use of plastic buckets for collecting pottery facilitates this step
and eliminates the need for rehandling.

After the pottery has soaked (at least two to three hours) it is
washed and set out to dry. Care is taken throughout to keep the basket
units absolutely separate. Washing procedures have undergone a number
of changes through the several excavation seasons. During the summer
of 1972, with the first season of Phase II work, the following steps
were involved:

a. Pottery was removed piece by piece from the soaked buckets and,
before washing, was carefully scrutinized for signs of paint, special
decoration, or writing.[8]

b. Sherds were then washed and placed in perforated plastic (shop-
ping) baskets. The original pottery tag was transferred to this
basket.

c. A second tag, designated the pottery "field-reading tag," was
prepared (Fig. 2). This involved the use of a special rubber stamp to
imprint the field reading form on the tag, then entering the basket
number, date, etc., as required.

d. The pottery was finally set out to dry in the plastic baskets,
accompanied by both the original pottery tag and the field-reading tag.
Field and Area groupings of materials were maintained throughout this
process.

This procedure proved satisfactory. As opposed to the previously
used method of spreading sherds to dry on straw mats, the use of shop-
ping baskets served to eliminate several steps in the handling of
materials (i.e., laying sherds out on mats, collecting them again,
etc.) and also eliminated the danger of mixing materials on the mats.
Moreover, use of these baskets enabled the earlier release of the pottery collection buckets for use in the field.

2. Reading the Pottery

At the heart of the field methodology employed at Gezer is the
routine daily analysis of pottery baskets. This process is intended

to provide a close watch on the progress of excavation in the several Fields and Areas, and to give a cross-check on stratigraphic developments. Not infrequently, this procedure warns of stratigraphic disturbances and intrusions (such as pits, etc.) and/or transitions into new chronological horizons. Such information enables the Area Supervisor to plan his excavation strategy more wisely and to control and record more deliberately what he digs. This regular feed-back is one of the most important regulating elements in the Gezer excavation system.[9] In the pottery shed, the daily routine runs as follows. (Again, Phase II procedures are represented, these being the latest adaptation of the basic technique.)

The analysis or "reading" proceeds on a regular schedule set by the Director. In addition to an expert in ceramic chronology, a reading session always involves either the Field Supervisor or the Area Supervisor responsible for the excavation of the pottery being reviewed. Ideally, both of these persons should be present to provide up-to-the-minute knowledge of excavation progress and to specify the precise provenance of each basket of pottery.

The pottery is spread, basket by basket, on a low table where it can be readily studied and sorted. Observations are made both of the "diagnostic" sherds (rims, handles, bases, painted or decorated wares, etc.) which provide clues to forms and types, as well as of the wares (the pottery fabric and color). Based on this study, a "call" or "reading" is given, indicating the period or range of periods represented by the pottery in the basket. This "call" is recorded in four places.

a. In the pottery field register. Pottery field-registration books are prepared for each Field and Area. Entries include the basket number, date of excavation, and the locus number, as well as the notations indicating the reading or "call" (Fig. 3).

b. On the locus sheets in the field notebook.

c. On the original pottery basket tag (Fig. 1).

d. On the field-reading tag (Fig. 2).

A kind of "short-hand" has been developed at Gezer over the years for recording pottery calls. The basic conventions used in this regard are outlined in Appendix A, "Gezer Pottery-Reading Notations."

After the "call" has been given and is properly recorded, the pottery is next sorted for "save" or "discard." This is done according to the possibilities of the materials for further study and publication. The normal practice has been to save generous samples from all stratigraphically controlled situations, but to discard materials from surface locations, dumps, etc.[10] Usually, all _diagnostic_ materials are

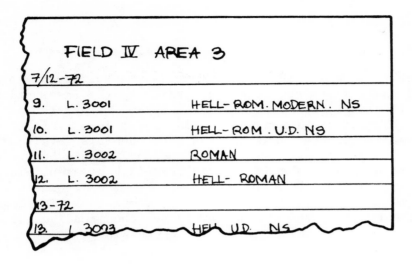

Figure 3. Pottery field register, sample page.

saved from especially significant locations, along with a generous
representative sample of the ware types. In some instances, e.g.,
where baskets are marked for restoration, all materials are saved. The
decision as to what is being saved is noted on the field-reading tag.
At the same time, this tag is marked to indicate what further steps are
required in processing the materials (registering and describing the
pottery, etc.; see below). The saved pottery is then bagged and boxed
as follows:[11]

    a. Baskets with only diagnostic sherds saved are put in a plastic
bag with the original pottery tag inside and the field-reading tag tied
to the outside. The bags are then boxed by Field, Area, and basket
number sequence, with markings on the outside of the boxes to indicate
contents.[12]

    b. Baskets with both diagnostic and body sherds saved are bagged
as follows: The body sherds are first bagged with the original tag
tied to the outside. Then this bag, along with the diagnostic sherds,
is put in a second bag, with the field-reading tag tied on the outside
of it. This bag is then boxed in sequence with other bags.

    c. Baskets marked "Restore" are bagged with both tags inside and then boxed individually with basket information marked on the outside of the box.

3. Pottery Registration

Subsequently, on a schedule worked out by the Pottery Registrar, the completed baskets are registered according to the instructions on the field-reading tag. The sherds in each basket (bag) are individually marked with registration numbers using India ink. References include season, Field, Area, basket, and sherd numbers (e.g., G72 VII. 1.3.1).[13] Sherd numbers are assigned in sequence within basket units. When marking is finished, sherds are replaced in bags as originally packed; and the "Date Done" is entered on the (outer) field-reading tag. This signals that registration work is completed. The bags are replaced in their boxes, and the materials are thus readied for movement to storage pending further study and processing.

II

THE PREPARATION OF CERAMIC MATERIALS FOR PUBLICATION

Gezer materials have all been kept in local storage in Jerusalem. A modest publication staff has been assembled to work in preparing materials for publication. A large part of the work of this staff involves the further processing (restoring, drawing, describing, etc.) of the saved pottery.[14] In what follows, the procedures and conventions adopted for this work are reviewed.

A. Pottery Restoration.

The first step in preparing saved pottery for publication involves the task of mending and restoring broken materials. As indicated, Gezer materials requiring this kind of attention have already been clearly identified in the field. At this stage mendable vessels are submitted for repair. Similarly, "Restore" loci are spread out and studied, and the repairable items are sorted out.[15] Such "pot-mending" requires considerable understanding of ceramic fabrics and types as well as technical competence. Accordingly, the Gezer Publication Staff has for some time included a professional formatore.[16] For this work, a modest laboratory has been developed at the Hebrew Union College (Plate I).[17]

It is not necessary to describe here the many technical processes and skills involved in this work, nor can the writer claim competence to do them justice. Suffice it to say that it involves more than

Plate I. Formatore's workshop; Phase II Director Seger and staff member
Seymour Gitin reviewing reconstructed materials. Photograph:
Zev Radovan.

simply gluing pieces of pottery together! It is important to observe
that the desired objectives of this (fairly expensive) work must be
carefully considered. For example, unless materials are being prepared
for display purposes, total reconstruction is not always necessary.
Except in cases where complete restorable vessels are clearly in hand,
reconstruction work on Gezer materials has normally involved repair
only to the extent that a complete (or as complete as possible) profile
can be constructed. From this, by geometric projection, the pottery
drawer can render the full form on paper. The use of supplementary
plaster is not employed extensively to recreate full forms but is used
where additional support is needed to stabilize the form reconstructed

117

from the original sherds. It has, in fact, been found to be of advantage at times for the drawer to have some remnant holes at strategic
points, especially in larger and/or closed vessels. These facilitate
the accurate measurement of ware thickness and other details.

B. Pottery Drawing.

Restored vessels and sherd materials selected for eventual publication are next submitted to the cartographic staff for drawing.
Again, a modest facility has been developed at Hebrew Union College
for this work. All Gezer materials are normally drawn at a 2:5 scale,
in preparation for one-half reduction to 1:5 in publication.[18] Drawing to this scale is aided by the use of a special drawing set-up originally developed by the Israel Museum (Plate II). It consists of a low

Plate II. Pottery drawing set-up; cartographer Yvonne Levy at work.
          Photograph: Zev Radovan.

metal stand with two movable upright measuring poles. These poles are calibrated at a special scale with segments equal to 2:5 centimeters (a "short-inch"). They are used in conjunction with special narrow metal rulers marked with a similar calibration. These measures provide for easy reduction to a 2:5 scale, by converting one "short-inch" on the uprights and rulers to one centimeter on the drawing paper. The drawing technique involves finding the correct stance of the sherd or vessel by aligning a rim or base section on a hard flat surface, and then establishing the vessel's diameter by use of a pattern board with measured concentric circles. The piece of pottery is then fixed with modeling clay in the set-up, on its correct stance, and is drawn in pencil on millimeter paper. The drawing is prepared according to a set of conventions established for Gezer publications work. These are described in Appendix B, "Gezer Drawing Conventions."[19]

When the basic drawing is completed the piece of pottery is marked with a red dot near the registration number, giving a convenient indication that it has been drawn. The registration number and the initials of the drawer are added to the drawing for identification, then both the drawing and the pot or sherd are passed on to be described and filed.

C. Pottery Description.

Describing pottery is one of the most problematic tasks faced by an archaeologist. It not only involves assumptions with respect to the complex technology of pottery making, but at the same time encroaches on the unsettled province of the ceramic typologist. Neither of these is a very accommodating sphere! In spite of the excellent work of Anna O. Shepard (or perhaps because of it!) there have not been established any generally accepted descriptive conventions for ceramic materials.[20] Each archaeologist or archaeological team still approaches the task of describing materials with relative independence. Little wonder that in Palestinian work "form" (a relatively more objective category) remains the principal basis for comparative study. Yet even here problems of nomenclature are all too pervasive, and a great deal of clearly subjective analysis exists.[21] In recognition of the complexities involved, the Gezer program for describing pottery evolved as something of a "middle-of-the-road" approach. The system used aims to be as purely descriptive as possible, but within fairly general categories and with carefully circumscribed intentions. The "Description Code" we employed is outlined in Appendix C.[22] A few supplementary notes are required, however, to underscore and elucidate some sections.

Section A. Form. The categories used are purposely broad. No final or rigid typology of materials is intended. Considerable training and advanced study are required to classify pottery within meaningful groups and traditions. This is left to the specialist(s) who will ultimately study the materials in detail. The aim at this juncture is simply to provide _functional_ groupings of materials according to generally predominant types.

Section B. _Technique_. Here a minimal basic listing is provided, but the system is open to additions.

Section C. _Ware_. Attempts to describe ware types without the aid of specialized, technical skills and equipment (such as a high-powered microscope and/or facilities for petrographic analysis, etc.) suffer severe disadvantage from the perspective of pure objective science. Special groups of Gezer materials are being subjected to such refined and specialized analysis by geologist Reuben Bullard. However, the bulk of the saved ceramic materials, of economic necessity, must be described without such aids. This implies distinct limitations which need to be acknowledged. Nonetheless, within certain boundaries a good measure of objectivity can be claimed for the processes and conventions used to describe Gezer materials. For example, the Munsell soil color code[23] is routinely employed for color description, as are standardized size and frequency measures for describing inclusions. On the other hand, there are obvious difficulties in classifying inclusions without the aid of specialized equipment, etc. While it can be noted that the five categories used do represent predominant types of grits found in ancient pottery, these types clearly _do_ _not_ exhaust the list of possibilities. They are employed precisely because they can be readily identified by the naked eye, or by the use of a hand magnifying glass. The classifications imply no more than that the materials appear, as presently seen, to be sand, limestone, etc. (Of course under more technical scrutiny they may prove to be something very different.) Similarly, these categories do not intend to imply anything about the nature or type of the materials originally used in constructing the pre-fired pottery. It is obvious that sometimes elements undergo radical changes in the course of the firing process. However, the analysis of such changes again lies in the province of the technical specialist.

Similar limitations must also be acknowledged for the conventions employed in describing the "firing" of wares. Without specialized study, details of firing technique (i.e., temperatures achieved in the kiln, baking speed, atmospheric context--whether oxidizing or under-reduction, etc.) can likewise only be approximated. Accordingly, the conventions for "firing" intend only to describe the resultant appearance of the pottery fabric, noting whether and to what extent carbon elements remain in the sherd section. Questions as to how the observed effect was in fact achieved are left for the technical analyst.

Finally the categories from "soft" to "metallic" used for measuring hardness are also somewhat general. However, as noted by Shepard, hardness is of limited value as a criterion of classification. Within types, materials will generally show a broad variation, while many types of groups display very similar ranges of hardness.[24] In any case the majority of materials fall into the "hard" category (4-6 on the Moh scale).[25] The "soft" and "metallic" materials represent the exceptional items which can usually be recognized without specialized testing.

The actual process of describing materials proceeds as follows. When the drawing is completed, the sherd and its drawing are passed on to be described. A punch card is prepared with the scale drawing attached as shown in Fig. 4. In the upper right hand corner of the card, the pottery field registration number is entered. Using a special rubber stamp, a form outlining the descriptive categories is imprinted on the card in a convenient place. This will usually be on the card's face; but depending on the size of the drawing, it may also be put on the reverse side. Next, the sherd is prepared so that a clear, fresh section of the pottery fabric may be seen. Where necessary, this may involve chipping or cutting off a corner or edge of the sherd with pliers. With whole vessels this step is eliminated, and only the ware surface is described. The description process proceeds using a Munsell Soil Color Chart, magnifying glass, millimetric calipers, and frequency charts as required. When this is finished, the drawing and description are given a final check, and the sherd is returned to its place in storage. The card is passed on to be punched and filed pending further selection for inking and publication.

D. The Filing System.

The descriptive conventions for Gezer ceramic materials were prepared for use in conjunction with a punch card system for filing and retrieval. The system is of a "hand-sort" type using a standard 8 by 5 inch (approximately 12 x 21 cm.) card (Fig. 4). Using the number banks (i.e., the units of 1 2 4 7 around the outer edge of the card) the categories of information are punch-coded either by direct numerical reference or by using a number reference key.[26] In general the verbal descriptions, especially for ware color, temper, and surface treatment, offer more detail than can be conveniently coded. However, the attempt has been made to code and record as much basic data as possible and to do this in such a way that it will assist in the recall of all stored information for further analysis.[27] As with other such punch card systems, the sorting is done with a thin metal rod or needle. This is inserted into a selected hole allowing the punched items to drop away for further sorting or reference.[28] Inasmuch as work in preparing these materials and files is still in progress, many of the anticipated advantages of this system remain untested. It should, however, provide an excellent permanent resource, useful not only in facilitating initial publication, but also in providing a significant resource for subsequent comparative research and study.

121

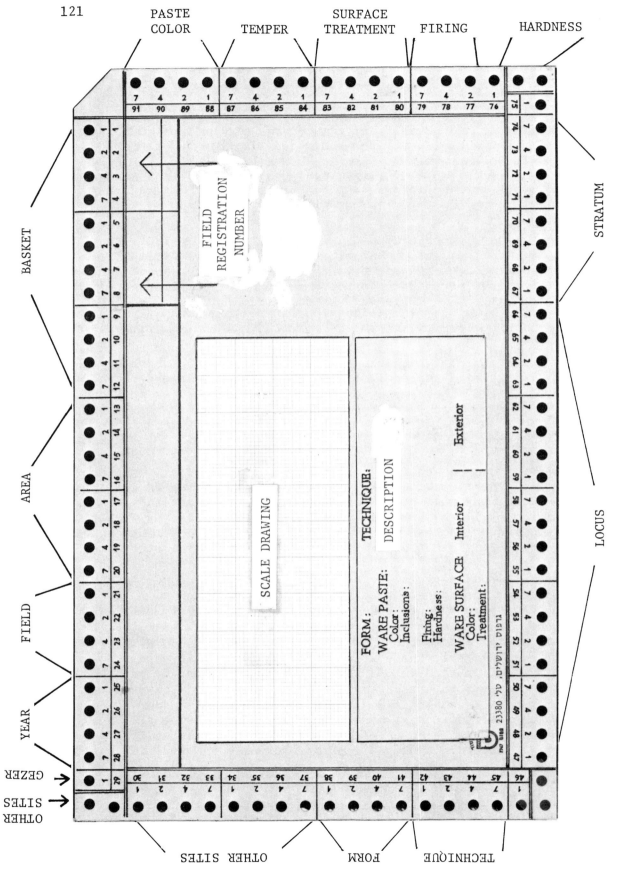

Figure 4. File card Reference Master.

E. Preparation for Publication.

At the appropriate time, selected materials are taken through the final steps in preparation for publication. This involves the process of inking the drawings and of laying them out on plates according to significant basket or locus groupings. As noted previously, Gezer materials are planned to be reduced one half in publication, i.e., normally to a scale of 1:5. The format adopted for use in report volumes is illustrated on Plates 26-35 in Gezer I, the first of such reports to be published.[29]

With publication, the processes of pottery handling are completed. As in all scientific enterprises, the final test of the systems and methods used for data recovery and processing lies in the accurate transmission of those data to the wider scientific public. We can only hope that the Gezer program for handling ceramic materials, as here outlined, will result in this kind of positive contribution to archaeological scholarship.

NOTES

1. Cf. W. F. Albright, The Excavation of Tell Beit Mirsim, Vols. I, Ia, II, III ("Annuals of the American Schools of Oriental Research," Vols. XII, XIII, XVII, XXI-XXII; New Haven: ASOR, 1932, 1933, 1938, 1943); G. E. Wright, Pottery of Palestine from the Earliest Times to the End of the Early Bronze Age (New Haven: ASOR, 1937); P. W. Lapp, Palestinian Ceramic Chronology (New Haven: ASOR, 1961). It is also worth note that no less than four of the original members of the Gezer Core Staff, (Cole, Dever, Holladay, and Seger) earned doctorates based on specialized research in aspects of Palestinian ceramic chronology and are now in the process of preparing their materials for publication.

2. This technique had already received favorable test in the course of the Drew-McCormick Excavations at Tell Balatah (Shechem) directed by Dr. G. E. Wright. Several members of the Gezer Core Staff received training as members of the junior staff of these excavations in the early 1960's. A considerable debt is to be acknowledged to the senior staff at Shechem for the experience and insight gained through this work.

3. Felt tipped "Magic Markers" were very successfully used at Gezer for preparing pottery tags in the field. Not only do these pens provide bold and easily read notations, but the use of different colors in the several Fields and Areas served to facilitate quick identification and easy arrangement of baskets for further processing. Care must be taken, however, to use quality pens with waterproof marking ink.

4. Credit for the preparation of the drawings for this chapter belongs to Miss Susan Moddel of the Gezer Publications Staff.

5. Chapter I above. See also H. D. Lance, Excavation Manual for Area Supervisors (Jerusalem: HUCBAS, 1967), pp. 5ff. This work provides the original basic statement on Gezer field methods.

6. It has likewise been found advisable not to reuse old tags. Multiple markings on a single tag, even where original numbers have been heavily crossed out, only lead to confusion.

7. See J. D. Seger, Handbook for Field Operations (Jerusalem, HUCBAS, 1972), pp. 36ff. Following the 1971 season, the members of the original (Phase I) Core Staff retired from active participation in the field. Phase II of the field work was initiated in 1972 under the writer's direction and with a new Core Staff.

8. This introduced a Gezer modification of the "sherd-dipping" process espoused by Dr. Y. Aharoni and others. As with Aharoni's work, the process was successful in helping to spot several possible epigraphs, as well as numerous jar handle stamps and other special materials.

9. As previously noted, this technique was first developed in a deliberate way during the Shechem excavation under G. E. Wright.

10. A broad estimate would indicate that approximately 60% of excavated pottery at Gezer has been saved. Some of our American colleagues, e.g., in the excavations at Tell el-Hesi and at Idalion on Cyprus, now save all excavated sherds. This would seem at first to be a most commendable procedure; and if significant additional data can be gleaned from this technique, it should be emulated. However, to date, this advantage has not been demonstrated. Inasmuch as the samples obtained by excavation are at best random, the additional time and expense involved in the handling, storage, and processing of the extra volume will require further justification before this approach will receive wide acceptance.

11. The system for storing pottery described here differs from that used in Phase I work at Gezer. Prior to the 1972 season each basket unit was stored in an individual cardboard box, 10 by 18 by 18 or 10 by 18 by 36 cm. in size. Registration information was marked on the face of these boxes and the pottery tag was placed inside with the sherds. This system had the advantage of providing for easy packaging and filing in storage. However, with the accumulation of several years, the volume of materials began to create severe storage problems. Moreover, the small boxes were not able to accommodate "restore" materials which were left in open, howbeit tagged, buckets. These suffered the obvious dangers of possible loss through spilling during transport and handling.

12. The bags used were of special heavy gauge plastic in two sizes, 30 by 30 and 30 by 60 cm. The boxes were of heavy cardboard 19 by 23 by 44 cm, large enough to hold one full plastic bag. The large bags and boxes were prepared so as to be able to accommodate one full pottery bucket.

13. In the Drew-McCormick work at Shechem, sherds were registered according to a master list with each receiving an individually discrete sherd number in addition to year, Field, Area, and basket designations. Where materials must be moved long distances and extensively rehandled, this procedure is indeed advisable. In working on Shechem materials, the writer has had numerous occasions to be thankful for this special registration process. Because Gezer materials have been held for study in Jerusalem, the need for this extra step in sherd registration has been considered unnecessary.

14. Having a year-round facility eliminates the need for the otherwise desirable expedient of trying to complete some of this work in the field. The field programs of several current American excavations (at Tell el-Hesi and at Caesarea) do include processes of pottery

drawing and describing as part of the regular routine. The Gezer procedures as described here could with minor accommodations also become part of the operation in the field. However, the advantage of working more deliberately with a regular professional staff would seem obvious. Moreover, the field situation does not usually provide ideal conditions for good cartography.

15. For "Restore" buckets the process of pottery registration is deferred until the completion of work by the Formatore. Then the reconstructed vessels are marked, and other materials are sorted for "save" and "discard" according to the regular routine.

16. All Gezer restoration work has been done by Mr. and Mrs. Moshe Ben Arie. Mr. Ben Arie is a technician on the staff of the Israel Museum.

17. All photographs for this chapter are by Zev Radovan, Jerusalem.

18. A technique of drawing at a 1:1 scale has been perfected by Mr. and Mrs. Wm. Ellinger of the Ai Excavation Staff and by other American archaeological teams. It is now being widely adopted. There are definite advantages in this method, especially because of the simpler, more direct drafting processes involved. One can also presume that it provides for more consistent and accurate rendition of forms.

19. These drawing conventions were codified for Gezer by the writer in the fall of 1969. They follow, with some modifications, conventions employed by the Israel Museum staff and generally by all Israeli archaeologists.

20. See Anna O. Shepard, Ceramics for the Archaeologist (Washington, D.C.: Carnegie Institution, Washington, D.C., 1965; Pub. No. 609).

21. A major step forward in clarifying this situation was taken with the publication of Ruth Amiran's Ancient Pottery of the Holy Land (Jerusalem: Massada Press, 1963 [Hebrew edition], 1969 [English edition]). In providing a general survey of Palestinian pottery types from the Neolithic period through the end of the Iron Age, it grapples with serious problems of terminology and has provided a widely accepted basis for further discussion of Palestinian ceramic typology.

22. These conventions for describing Gezer pottery were originally outlined by the writer with the assistance of A. Walker in August, 1969. A further draft with some additions and revisions was prepared by W. G. Dever and J. S. Holladay, Jr. in the fall of 1970. Some of these later suggestions have been incorporated into the code as presented here.

23. Cf. <u>Munsell Soil Color Charts</u> (Baltimore, Md.: Munsell Color Co., Inc., 1954).

24. Cf. Shepard, op. cit., pp. 115ff.

25. Moh's scale is a scale of hardness for minerals rated from 1-10 as measured against each other on the basis of which mineral scratches which. Diamond at 10 is the hardest. Diamond scratches corundum which is 9. Others are topaz (8), quartz (7), orthoclase (6), apatite (5), fluorite (4), calcite (3), gypsum (2), and talc (1). For rule of thumb, something that a pocketknife will scratch is 5. A copper penny will scratch a 3, and a thumbnail a 2. For more see most basic geological books, e.g., J. Gilluly, A. C. Waters, and A. O. Woodford, <u>Principles of Geology</u> (2nd ed., San Francisco: Wh. H. Freeman and Co.), pp. 490f.

26. See Fig. 4. By employing a combination of the numbers in a given bank, one can have number references from 1 to 14. For example by punching holes for 2 and 7 one has 9; punching 2, 4, and 7 one has 13, etc. These number references are used in conjunction with a key to provide for information storage. Thus with reference to the "form" category, 1 = jars, 2 = jugs, 3 = juglets, etc. For direct coding of numerical references (e.g., year, Field, Area, baskets, loci, etc.) several banks are employed in a series. Each bank represents a unit of tens. Combinations only of from 1-9 are used in each bank. Thus the first bank represents units 1-9, the second bank, 10-90, the third bank 100-900, etc. The last bank used may be extended to utilize all fourteen combinations. Thus two banks provide a possibility of reference up to 149, three banks to 1499, etc.

27. Although this is a primitive type of "computerization," the materials are nonetheless made quite available for reference and comparative study. Until such time as computer programs can be devised to provide accurate objective recall of form types, some advantage can be argued for this system in that it <u>does</u> provide for retrieval of complete information, including the forms themselves, i.e., the drawings.

28. For further detail on uses of this type of system, cf. Shepard, <u>op. cit.</u>, pp. 322ff.

29. See W. G. Dever, H. D. Lance, G. E. Wright, <u>Gezer I: Preliminary Report of the 1964-1966 Seasons</u> ("Annual of the Hebrew Union College Biblical and Archaeological School," Vol. I, Jerusalem: HUCBAS, 1970); W. G. Dever, H. D. Lance, Reuben G. Bullard, Dan P. Cole, J. D. Seger, <u>Gezer II. Report of the 1967-1971 Seasons in Fields I and II</u> ("Annual of the Nelson Glueck School of Biblical Archaeology," Vol. II, Jerusalem, NGSBA, 1974).

Appendix A

GEZER POTTERY READING NOTATIONS

The system of notations used for pottery calls includes the following conventions:

a. Pottery periods are referred to by the following abbreviations (parentheses indicate that the period is not well represented at Gezer):

Notation	Pottery Period	Dates
Chalco.	Chalcolithic	3500-3200 B.C.
EB I	Early Bronze I	3200-2900 B.C.
EB II	Early Bronze II	2900-2600 B.C.
(EB III	Early Bronze III	2600-2300 B.C.)
(EB IIIB	Early Bronze IIIB	2300-2200 B.C.)
(MB I	Middle Bronze I	2200-1950 B.C.)
MB IIA	Middle Bronze IIA	1950-1750 B.C.
MB IIB	Middle Bronze IIB	1750-1650 B.C.
MB IIC	Middle Bronze IIC	1650-1550 B.C.
LB I	Late Bronze I	1550-1400 B.C.
LB IIA	Late Bronze IIA	1400-1300 B.C.
LB IIB	Late Bronze IIB	1300-1200 B.C.
Iron IA	Iron IA	1200-1100 B.C.
Iron IB	Iron IB	1100-1000 B.C.
Iron IC	Iron IC	1000- 900 B.C.
Iron IIA	Iron IIA	900- 800 B.C.
Iron IIB	Iron IIB	800- 700 B.C.
Iron IIC	Iron IIC	700- 586 B.C.
Pers.	Persian	586- 330 B.C.
Hell.	Hellenistic	330- 100 B.C.
Rom., Early	Early Roman	100 B.C.-100 A.D.
(Rom., Late	Late Roman	100- 400 A.D.)
(Byz.	Byzantine	400- 700 A.D.)
(Arabic	Arabic	700-)

b. Pottery from periods in a series, e.g., from MB IIC, LB I, and LB IIA will be noted as MB IIC-LB IIA, using a dash (-) to signify continuity.

c. Pottery from scattered periods will be recorded with a comma separating the notations, e.g., EB I, LB II, Hell.

d. Pottery from transitional periods, e.g., from the end of the MB IIC and beginning of the LB I periods, will be recorded with a slash (/) dividing the notations, e.g., MB IIC/LB I.

e.   Other special conventions include:

Notation	Definition
Ns	Not saved
All saved	All saved
Ud	Undistinguished (ordinarily used together with a period abbreviation as, e.g., EB Ud)
RST	Restore
Mend	Mend
* (starred)	Starred basket numbers indicate that the pottery is of special significance, usually having to do with its provenance.
Delicate	Fragile items or materials with paint, etc.

Appendix B

GEZER DRAWING CONVENTIONS

1. Measurements:

   a. All vessels up to 75 cm. are drawn at a 2:5 scale.
   b. Vessels larger than 75 cm. are drawn at 1:5 scale.
   c. Store jars larger than 1.00 m. are drawn at 1:10 scale.
   d. The following are drawn at 1:1 scale:
      1. Body sherds with decoration or inscriptions
      2. Lamps
      3. Small delicate objects
      4. Sculpture and reliefs
      5. Bronzes (up to 10 cm.; over 10 cm. at 2:5)
      6. Glass
      7. Figurines and statuettes
      8. Jewelry (if very small 2:1)
      9. Scarabs
     10. Wooden objects

2. Pottery Illustration and Decoration:

   a. The right-hand side of the drawing shows the cross-section of a vessel as well as the signs, markings, and/or other decorations on its inside.

2:5

   b. The left-hand side of the drawing shows the outer view including signs, markings, etc. on the outside.

   c. The rim or lip of a vessel is drawn thus:

2:5

   d. The base is drawn as follows:

2:5

e. Body sherds are drawn (at 1:1 scale) in profile and face-on (with decorations, etc.) as follows:

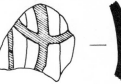

f. Outside decoration is illustrated as follows: 1:1
   1. All decoration in brown or black is shown in solid black.

2:5

   2. All decoration in red, orange, or yellow, is shown with hatched lines.

2:5

      Thus, e.g., decoration in red and black:

2:5

g. Interior decorations are illustrated via the same conventions. However, when interior decoration (on the right-hand side of the drawing) conflicts with the clarity of the section drawing, special conventions must be sometimes applied and special notice of the circumstances must be added in the written description.

3. Directions and Perspectives of Drawing:

a. All vessels are drawn from the front except in the following cases:
   1. Lamps are drawn from above and from the side (at a 1:1 scale).

1:1

   2. Handles are drawn from the front or side and in cross-section.

2:5

3. Juglets are drawn from the side and from above if the rim is not round.

4. Small delicate objects are drawn complete and in a realistic manner (showing three dimensions in perspective) with a cross-section next to them.

5. Figurines are drawn from front and side and in a realistic manner with shadows and a cross-section according to need.

6. Rings are drawn from above and from the side with a cross-section.

7. Nails and scales (of coats of mail) are drawn from the front, but with 2 or 3 cross-sections as needed.

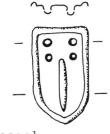

b. A view from <u>above</u> is drawn in the following cases:
   1. When the rim is not round (cf. a.3 above).
   2. When there are an unusual number of handles on a vessel.
   3. When there is decoration or engraving on the rim.

   Note: Such a drawing is always placed <u>above</u> the drawing of the vessel or object.

c. A view of the <u>bottom</u> is drawn in the following cases:
   1. When there is a special drawing, marking, or design on the base.
   2. When there is a stamp or seal impression on the base.

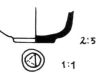

3. When the base itself is of unusual or irregular design.

   Note: Such drawing is always placed <u>below</u> the drawing of the vessel or object.

d. An enlarged drawing (at scale 1:1) is done for seal impressions or unusual decorations on the rim or handle of a vessel.

   Note: Such is always placed on the <u>right</u> of the drawing of a vessel.

2:5   1:1

e. Miscellaneous notes on routine processing of materials:
   1. Every drawing must be identified according to the registration number on the sherd, vessel, or object.
   2. When the scale is other than 2:5 it is given next to the drawing or immediately below it.
   3. The initials of the person doing the drawing are put next to the registration number on the drawing.
   4. When the drawing is completed a red dot is put on the sherd or vessel next to the registration number.

4. Symbols for composition of artifacts:

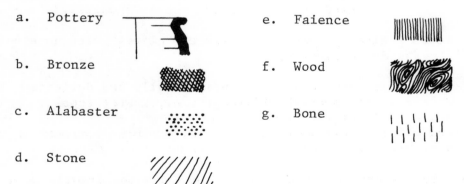

   a. Pottery   e. Faience

   b. Bronze   f. Wood

   c. Alabaster   g. Bone

   d. Stone

Appendix C

GEZER POTTERY DESCRIPTION CODE

All ceramic materials are to be described according to the following categories and canons:

A. <u>Form</u>:

An initial classification of form according to broad and general categories of vessels will be assigned in the initial description process according to the following designations. This is designed only to give a broad separation of items. Detailed study is necessary for final classification, etc. of materials. The categories used for this initial classification are:

Jars - All large two-handled (or no-handled) vessels, with handles on the shoulder and with wide mouths. The neck is narrower than the shoulders.

Jugs - Smaller one-handled vessels, with handle from lip or neck to shoulder, wide mouth, neck narrower than shoulder.

Juglets - Very small jug types (dippers, piriforms, etc.)

Flasks or Bottles - Very narrow-necked vessels with two (or no) handles from lip or neck to shoulder.

Platter Bowls - Wide open-mouthed bowls or "plates" with no shoulder carination.

Deep Bowls - Large open bowls with upright walls and definite carination or shouldering, i.e., krater types.

Bowls - Bowls with closed mouths, i.e., with mouths narrower than shoulder.

Cooking Pots - A "functional" designation for vessels with heavy grits used in preparing foods. Included as a special category because it is a common and usually obvious vessel type.

Lamps - Another "functional" but obvious type.

Imported Wares - May be any of the above but separated as a potentially useful grouping of materials.

Miscellaneous Forms - Other types and oddments exclusive of items registered as "Objects."

B. Technique:

According to technique of manufacture materials are described as:
1. Hand-made
2. Wheel-made
3. Hand-and-wheel-made (with description of distribution, e.g.,
    hand-made body, wheel-made rim)
4. Mold-made

C. Ware:

Ware is described according to the following outline of categories
and conventions:

1. Paste:

    a. Color - This means the color of the sherd section!
            Description is given via Munsell soil color code.

    b. Inclusions (temper) - Inclusions are described according
            to type, size, and frequency in terms
            of the following categories:

    1.) Type -- Sand - Sand. (To the naked eye these appear
            as sand-type grits. A sub-group of
            this category involving larger par-
            ticles may be noted as "wadi gravel.")

        Limestone or Lime. - (CaO, calcium oxide).
            (To the naked eye these appear as
            white chalky grits.)

        Ceram. - Ceramic particles or "grog." (To
            the naked eye these are usually
            angular red or black fragments.)

        Crystl. - Crystal (SiO_2, silicon dioxide) or
            quartz. (To the naked eye these
            appear as angular translucent frag-
            ments.)

        Organic - Straw or shell fragments, etc. (To
            the naked eye evidence of straw grits
            often remains only as patterns in the
            fabric or as carbon deposits.)

        Other - Miscellaneous types not included in
            the above.

2.) Size -- Gezer Code   Wentworth Scale

        (1) large 2-1 mm.   = Very coarse
        (m) medium 1-1/2 mm.   = Coarse
        (s) small 1/2-1/4 mm.   = Medium
        (ss) very small 1/4-0 mm. = Fine

3.) Frequency -- few   = density below 15%
               some   = density between 15% and 30%
               many   = density between 30% and 50%
               very many = density above 50%

    Note: scales below for 15% and 30% density copied
           from Robert J. and Linda S. Braidwood,
           Excavations in the Plain of Antioch (Chicago:
           University of Chicago, 1960), Fig. 16, p. 33.

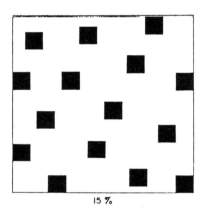

15 %

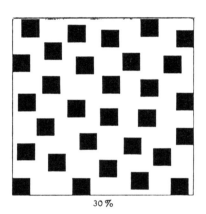

30 %

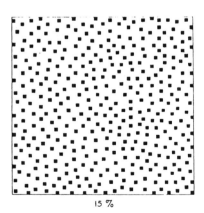

15 %

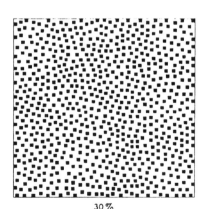

30 %

c. Firing – Because of variables in firing (i.e., faster and slower exposures with more or less oxygen present, etc.) descriptions are given to represent only the darkness of the core indicating the extent to which the carbon properties have been reduced. Four gradations are to be noted:

Dark grey core
Grey core
Light grey core
(No core)

In the descriptions no notation on firing is given where the carbon reduction is complete, i.e., (no core is evident).

d. Hardness – The hardness of the paste fabric is described according to three gradations as follows:

		Moh's Scale
soft	– As the chalky paste of e.g., Chalcolithic materials	3
hard	– As most normal sherds	4-6
metallic	– As e.g., base-ring ware. Very hard ware that "clinks."	7

2. Surface: (Note: Descriptions in this category may pertain either to inner or outer surfaces as relevant and as so indicated. Where distinction is not given, descriptions can be assumed to refer to both alike.)

a. Color – Given via Munsell only if different from paste section.

b. Treatment – The following classifications are used:

Wash – Application of paste solution after firing. Color description is given via Munsell.

Slip – Treatment of paste solution applied before final firing. Color reference is given via Munsell only when the color is different from paste section or surface color designations.

Burnish – Smoothing of pores of vessel while in the drying process with a hard tool (bone, stone, shell, etc.). This is done just before firing. Color

 is given via Munsell Code. Technique is described according to the following conventions:

Chordal - Crossed or fabric-like pattern of strokes, frequently along the chord of a vessel, on the inside bottom or on the base.

 Circular - Spiral or circular pattern of strokes around or inside vessels. Always horizontal. Classified as hand- or wheel-made.

Radial - Pattern of strokes radiating from a central focus.

  Continuous - Pattern of closely packed continuous strokes. May be classified as vertical or horizontal strokes.

Random - Patternless strokes. May be classified as vertical or horizontal.

 Polished - Treatment so well done that lustrous overall polish results in which burnish marks do not show as distinct entities. (Not to be confused with sintered items: see under C.2.c below.)

Paint - Color is given via Munsell Code.

- Type classification is given as follows:

Oxide - Inorganic paints applied in suspension, occasionally forming a raised coating on the vessel.

Organic - Soluble paints presenting no relief on the vessel surface.

c. Other Miscellaneous Treatments of Surface

Combing - Patterns of regularly spaced fine lines, incised.

Incising - Other incised decor.

Molded - Relief designs applied through molding to the vessel surface (as often on mold-made pottery).

Knife-paring – Shaving of excess clay from the vessel with a knife before firing.

Appliqué – Relief designs applied secondarily to the vessel surface.

Stamping – Stamping of the leather-hard clay with a patterned stamp before firing.

Rouletting – A stamped design rolled on to the leather-hard clay with a patterned wheel.

Cross-wiping – Wet-smoothing of the pre-fired clay with a rough cloth producing a "basket-weave" effect.

Sintered – Polish, or semi-glaze effected by application of special slip solutions as in later Hellenistic and Roman wares.

Chapter VI

FIELD SURVEYING AND DRAFTING FOR THE ARCHAEOLOGIST

William G. Dever

"Scholarship is by no means all that is wanted; the engineering training of mind and sense ... will really fit an archaeologist better for excavating than bookwork can alone." W. M. F. Petrie

This chapter is not concerned with the general theory of surveying nor with archaeological drafting as a whole. It is rather a discussion of these disciplines as they can be adapted to the specific problems the archaeologist is likely to encounter in the field. Since this Manual is primarily a description of what was done in actual practice at Gezer over the years rather than a discussion of theory, it may be helpful to begin by setting our practice in surveying and drafting over against more traditional approaches.

A classical statement of the latter is that of A. H. Detweiler in his Manual of Archaeological Surveying. Here standard procedures of professional surveyors and architects were admirably adapted to archaeology in the light of the state of that art in the 1930's.[1] But the conception of archaeological method in this Manual must now be regarded as antiquated, as seen from the following statements: "The first and ideal method consists of clearing each occupational level completely before going on to the next level below it" (p. 10); "When once the width of the wall is determined it is a comparatively simple matter to dig in both directions along the inside and outside faces of the wall" (p. 13); "The condition of the debris between the floors will sometimes give important information" (p. 26; italics all mine). Here the orientation is obviously architectural rather than stratigraphic. The description of the role of the Architect on the expedition staff is even more revealing: "He is responsible for establishing the loci of all non-architectural objects that are found" (p. 6). "The architect must assume a great share of the responsibility for supervision during the actual digging" (p. 11). "When the buildings on any level have been completely cleared and surveyed, they must be removed under the direction of the architect" (p. 26). Here the assumption is that the staff comprises principally the Director and the Architect, with the latter second in command; no place is accorded the stratigraphers, the Field and Area Supervisors who make up the bulk of a modern excavation staff.

In comparison with the staff presumed by Detweiler for an expedition in the 1930's, the Gezer staff in a typical year included, besides the Director, five professional archaeologists or "Field Supervisors," 14 trained stratigraphers or "Area Supervisors"--and no Architect! The architectural recording was done by a single draftsman who had good general background in art and was skilled in the mechanical aspects of the task but was not a professional architect. This situation is more or less typical for modern excavations in Palestine (with the possible exception of classical sites with more impressive architecture), and it illustrates as perhaps nothing else how radically the balance of architectural vs. stratigraphic concerns has shifted in the last generation.[2] This shift must be borne in mind in the discussion that follows, or the reader will be inclined to dismiss the proposed surveying and drafting techniques as amateurish. The point is that stratigraphy, not architecture, now prevails, and both staff and field methods are being adapted accordingly.

I

ARCHAEOLOGICAL SURVEYING

A. Objectives.

The objective of an archaeological survey of a site is simply: (1) to place the site on the map and to record for publication the physical appearance before excavation; and (2) to bring together the various excavation areas in a geometric relationship, so that permanent records can be kept and accurate architectural plans drawn for publication as the various strata are cleared and removed.

1. Map Coordinates and Contour Plan

For the first aspect of this task, a contour plan is prepared, using standard surveying techniques. These will probably involve the services of a professional surveyor, or more likely a team of survey-ors, especially if the site is a large one. More recently techniques of aerial photographic surveying have been sufficiently perfected that they may be employed in conjunction with a simple ground survey at a great savings in time and even in cost.[3] Contours are commonly drawn at five-meter intervals; or, if the site is quite small and detail is required, at intervals up to one meter. The elevations will be given in meters above (or below) Mediterranean sea level, determined from bench marks set by a reliable national or regional survey. In Pales-tine (principally modern Jordan and Israel) the basic survey is the Cadastral Survey done in the 1920's by the British Mandatory Govern-ment, the bench marks of which may be located by referring to the 1:20,000 survey maps, for instance, where number, grid references, and elevations are given.[4]

The contour plan should show any bench marks on the site or nearby, and it should be clearly located in relation to both longitudinal and latitudinal map coordinates on the national survey or ordnance maps. It is helpful if some natural landmarks or modern structures are in-cluded. Of course scale (in meters and miles) and magnetic compass bearing must also be clearly shown. Fig. 1 shows a typical contour plan with map coordinates. The scale of the original drawing may be 1:1,000 or 1:500 for smaller sites, though this will undoubtedly be reduced in publication. Needless to say, this plan and all other orig-inal plans should be inked on a good stable tracing linen (or plastic

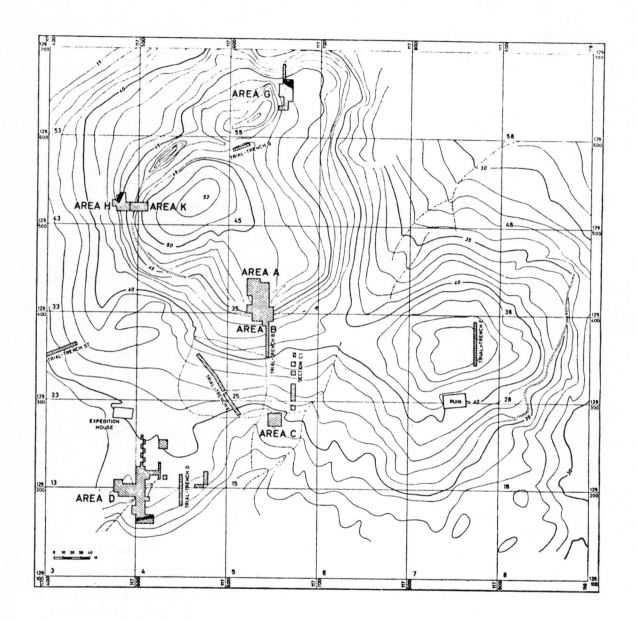

Figure 1.   Topographical map of Tel Ashdod showing
excavation areas (seasons 1962, 1963, 1965).

(From M. Dothan, Ashdod II-III. The Second and Third Seasons of
Excavations, 1963, 1965, Jerusalem, 1971, p. 16; used by permission.)

drawing film such as "Permatrace"), protected by bound edges, and safe-guarded as part of the permanent records of the expedition. The contour plan should be completed before actual excavation begins if at all possible, since excavation and dumping in particular will change the appearance of the site appreciably.

2. Coordinate Grid

The second objective of the archaeological survey of a site is to link together all areas to be excavated. Ideally this is done by laying out a "coordinate grid" over the whole site, beginning with the trigonometric points used in establishing the longitudinal and latitudinal coordinates for the national survey, if these can be located, or at least in relation to a bench mark nearby or on the mound itself which can be related in turn to this survey. If only certain areas of the mound are to be excavated, a "triangulation grid" rather than a complete grid will be sufficient to link them together.[5] The grid lines should be extended north-south-east-west, using magnetic compass bearings and giving information to calculate the angle of declination. It will probably be sufficient if the surveyor will set permanent grid stakes in the areas to be excavated at intervals of 50.00 m., assuming that the module of the grid is 5.00 m. as is often the case; smaller units can then be laid out by amateur surveyors wherever it is decided to excavate. However, if the site is small, grid stakes every 10.00 m. or so will be found convenient. A problem at every Middle Eastern archaeological site is that villagers or beduin will pull up these stakes for the wood or metal in them, so they must be set as securely and permanently as possible. A two-centimeter iron rod, a pipe, or a steel angle iron is ideal; these grid stakes should be set at least 75 cm. deep, in concrete. Fig. 2 shows several ways of preparing the grid stakes. It will be convenient if reduced elevations are calculated from the basic bench mark and painted on or cut into the concrete at each of these stakes, since this will save time later.

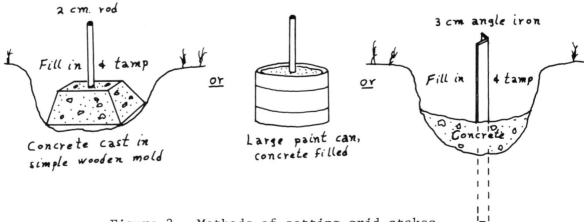

Figure 2. Methods of setting grid stakes.

The lines of the coordinate grid should appear on the master top plan, along with the contours already established. Some simple and convenient scheme of enumeration must be devised to designate any areas which may be later excavated. A time-honored scheme--used by Tell Beit Mirsim, for instance, and still favored by American excavators--is to divide the mound into quadrants, beginning at a point roughly central. The quadrants are labeled "Northwest," "Northeast," etc. Within each quadrant the squares may be given numerical designations running out both horizontally and vertically from center, or numerical designations in one direction and alphabetical designations (omitting I and O) in the other. This scheme allows each quadrant to expand almost indefinitely, a considerable advantage if the extent of the site is unknown in the beginning or the areas to be dug have not yet been determined. Illustrations of such a grid are given in Fig. 3. The excavation

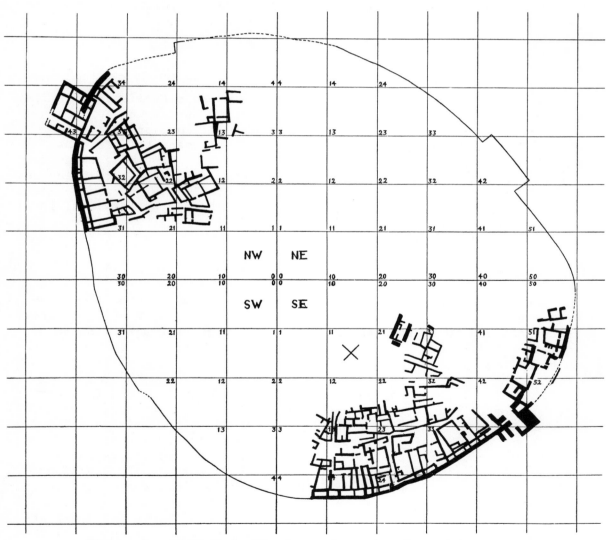

Figure 3. Tell Beit Mirsim; schematic plan with walls of Str. A in outline.

square marked with an X, for instance, is referred to as "SE 11." Any
one of several schemes may be used satisfactorily, as long as the major
requirements are satisfied; (a) it is unambiguous in locating excavating areas; (b) flexible enough to allow for expansion; and (c) logical
and convenient for reference by excavator and reader alike.

At old sites being re-excavated, a coordinate grid may be established; but it will not be found as useful as on a virgin site, for the
simple reason that at the latter, Fields will probably be laid out in
relation to the architecture already known rather than laid out arib-
trarily north/south. This was the case at Gezer, where none of our
Fields corresponded exactly to the grid. However, the grid did prove
useful in locating or referring to various Fields; and it could certainly prove useful to future excavators who might choose to excavate
untouched areas of the mound and who would need to relate them to both
the areas that we had dug and those dug by Macalister.[6]

B. Staff.

Once the contour plan and coordinate grid are established, a full-
time professional surveyor will probably not be needed on the excavation staff, since the typical surveying problems encountered on an
excavation can be handled by the Architect/Draftsman--or, for that
matter, even by someone with little or no previous surveying experience
who will take the trouble to master a few simple items of equipment and
equally simple techniques. (The occasional problem which cannot be met
in this manner can always be handled by calling in a professional local
surveyor on a contract basis.)

C. Equipment.

Let us look first at the equipment required and then at the techniques to be employed--recalling again that on the basis of long experience both can be adapted and simplified as suggested here. Basic
equipment which should be purchased by any expedition at the outset
must include (quantities not specified):

1. Theodolite or engineer's transit with heavy tripod, for measuring horizontal and vertical angles, as well as for leveling; should
have a compass and a vernier which reads at least to 1 minute. The
instrument should have a powerful telescope for long-distance readings;
an optical device for centering over triangulation points is useful;
optional but extremely useful are stadia hairs for measuring distances.
The instrument should be of a reliable brand (Gurley, K and E, Wild,
etc.), but it need not be the most elaborate or expensive model; in
fact, a simple instrument is more easily used and maintained under the
difficult conditions usually prevailing in the field.

2. Dumpy level: optional for smaller excavations, since the theodolite can also be used for leveling.

3. Level rod: at least four meters long; since target will not usually be required, may be of the folding type, but should be sturdy; special readings for stadia hairs may be desirable for long-distance sighting.

4. Plane table with tripod, and alidade: useful for very large architectural complexes or for planning elaborate and well-preserved classical buildings, but optional for most expeditions; plane table should be nearly 1.00 m. square, with a quick-lock head such as the Johnson head, and with a plumbing arm or other device for centering the table over a triangulation point. The alidade may be of the simple, non-optical type, although one ought to buy a good telescopic alidade if the transit is first-quality; it will be more useful if it has bubble levels and vertical arcs on the tube and stadia hairs in the eyepiece.

5. Fifty- or thirty-meter reel-type surveyor's steel tape of best quality, in a case of the sturdiest type: metallic-reinforced cloth tapes of twenty and ten meters will be useful for smaller areas and for less critical layouts.

6. Plumb bobs: these should be slim-tapered and sharply pointed for accuracy in sighting, and heavy enough to settle quickly in high wind.

7. Three-meter steel tapes in sturdy, instant-recoil cases: a lock clamp for the tape when extended and a belt-clip will be useful.

8. Surveyor's ranging poles, 2.00 m. long.

D. Field Problems and Techniques.

The most frequent situations calling for the use of surveying techniques by the field archaeologist or an amateur surveyor on his staff are: (1) laying out and locating smaller areas to be excavated within the coordinate grid; and (2) taking elevations for inclusion on the architectural plans of each stratum.

1. Laying out Excavation Areas

The first task, that of laying out Fields and Areas (or "Sites," as the British term them) is simple enough in principle, but there are several pitfalls to be avoided. It cannot be stressed too strongly that absolute accuracy is desirable in establishing excavation areas, especially in the system we are advocating, where planning will be done by constant reference to the grid stakes of individual squares, rather than by plane table surveying. A little extra care in laying out squares will save shifting of balk lines and consequent headaches later! Three things are essential: (a) as near absolute accuracy as possible for the grid stakes, ideally within two or three cm.; (b) stability of these stakes, especially those <u>outside</u> the extreme limits of excavation, which will serve as the permanent control for the inner stakes when these are removed and re-established as balks are lowered; (c) accuracy as well as safety and convenience of use in the balk lines which are established from the grid stakes for each excavation square.

The first two requirements are met when the lines of the coordinate grid already established by the survey are extended to cover the entire area chosen for excavation, with similar steel stakes set in concrete, at the intersection of lines every six meters (or other figure, as the module requires) north-south and east-west.[1] This is best done by leveling the transit exactly over the nearest grid stake on one side of the new Field and sighting another stake on the opposite side of the field somewhere across its center, for instance on a north-south line. The steel tape is pulled from the first stake and points are marked every six meters on the line of sight--being sure that the tape is as nearly horizontal and stretched as tight as possible to avoid inaccuracies. Either a plumb bob is used and the transit sighted on the string of that, or the transit head is tilted to ground level, to make sure that the points are exactly on the line of sight. When this line of points is complete, a transverse east-west line is similarly established. If no grid stakes are convenient, the transit can be swung 90° to establish the base line for these points. If no transit is available, the "3-4-5" method of finding a right angle to the base line may be used, as in Fig. 4. With one base line and a line at right angles, it is then a simple matter to complete the grid with tapes only, running parallel lines and marking these also at six-meter intervals.

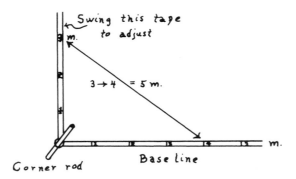

Figure 4. One method of finding a right angle.

The stakes should then be permanently set, protruding only a centimeter or two above ground level, both to discourage tampering with them and to guard against people tripping over them when the inner balks are used for traffic (as they often must be). These stakes may be iron rods of only one centimeter which will give slightly greater accuracy in measurement than the larger rods. It will be convenient if levels are also run on each of them (below), and the value painted on or incised in the wet concrete--making sure that it is indicated whether the point taken was at the top or the base of the rod.

The third requirement is met when the actual excavation squares are laid out within the grid. Since the grid stakes are usually set at six-meter intervals, one must measure in 50 cm. on each side to end up with a one-meter balk and excavation areas 5.00 by 5.00 m. With grid stakes at every corner, this is fairly simple and can be done with nothing more than three-meter tapes. Accuracy is of course important, or the care in establishing the grid stakes will have been wasted. Experience has shown that the best system is one that permits the balk lines to be taken down (for safety's sake) once the balk has been well begun and accurately cut, but re-established at any time for checking. Fig. 5 suggests an easy method for setting stakes beyond the square so that they will not be removed when the corners of the balks are cut.

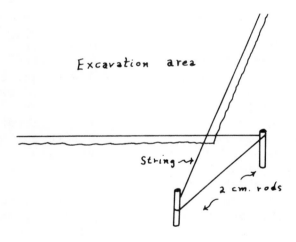

Excavation area

String →

2 cm. rods

Figure 5.   Setting corner stakes.

We shall see presently that accurate layout and subsequent cutting of the balks to very close tolerances is not merely "cosmetics"--it is essential for the recording system we are describing. (No matter what the system, it ought to be done anyway.) A few suggestions may sound picayune, but experience has shown that they make life much easier for the Area Supervisor--and for the Director, too, since only what is made convenient will actually get done as the dig wears on! Stakes may be large 15-20 cm. spikes. String is important: it should be fine enough to give a clean datum line (not fuzzy), but heavy enough to be clearly visible; strong enough not to break easily but capable of snapping if someone trips over it; just stretchy enough to slip on and off the stakes but not so stretchy that it sags. Nylon or synthetic string might seem ideal, but some of it does not stretch or tie well, and it may tangle too easily; light cotton string of the type usually sold as carpenter's "chalk line" is preferable. The strings can be tied permanently to one end of the balk stakes and a loop tied in the other end so that they can be slipped on and off the stakes. If these suggestions are followed, even though they require a bit of extra care in setting up, squares are apt to be kept more accurate and balks more carefully cut as the work proceeds, especially when excavation reaches several meters below ground level where the eye cannot be trusted and accuracy becomes more and more difficult to obtain.

2. Taking Elevations

The second job of the amateur surveyor will be to "run levels." This requires the theodolite or dumpy level, the level rod and an assistant. Only the bubble levels of the instrument are used in this operation. The instrument is set up in a convenient position and leveled by means of the leveling screws and the bubbles in the base plate and/or telescope. The position should be chosen to provide: (a) safe location outside the area of traffic; (b) a roughly equal distance to backsight point and to as many of the main points as possible for foresights (below), but not less than 10.00 m. distant if possible (the rod is hard to read at close range); and (c) a height of instrument (below) at least as high as the highest point to be taken but not more than 4.00 m. above the lowest point. (Several setups may be necessary to get readings on all the points.) Level the telescope with the tube in one position, and then rotate it 180° and take out <u>half</u> of the error; then rotate the tube <u>90°</u> and start over with the whole operation; finally check against the original position of the tube. The instrument is ready when the bubble remains level throughout the 360° swing. This should take no more than two or three minutes with experience. Throughout this operation and subsequent use, it should be ascertained that the tripod is <u>firmly</u> set and that the operator does not lean against or even touch it; after an interval of disuse, the set-up should be re-checked and adjusted if necessary before another series of levels is run. A slight error here will mean several centimeters of error in the readings!

The level rod is rested by the assistant on one of the bench marks of known value, i.e., the grid stakes, making sure that it is held vertically. (The person at the transit can check this against the vertical crosshair in the telescope and give hand signals for corrections.) In what is called the "backsight," the rod is sighted through the cross-hairs of the telescope on the transit and read to the nearest centimeter. This figure is <u>added</u> to the elevation of the bench mark and becomes the "height of instrument" (conveniently HI), which will be used for all readings as long as this setup is maintained. Points for which the reduced elevation is desired are then selected and a series of "foresights" are taken. The rod is held on each point and read through the telescope, the "foresight" readings being subtracted from the "height of instrument." The result is the "reduced elevation" or height in meters above (or below) Mediterranean sea level. The technique can be learned by nearly anyone in a few minutes, and thereafter nothing but a little care is required to get the same results that a professional surveyor would get. The following tips may be helpful: (a) one person (or perhaps one person with one transit for each Field) should be trained and made responsible for running levels to insure consistency; (b) readings should be practiced until one is absolutely familiar with the rod, since rods differ, and especially at extremely close or distant ranges it is easy to misread; (c) it should be agreed whether readings are to be rounded off to the nearest high or lower centimeter; (d) the same basic bench mark, or one checked and double checked against it, should always be returned to for the backsight; (e) a survey book should be kept, listing in column form all points read (probably by Field, Area, and locus number), all readings, the date, and showing all arithmetic (Fig. 6); (f) when reduced elevations have

	No.	Backsight (HI)	Foresight	Reduced Level	Description
	49	224.90	2.48	222.42	VI.NE.3 Wall 3014, N
O	50	"	2.52	222.38	" , middle
	51	"	2.46	222.44	" , S.
	52	"	2.42	222.48	Wall 3015, W.
O	53	"	2.36	222.54	" , middle
	54	"	2.47	222.43	" , E.
O	55	"	2.89	222.01	" , founding level at E. end
	56	"	2.78	222.12	Surf. 3017
O	57	"	2.72	222.18	Cobbles 3018
	58	"	2.69	222.21	Bench 3020, top
	59	"	2.92	221.98	" , founding level
O	60	"	2.71	222.19	Mortar 3022, top
	61	"	2.84	222.06	" , founding level

Figure 6. Sample page from surveyor's notebook.

been calculated and called out by the surveyor to the supervisor or draftsman, they should be repeated to insure that they have been heard and transferred to the plan correctly.

Although these simple surveying techniques will ordinarily suffice, it must not be assumed that they will necessarily cover all field problems encountered by the archaeologist. For instance, isolated one-period settlements or large cemeteries not connected with a _tell_ pose a problem, and they will probably require a professional survey to relate them to known landmarks or national surveys. If clearance of such areas must be done without time for a preliminary survey, as is often the case with salvage operations, it is best to select several points to serve as triangulation points and to establish a triangulation grid if possible (above). It will also be necessary to select a temporary bench mark which may be given an arbitrary elevation. The foregoing survey techniques can then be applied and all excavated remains related to these temporary reference points which may then be located later by a professional survey. In fact, nearly _any_ field problem can be solved in this rather make-shift way, provided that a proper survey can be done later. It is essential, however, that _several_ points are selected, spread over a fairly wide area surrounding the excavation area, and that these points are clearly marked and permanent enough to be located later.

For more advanced surveying techniques, the field archaeologist should consult a standard text. The field archaeologist, especially if he intends to direct his own excavations, or if he wishes to be flexible enough to cover unexpected or unusual opportunities for excavation, should make himself acquainted with elementary surveying. Ideally, he ought to be capable himself of doing any routine surveying that may be required as well as understanding at least in theory the more complicated surveys necessary in special situations. At the very least, he must be equipped to communicate with those doing the surveying, to evaluate their work critically, and to insure that their results are accurate and well integrated into the total framework of his archaeological enterprise. It is no exaggeration to say that surveying is one of the most basic and useful technical skills required for field archaeology.

II

ARCHAEOLOGICAL DRAFTING: ARCHITECTURAL RECORDING

A. Objectives.

Here we do not attempt to cover the general topic of drafting for the archaeologist, since this extends to much broader areas than those

with which we are concerned, i.e., field problems. The primary need
in the field is the recording of the architectural remains that are
brought to light and then must be dismantled as the excavation proceeds
downward stratum by stratum. Apart from the verbal description in the
supervisors' notebooks and the photographs, there will be no other
record of what is in fact the major evidence upon which the reconstruction of the history and material culture of the site will rest. It is
assumed in this Manual that proper digging technique stresses debris
layers first of all. As the debris layers are untangled, architecture
will of course emerge of its own; but the understanding of these layers
will almost automatically bring the understanding of the various building phases. This means that as the major objective of archaeological
digging, architecture has been replaced in modern method; nevertheless,
architecture remains a major objective of archaeological recording, and
no apologies need be made for the concentration of much of the expedition's resources on this responsibility. It is fair to judge an excavation by the architectural plans it produces: amateurish or careless
work at this point almost certainly means an irresponsible excavation
and one whose results are not to be trusted in detail.

B. Staff.

    Let us take the older approach once again as a point of departure
for suggesting somewhat "streamlined" procedures in selecting staff and
doing architectural recording. For instance, Detweiler's Manual
assumes, as we have already noted, that a key member of the excavation
staff will be a full-fledged Architect; that he will do all the architectural recording and even much of the supervision of the clearance
and removal; and that he will also do detailed theoretical reconstruction on the spot as well as in the form of rendered perspective and
isometric drawings. It is difficult to quarrel with such a staff
arrangement, provided that: (1) a competent professional architect is
available; (2) the exposure of architecture is on such a large scale
as to require detailed planning and reconstruction of large building
complexes; and (3) the quality of construction and state of preservation of the building merit sophisticated treatment. In actual practice
on excavations with which we are familiar in Palestine, none of these
conditions is normally met!

    With a few notable exceptions, professionally-trained architects
who will devote themselves to archaeology simply cannot be found these
days--certainly not for the pitiful architectural fragments we ordinarily turn up in Palestine! Thus most of us make do with draftsmen
who are skilled in the purely mechanical aspects of planning and
recording the architecture. The archaeologists themselves attempt to
supply the guidance the draftsmen need in planning these buildings and
in representing structural details, drawing upon their experience of
ancient building techniques as well as observations of their modern
adaptation in the Middle East. We also supervise the clearance and

removal of the buildings, relying more on the empirical evidence of debris layers than on theoretical architectural principles for the reconstruction of building phases.

In this as in other cases, the best method is that best suited to the distinctive character of the material; simple architecture does not require elaborate treatment. In fact, the plans produced by a professional architect may be drawn with such style and elegance that they convey a misleading impression of the rather crude architecture we usually bring to light. What is required is simply accurate representation of the building remains. There should be as few preconceptions as possible, and what interpretations there are should be deliberate and should present an interpretation which is archaeologically intelligent and represents the consensus of the archaeologists themselves. In short, both extremes are to be avoided: the "artistic" plan which is more style than substance, and the mindless drawing which purports to be simply a record of "what was there." Any drawing is an interpretation: let it be a defensible one!

C. Equipment.

The following are field-tested "shortcuts" to architectural recording. The equipment needed in the field is of the simplest sort, but it should be of the best quality obtainable. In addition to the surveying equipment required and already on hand in any case (above), one needs only the following (quantities not specified):

1. Drawing boards at least 30 by 30 cm. The most convenient are of plastic, with a built-in paper clip, a pocket for lead holders and other equipment, and a protective cover for the drawing (several commercial brands are available); each draftsman should have his own drawing board.

2. Quantities of the best grade of millimeter paper, sheets ca. 30 by 30 cm. as well as rolls of larger sizes. Blue is preferred, since the millimeter lines drop out in photo or mechanical copying; the paper should be thin and translucent so that overlays and tracings are easily done.

3. Triangular drafting scales, with at least 1:25, 1:50, and 1:100 scales.

4. Small dividers with provision for a drawing lead.

5. Leadholders of the best quality, with strong non-slip clutch and comfortable grip.

6. Drawing leads. They should be hard enough to take and hold a fine point, but soft enough to erase easily; brands vary, but 2H, or occasionally HB leads, have been found most satisfactory.

7. Lead sharpeners, preferably of the small disposable plastic type.

8. Gum or plastic erasers.

9. Metal-reinforced cloth meter tapes: 10.00 m. lengths are convenient; it is important that they should have a loop end which reads from zero.

10. Miscellaneous string (as above), large spikes, several clothespins.

11. Plumb bobs and 3.00 m. steel tapes as above.

12. For the fieldhouse, a large tilt-top drafting table (not necessarily with attached drafting instrument), and a large light-box for overlaying and tracing plans.

D. Field Problems and Techniques.

1. Plane-Table Surveying

It will be seen that the plane-table--considered the basic item of equipment in surveying manuals--is conspicuously absent in the above list, and this is deliberate. There are drawbacks in the use of the plane table for several reasons: (a) the equipment is cumbersome and expensive; (b) plane-table surveying may require professionally trained personnel not available, and in any case is too sophisticated for the simple planning our excavations usually require; (c) despite its "professional" appearance, plane-table surveying has considerable built-in error, especially when used by amateurs.

However, the real reason the system we are advocating avoids the use of the plane table is not because of its difficulty but because modern excavation methods based on extensive use of balks have made it largely obsolete. It is far simpler--and more accurate--to use the grid and balk lines as datum lines and to draw all architectural elements in each square by relating them to the square itself. These drawings can then be easily linked together to form larger complexes. This has several advantages, chiefly that it eliminates the plane table, with the difficulties we have already noted. It should be stressed that plane-table surveying was a classic technique before excavation was confined to trenches and 5.00 m. squares which were accurately located within a grid and employed balks. But the introduction of modern systems of excavation automatically replaced the triangulation grid and base lines needed for plane-table surveying with more accurate and more convenient grid lines which can serve as datum lines.

2. An Alternate System Using the Grid for Datum Lines

Using our system, an inexperienced draftsman with the simplest
equipment can be trained in a surprisingly short time to produce plans
that are drawn quickly, and to a tolerance within 2 cm.--no more than
the width of a pencil line at the usual published scale of 1:50. The
basic principle is simply to set up strings at measured distances
parallel to the grid lines and to draw using these as datum lines. A
typical setup is shown in Fig. 7. A string is stretched across the top

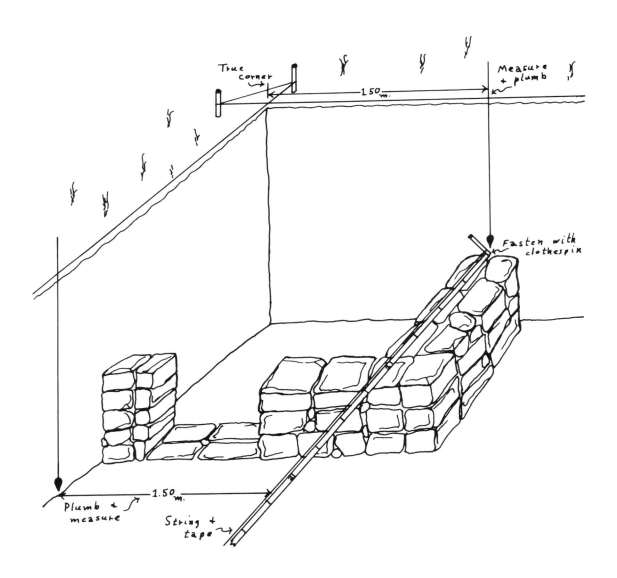

Figure 7. Setup for drawing a stone wall.

of the wall or other feature to be planned, running exactly parallel to
one of the balks at a predetermined distance out from the balk. A
cloth tape is strung up under this line; the zero point is determined
not from the balk as cut but rather from the balk line up at ground
level (or from the grid line if the balk line is not trusted), by dropping a plumb bob as shown. Long spikes or iron rods are firmly set so
that the line and tape can be stretched as taut as possible (especially
important when drawing in the wind), the tape being secured with a
clothespin. If the tape can be stretched sufficiently, the string may
be dispensed with and the tape itself used as the datum line, measuring
out from the center of it (below).

Several hints are offered for setups which will make the drawing
both faster and more accurate. (a) The datum line should be deliberately placed so that it falls at an even interval on the graph paper if
possible (i.e., not an arbitrary 1.31 m. but 1.25 m.); (b) the datum
line should be parallel to one balk if at all possible, since if it
runs at an angle, points cannot be counted off on the graph paper and
every one will have to be plotted with the drafting scale. (This is so
important that it should be attempted even if the wall runs somewhat
obliquely to the balk lines; of course, a wall at an angle of 30-45°
will require an oblique datum line, which can be plotted either by
measuring or triangulating (below). (c) The datum line should bisect
the most obvious features of the structure, allowing as many points as
possible to be read by the Draftsman directly from the tape. (d) The
datum line should run quite horizontally, and preferably just across to
the top of the main features of the structure. If a wall, for instance,
is preserved in "steps," it may save time and error to move the tape up
or down and re-establish it several times--always making sure, of
course, that the axis is the same and that zero begins at the same
point (using a plumb bob).

The actual drawing is done with an assistant, who calls off the
measurements for the points the Draftsman indicates he wishes to plot.
A three-meter tape is held at right angles to the datum line and the
measurement is given with some such formula: "At 1.35 on the datum
it's 47 centimeters out." Measurements should be rounded off a centimeter or so to coincide with the scale of the graph paper, on which at
the scale of 1:25 one square = 2-1/2 cm., i.e., not "1.36" but "1.35"
or "1.37-1/2." Remember that even 2 cm. is less than the width of a
pencil line at the published scale of 1:50! The drawing will progress
faster if the draftsman walks along the top of the structure as he
draws, looking directly down at the stones. This enables him to check
the points being called at a glance (the measurer is often too close
for good perspective), and it gives a good enough view so that with
practice many points, especially those bisected by the tape, can be
read directly without measurements and details can simply be sketched.
For points below the plane of the tape, or for protruding lower courses
of a wall, a plumb bob will be required as shown in Fig. 8. The structure should be drawn as the top course appears, emphasizing this and

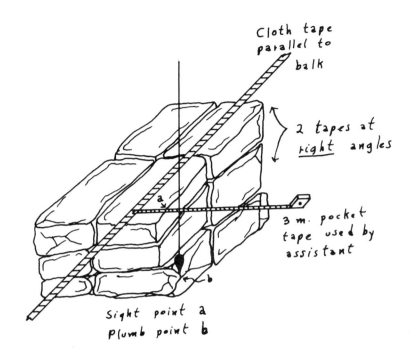

Figure 8.   Detail of wall setup.

other features such as thresholds with a bold line; protruding lower courses should be sketched in a lighter line.   Contours of stones can be quickly sketched by eye; and, while not strictly necessary, they give a plan a "three-dimensional" effect that lends style and may also indicate details of the masonry.   It may be personal prejudice, but we much prefer to look at a stone-for-stone plan which has contours; and we suspect that a drawing which is careful in such detail will be found more trustworthy in other respects.

Experience has shown that several factors make for a rapid and accurate drawing: (a) a convenient and accurate setup (above); (b) a draftsman who can spot and indicate at once the minimum essential features of a stone, from which the general configuration can be easily sketched; (c) a good measurer, who has sufficient "feel" for the architecture to anticipate the points the draftsman will want and can call them off rapidly.

When the drawing is completed, the Draftsman--probably in conjunction with the Supervisor or Director--should choose the spots where elevations are to be taken and mark them with an "X" and a number on both the actual stones (in chalk) and on the plan.   Points should include the tops of representative stones, especially where they are appreciably higher or lower; all other significant structural details; and several founding levels, usually shown with a squiggly arrow on the plan. (The latter may have to wait until dismantling of the structure, but they must not be overlooked.) Readings are taken with the transit (above), and reduced elevations are given to the draftsmen to transfer directly to the drawing. Elevations should be called back to the transit operator as they are given to double check them. Of course, the legend of the drawing should give Field, Area, and locus information; scale; and date and initials of the draftsman. It is exceedingly important that a north arrow be placed on the drawing. Even more important (and often overlooked!) is making sure that the balk lines are drawn in relation to the datum line (and hence to the structure itself), or otherwise the structure is "floating" and cannot be placed on the grid as the drawings are pieced together later to form larger and larger architectural units.

Once the principle described here is understood, a bit of imagination and ingenuity will enable one to solve virtually any drafting problem encountered in the field. All that is required is that the datum lines be accurately related to the grid. The following figures illustrate how several typical features found in excavation may be set up for drawing, using a transit and plumb bob to establish one or more datum lines, and then drawing by the method described above.

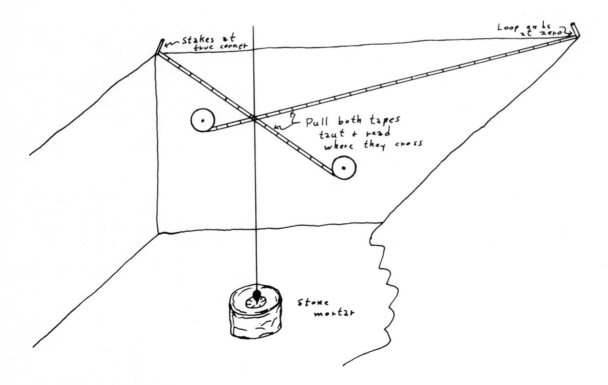

Figure 9. Triangulating to position isolated feature.

In Fig. 9 a stone mortar is being plotted in relation to the grid by triangulation from the grid stakes to the center of the mortar which can then be sketched by measuring several points with a three-meter tape. Note that _two_ triangulation setups may be needed to insure reasonable accuracy, especially if one angle is quite acute; in an especially critical situation, even three setups may be needed. The technique in this and other triangulation setups is essentially the same. Here two cloth tapes are looped over the grid stakes (thus the need for tapes reading zero at the _end_ of the loop, as specified above) and pulled until they cross exactly where the string of the plumb bob hangs when centered over the point to be plotted. The small dividers are set at the measurement of one tape, using the triangular drafting scale, and an arc is lightly sketched on the plan. The second measurement is transferred in the same way. The point at which the arcs cross on the plan is the datum point. The second or third setup is used for a check; in case of a substantial error (more than 5 cm., for instance) the datum point is drawn roughly in the center of the maximum crossing points of the arcs. Note that any single point or isolated feature which can be drawn from a single datum point can be dealt with by simple triangulation. If zero loop tapes are used, the setups are fairly quick and can even be handled, plumb bob and all, by one draftsman with no assistants.

Fig. 10 shows one way to draw a cistern. The basic datum line a-b is established in the usual way and the stone-lined mouth of the cistern is drawn. Then the same datum line, which will be on an exact E-W axis (if the grid is oriented to magnetic north), is then lowered into the cistern by dropping a plumb bob from point 'c' on the datum line to point 'd'. The transit is set up over the latter point (or only the head is used, if there is insufficient height) and the compass adjusted for north then rotated to a bearing of N 90° W. The telescope is tilted, and point 'e' is marked. Rotate the telescope 180° to a bearing of N 90° E and establish point 'f' similarly. A second datum line at right angles can also be established if needed. If the datum line e-f is set at the same time at a known vertical distance from datum line a-b (the reduced elevation of which is known), then it can serve as a datum line for _both_ the plan and the section, which will be convenient. When the plan of the underground cistern is drawn (probably at its maximum circumference), the cistern can be dotted on the top plan by "swinging" the drawing onto the plan of the square or Area, using point c-d and aligning datum lines a-b and e-f.

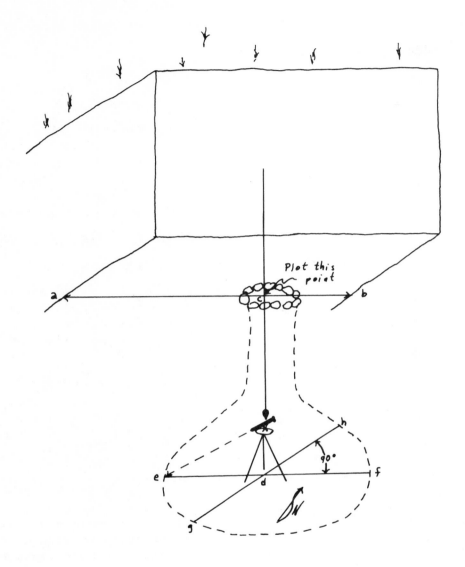

Figure 10. Setup for drawing a cistern.

Drawing caves and rock-cut tombs of various sorts is basically similar to the procedure for drawing the cistern described above. Fig. 11 shows a setup for the plan and section of a shaft tomb with a single lateral chamber. The basic datum line is a-b, established arbitrarily to suit the configuration of the tomb but _leveled_ by means of a spirit line-level. Point a is marked by a permanent pin, which will later be surveyed with transit or plane table; this, in conjunction with the compass bearings to be taken on datum line a-b, will serve to swing the tomb plan onto the master top plan. It will also automat-

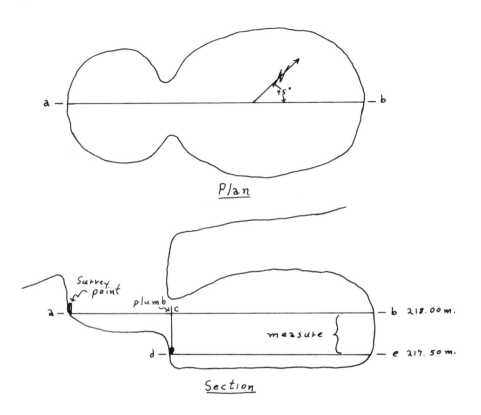

Figure 11.   Setup for drawing a shaft-tomb.

ically give the reduced elevation of the section. Datum line a-b is
lowered as needed for the chamber floor by transferring it with a
plumb bob to d-e; note that the same zero point must be maintained by
dropping a plumb bob at c. Of course, for the section, a-b and d-e
must not only be exactly aligned, but the vertical distance between the
two (c-d and b-e) must be measured so that the lower datum string is
level. We have learned from experience that a little time taken to
establish the several horizontal datum lines at even intervals is worth
the trouble, as the bold lines of the graph paper can be used to better
advantage and points plotted much faster. Note that the datum line can
also be raised to get the slope outside the tomb, using the transit
tripod if necessary to support one end of the line, and again using the
line-level for leveling.

When all tombs are planned, a plane table can be used to locate the
survey pins as shown in Fig. 12. All individual tomb plans are swung
by their survey pins onto the survey sheet, using the north bearing on
each plan to align them. Thus the plan of the whole cemetery is

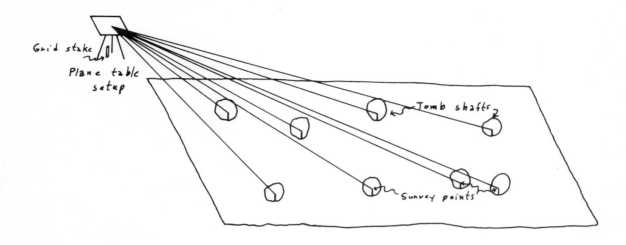

Figure 12. Using a plane table to plan a cemetery.

completed. If a plane table is not available, the survey can be done
with a transit, using it to measure the horizontal angles and a steel
tape to measure distances. The principle is exactly the same, but this
technique has the disadvantage of producing a series of calculations
which must be used to draw up the plan later, rather than a finished
sketch on the spot.

Fig. 13 illustrates how to set up for drawing a large cave. The
principle is exactly the same as for the shaft-tomb, except that
several horizontal datum lines will be required, running at various
angles to connect up the chambers of the cave, i.e., a-b, c-d, f-g,
etc. All that is necessary is to know the exact angles and distances
which these datum lines intersect, as for instance angle a-d = 90°,
angle c-f = 120°, etc. These datum lines can be arbitrarily set and
measured later, but it may be better to set them with the transit at a
predetermined angle. For the section, any raising or lowering of these
datum lines will also have to be plumbed, measured, and leveled.
Again, the plan is swung onto the top plan by surveying point a and by
using the compass bearing on datum line a-b. By extending datum lines
at measured angles and elevations, virtually any cave, no matter how
complex, can be planned from a single survey point.

163

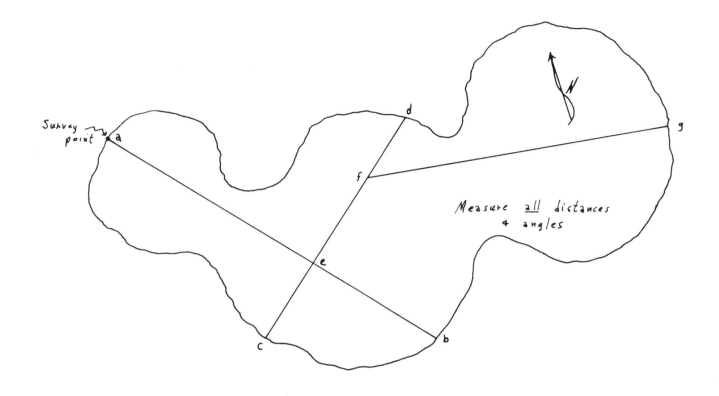

Figure 13.   Steup for drawing a large cave.

The kind of archaeology that we usually do, dependent upon maintaining temporary or even permanent standing balks, often leaves a building distributed over several excavation squares and brought to light at varying stages. Thus the complete architectural plan must be "built up" with many individual drawings--awkward-sounding, but in fact with a good grid more accurate than plane-table surveying, and with the added advantage of not holding up the excavation in any sector (except for checking, see below). The architectural plans which have been drawn square by square should be linked up by laying out the grid to scale on a large sheet and tracing off the individual plans to form larger architectural units. (If portions of walls remained in the unexcavated balks, they must be added later.) This should be done in the field under the direct supervision of the archaeologists, since they will have to decide which phases go together. However, the large-scale plans can be simply block or schematic plans, leaving the final inked stone-for-stone-plans to be done later. One reason for promptness is to provide the archaeologist with working plans for checking in the field, while any remaining problems can be spotted and solved.

Another reason is to allow for checking the accuracy of the plan of a particular building or building complex as a whole. (Of course, a plane-table survey would automatically produce such a plan--one of its advantages.) Checking can be easily done by measuring and especially by triangulating between key points such as corners of the building, etc. Here a plane table may also be used, if available, for checking, although it will usually be found that the pieced-together plan will be more accurate than a plane-table survey.

The system we have described here assumes that the services of a professional Architect will often not be required during the excavation itself if the architectural recording can be done sufficiently by draftsmen trained in the techniques above. However, two cautions must be sounded: (a) the Director himself must be sufficiently trained as a draftsman to coordinate all recording and to give continuity in style, and he must make the checking of the plans as they are linked up one of his major preoccupations; and (b) the services of a professional architectural consultant may be required when it comes time for preparation of the final plans for publication, both to check structural details and interpretations, and to prepare reconstructions such as isometric projections, which will be most helpful to the reader. Of course on a classical site a full-time professional Architect will almost certainly be required. Again we stress that it might be ideal to have on every excavation staff a fully trained Architect, provided that he were also an experienced stratigrapher; but in the absence of that desideratum the system advocated here, followed consistently under the control of a responsible Director, has proven its ability to produce architectural plans equal to the very best.

III

DRAWING SECTIONS

In modern field archaeology stratigraphic work is so dependent upon sections and measured section drawings that we must devote a special treatment to the drawing of sections.

A. Objectives.

It is axiomatic that on a modern excavation frequent cross sections of the stratified debris must be cut, observed, and recorded. In practice this means that with a grid system a measured section drawing should be made of all four sides of every excavation square. It should be stressed that this is not merely a record for publication--though it is that, and such a graphic and readily intelligible means of presenting the evidence that section drawings would be justified on this basis alone. Perhaps even more important is the element of <u>intellectual discipline</u> that is forced upon the excavator who knows that not only will he have to cut sections, but finally he will have to give an interpretation that will enable an intelligent drawing to be made of every debris level and its relations to any architectural remains. The expectation, then, of producing a final section drawing upon which most of the presentation of the evidence will rest informs the digging from the very beginning. Obviously, the drawing itself is in one sense the "point" of the whole enterprise, and we need not apologize for giving considerable attention to it. In this chapter we confine ourselves to the purely <u>mechanical</u> aspects of this task, while readily acknowledging that the fundamental aspect is the interpretive one (see Chapter III). Once the balk is properly prepared and the interpretation is agreed upon by the Area and Field Supervisors in consultation with the Director, how is the drawing to be done?

B. <u>Staff.</u>

1. There are differences of opinion as to who should be responsible for doing the section drawing. On many British and American excavations the Area or "Site" Supervisor is required to do his own sections, though it is usually assumed that he will have the benefit of the Director's counsel (or that of another experienced stratigrapher) on the interpretation preceding the drawing. At Gezer the "team" orientation of the work was carried far enough that ideally three people were involved in producing the section: the Director, who drew many of the sections himself in the early years and continued to be responsible for continuity of style; the Field Supervisor, who was responsible for four to six Areas and would be writing the field report; and the Area Supervisor who oversaw the actual digging. Only when all had agreed were lines finally settled upon and scratched in preparation for drawing. It could almost be said that the drawing, after this procedure, was a mere mechanical process. Indeed, we did find that relatively inexperienced Area Supervisors could then draw their own sections; but for the most part the drawing was done by the five Field Supervisors, with the assistance of Area Supervisors. These drawings in turn were gone over by the Director, so that the finished products were not only the result of consultations between several experienced people, but they were sufficiently standardized in style that a draftsman who had not been at the site could easily trace them off later to form continuous sections ready for publication. We would stress two things: (a) the interaction of several people in the interpretation of what can be seen and drawn, at least some of them stratigraphers as well as draftsmen; and (b) the overall supervision of one person, which lends continuity. With a system like this there can be no question of such a criticism as that of Franken, who claimed (mistakenly) that at one site "it is not the excavator who has drawn this section...but the architect at the end of the season's work."[8]

Behind this approach lies a conviction which should be frankly stated: the drawing of a section is <u>not</u> merely a mechanical task--as one reputable excavator has put it, "the empirical record of stratified digging."[9] We are convinced rather that "the purpose of a drawing is to provide a graphic summary of relevant data, to demonstrate the processes and results of interpretation."[10] A drawing is by nature subjective and selective; it is a dangerous illusion to suppose otherwise. If this is so, then our "team" approach to section drawing, involving as it does the criticism of several people, is sound, for it provides some control.

2. The question of who draws the section is related to the question of when, and the same fundamental presupposition underlies our answer. If a drawing is a considered intellectual appraisal, then time and distance must be allowed for this appraisal. This means that lines in the section cannot be drawn every few days to keep the section absolutely current--which one might suppose to be the prime consideration, to hear some field archaeologists. Of course, one does not want to get behind, so that sections are postponed to the end of the excavation and must be drawn in haste. It is true that the soil dries out quickly, and that color and texture become increasingly difficult to distinguish. And drawing a section is awkward if one is too far below to reach and measure the layers being drawn with ease. But these problems are not the <u>primary</u> consideration--a defensible interpretation is, and that requires perspective.

We would argue that a stratum cannot be intelligently understood until one is well into the stratum below, so that one can be sure that the earliest phase of the stratum at hand has been reached and that it can be related to what preceded it. Of course, debris layers are separated, they are tagged as one digs through them, the section is given careful scrutiny over a period of several days in varying lights, and the main lines are probably scratched in lightly. But before one commits oneself irrevocably to paper--and a final interpretation--much more needs to be seen.

One thing more needs to be said if a section really is an interpretation, and that is that there is no reason to hesitate in changing a line if a later perspective makes the line clearer. To draw a section "as it was dug," with precisely the separations that were discerned at the time of digging when only two of the necessary three dimensions were visible, may be simply to perpetuate a mistake that had better be admitted and changed. Loci may have to be subdivided and pottery baskets and objects redistributed; but precisely the value of the system advocated in this <u>Manual</u> is that this can be done with confidence, and errors in stratigraphy--which <u>all</u> excavators make, whether they recognize them or not--can be corrected. One of the reasons for having those other than the Area Supervisor who dug the material involved in the interpretation and drawing of a section is that new insights are often provided by critics who have nothing at stake. In the attempt to defend the section "as dug" and the resultant exchange of views, a synthesis is likely to emerge which has already been severely tested and can be published with some confidence.

Of course, if one supposes that the drawing is the "empirical record," none of the above will be needed and section drawing can be greatly simplified. But in long and earnest disputes among experienced stratigraphers who in all honesty see things in a section quite differently (all of whom offer plausible explanations for the phenomena they believe they see!) we have learned that one cannot simplify the process without being simplistic.

C. Equipment and Technique.

No equipment is required for section drawing beyond that already listed for surveying and architectural recording: iron rods or large spikes, datum string, plumb bob, three-meter tape, and simple drawing equipment. The rods or spikes are driven into the corners of the square at predetermined reduced elevations, preferably in even numbers above Sea Level, using the transit and level rod. (Setting the spikes at both ends with the transit is more accurate than setting only one end and leveling the other with a line or spirit level.) Thus if the rod-reading at point a gives an HI of 243.56 m., the rod is lowered into the corner of the square until point b reads 3.56 m., and the datum line for the section drawing will be 240.00 m.

The datum string is stretched, making sure that it is tight enough not to sag. A cloth meter tape is fastened to both spikes with clothespins, checking that it is out from the datum string and does not ride on it at any point; if necessary, the tape can be supported at several points with nails or surveyor's pins. Note that the tape is not started from the spike, which will almost certainly be slightly in from the true corner, but is begun at a point indicated by dropping a plumb bob from the balk or grid line up at ground level, as in Fig. 7. Both a correct zero point and an accurate reduced elevation are important, especially if the section is to be continued in subsequent seasons and the new drawing must link up with the old (below).

The actual process of drawing a section is like that of drawing a wall (illustrated in Fig. 14). An assistant uses a three-meter tape to measure and call off points to be plotted. The only difficulty is making sure that the two datum lines--the string and the small tape-- are at right angles. Here is where a lock-device on the tape is helpful, because it permits it to hang as a plumb bob. The assistant must also make sure he is eyeing the point nearly dead on, to prevent a distorted view, even if this means looking like something of a contortionist! Each point is plotted on the graph paper by the draftsman, and the points are connected into continuous lines. The drawing proceeds point by point in this fashion. Of course, it is not quite that

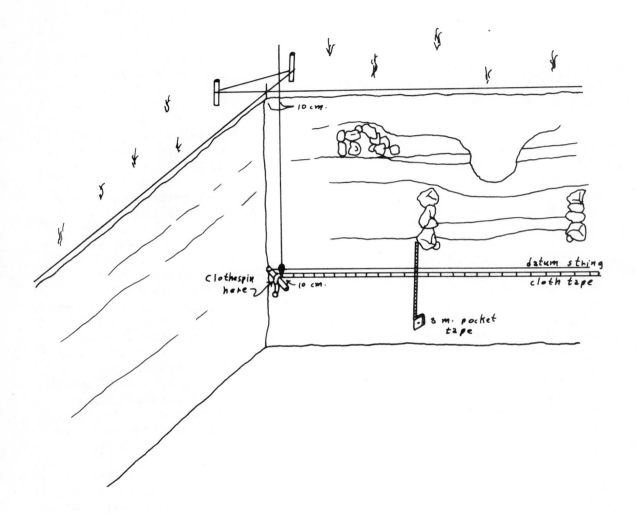

Figure 14.   Setup for drawing a balk.

simple, and we are encouraged by trial and error to offer the following
suggestions to the archaeologist or draftsman who wishes to facilitate
section drawing.

   1. Save time by thinking through a convenient setup, i.e., establish the datum at an even meter, half-meter, or quarter-meter elevation
if at all possible, so that the blocks of the graph paper can be used
for rapid sighting and millimeter squares do not have to be counted.

2. Double-check the elevation and zero point, especially if you are adding on to last season's drawing, and replot a few key elements on the old drawing to be sure you are properly aligned before proceeding. The ideal here, as in the architectural drawings, should be to keep errors within a tolerance of about 2 cm.

3. Pause to set up a new section drawing properly on the paper, i.e., allow for all possible future expansion laterally or vertically; make sure the reduced elevation of the datum line is clearly written on the drawings; etc.

4. Get yourself placed confortably on a low stool well back from the balk to be drawn, at approximately eye-level to the major features. Such perspective is extremely helpful since it provides an overview in which to fit details, provides a ready visual check on the assistant's measurements (who is often too close and gets a distorted view), and provides opportunity for a good deal of sketching from various reference points.

5. Draw in the larger features first, such as walls, prominent stones, main tiplines, so that they can serve as reference points. Speed up the drawing by learning to size up a stone, a configuration of lines, a pit, etc., and to spot those few significant points from which they can be most easily and accurately drawn. At the same time learn to think of the graph paper in "blocks" according to the scale being used, and when simply running tip lines call for points at even intervals, i.e., for a scale of 1:25, at intervals of 12-1/2 or 25 cm. Learn to pick out and plot strategically located points and to sketch surrounding detail from them. Learn to run several parallel lines at once, if they are uncomplicated, by plotting a number of vertical points at, say, every 50 cm. Learn to sketch contour lines on stones quickly.

6. In terms of simple mechanics, keep needed items such as erasers and sharpeners readily at hand. Keep the drawings clean, especially in heat and dirt, by resting the drawing hand on a plastic triangle or the like. Use light, flowing lines to sketch between plotted points, and then firm them up to avoid the "connect-the-dots" look which makes even a fairly accurate section appear amateurish.

7. Strive for a "neutral" style which a draftsman can combine with other drawings, and for a clean unambiguous line which can be clearly traced later. Definitely to be avoided are fuzzy, "impressionistic" section drawings; the ideal line is that of a man who has made up his mind and knows what he wishes to state!

8. Be sure that all information is included, i.e., Field and Area designation, scale, datum and elevation, north orientation, all locus numbers possible, soil color and texture descriptions (with Munsell designation, if especially crucial).

9. Check the section as soon as possible by placing it on a light box and trying for alignment with all section drawings which impinge upon it, as well as by juxtaposing it with the architectural plans of walls which also appear in the section. Better to discover errors in placement now!

There are several special problems likely to be encountered in drawing sections. One is the problem of scale. A scale of 1:50 is sometimes used, and it is probably the scale at which one will publish the section drawings. But a scale of 1:25 is vastly superior, both because it allows for much more detail, and because it makes for tighter lines when the drawing is done outsize and then reduced for publication. (A scale of 1:20 is sometimes used.) It is strongly urged that in any case the scale of both plans and sections be standardized, as to the same scale. Only in rare cases should deviations be allowed, as for instance when a crucial detail in a subsidiary balk is drawn to 1:10.

Then there is the question of conventions. At Gezer we have adopted certain conventions for representing debris layers or other features which are differentiated but cannot actually be drawn in detail, i.e., hatched lines for built-up earthen surfaces; dots for plaster; broken slashes for ash; cross-hatching for bedrock; dotted lines for surfaces that cannot be traced any farther; etc. But these are never used to produce schematic sections, which we think undesirable (although they are often seen, for instance, in British publications). Even stone-falls and fills are represented as accurately as possible, in the conviction that a section drawing should be as detailed and even as "objective" as the scale permits. After all, the drawing can always be schematized for publication, but detail which is omitted--which might have given critics the possibility of an improved interpretation --can never be added later.

There is also the question of whether or not a section drawing is to be understood as the representation of exactly what would show in a perfect cross-section if that were possible. Here we suggest a compromise, since the drawing is a deliberate conclusion regarding the evidence. For instance, we would recommend at least dotting in the position of a wall which does not quite reach the balk, since the absence of the wall on the section drawing would be technically correct but actually misleading. Similarly, a wall robbed down to its foundation course can be dotted up a course or two to show its relation to higher surfaces, although of course nothing really shows in the section. Walls in the balk probably cannot be shown exactly in section and a slightly schematized version may convey more accurately the actual character of the wall. The question of contours is relevant here. Strictly speaking, there could be no contour line on stones in the section, since the projected section-line would bisect them. But we prefer to sketch in the main contour lines, both to give an impression of the masonry, and also to avoid the curiously "flat" look of many sections. Again, it is a matter of taste and judgment; but the criterion must always be whether the drawing obscures vital information, or whether it conveys the picture the archaeologist wishes to leave with the reader who has not been privileged to see the actual material.

Certain mechanical problems occur when a very large field of squares is being recorded and all four sections are being drawn in every square. The only way to end up with sections that go all across the field with no lacunae in them is to draw all four sections in each square; to take down the balk, leaving standing stubs one meter square; and then to piece onto the drawings the four faces of these stubs. It will be seen that at each such stub four long sections actually cross, and eight section drawings come together within a one meter area. So accuracy is called for. The best way to insure alignment, since the square balks will have been removed and cannot be rechecked, is to overlap on the light box the four sets of drawings that form each corner, checking each pair carefully for alignment; to tag the main lines in the corner of each square before the balks are taken down; and to juxtapose the two drawings on either side of the one-meter lacuna to be filled in from the remaining stub, and to pencil in lightly the connections that have to be looked for and drawn. Of course, absolute accuracy in maintaining the grid when removing the balks and in establishing the reduced elevation of the datum lines is also required. With these fairly routine precautions, we have managed to draw all 104 sections of the 26 squares in Field VI at Gezer, some of them from surface to bedrock. All sections link up, and where the balks have been removed the sections are continuous clear across the field.

A related problem is that of managing the section drawing when balks are removed stratum by stratum, down to each consistent architectural horizon as it is reached and cleared completely. (Despite its problems, we think this is a much more desirable procedure than leaving balks standing and excavating in small, isolated "boxes" where architectural plans are never completed and large-scale photographs are impossible.)[11] Here all that is required is absolute accuracy in laying out squares; enough permanent grid stakes to return to for the new layout after balks have been removed; care in re-establishing datum lines for sections, and the presence of mind not to remove the lowest levels of the balks before lines are all on the section drawing and checked. With care, balks can be drawn, lowered, drawn, lowered again, etc., repeatedly.

One "trick" to cutting and drawing sections is to remember that section drawings can be reversed on the light box or when traced. In this way it is possible to cut to a longitudinal section line from either side, or even from alternating sides in different squares, and still end up with a continuous section drawing by reversing and piecing together several individual drawings. All that is required is care in the setup. This procedure was, in fact, followed with great success in the drawing of the main section in Field V, the famous Gezer "High

Place," where logistics made it impossible actually to dig a continuous section.

Since this Manual is concerned primarily with field technique rather than with preparation of the material for publication, we only remark in passing that some differentiation in lines at the time of drawing in the field will be most helpful later on. Surfaces, wall-faces, pits, etc., should be given a bolder line, with tip-lines and secondary features less emphasized. It should also be absolutely clear which lines or features a locus number refers to, i.e., the locus number should not appear on a line demarcating two fills (since properly speaking a non-dimensional line cannot be a locus), but clearly on one or the other of the fills. Similarly, locus numbers of walls should be on the wall, not merely nearby; surface numbers actually on the surface, or keyed to it by an arrow, etc. Again, the object of the drawings is a consistent, clear statement which, whether it is agreed to or not, can be understood by the reader.[12]

NOTES

1. See A. H. Detweiler, Manual of Archaeological Surveying, "Publications of the Jerusalem School: Archaeology," Vol. II, New Haven: American Schools of Oriental Research (1948), p. vii.

2. See G. E. Wright, "Method in Palestinian Archaeology--An American Interpretation," Eretz-Israel, 9 (1969), pp. 120-33; also the writer's article, "Two Approaches to Archaeological Method--The Architectural and the Stratigraphic," in Eretz-Israel 11 (1973), pp. 1-8.

3. For a recent treatment of aerial surveying, see J. K. S. St. Joseph, ed., The Uses of Air Photography (London: 1966).

4. The 1:20,000 cadastral survey of the 1930's was originally projected over the entire country north of Beersheba and was intended to be the first completely modern, accurate survey. However, it was not completed until after the British Mandate ended, and the various portions are of uneven accuracy. A 1:100,000 topographic survey was begun by the British in the 1930's and completed by the Israelis after 1948; and the Israelis have also completed a 1:50,000 survey of the whole country. On these maps and cartography in general, see now the excellent Atlas of Israel, edited and published by the Survey of Israel (Jerusalem, 1970).

5. For the procedure in establishing a "triangulation grid," see Detweiler, op. cit., pp. 7-10. Such a grid is not necessarily required, but it may be useful for small areas of excavation, for locating features already exposed, or for general Plane Table surveying.

6. See further W. G. Dever, H. D. Lance, G. E. Wright, Gezer I. Preliminary Report of the 1964-66 Seasons (Jerusalem: HUCBAS, 1970), p. 10.

7. The following procedure is designed for use when the coordinate grid is being used; when Fields are laid out arbitrarily or in relation to existing architecture, as at Gezer (above and n. 6), it may be easier to lay them out using the following procedure generally, and survey them later for placement on the top plan vis-a-vis the coordinate grid.

8. H. J. Franken, A Primer of Old Testament Archaeology (Leiden: E. J. Brill, 1963), p. 12.

9. Paul W. Lapp, "The Tell Deir 'Alla Challenge to Palestinian Archaeology," Vetus Testamentum, Vol. XX (1970), p. 255.

10. Brian Hope-Taylor, "Archaeological Draughtmanship: Principles and Practices: Part II," Antiquity, XL, No. 158 (June, 1966), p. 108; see also reference to an earlier article in this series by Stuart Piggott.

11. See further article by Dever cited in n. 2 above.

12. The writer of this chapter is indebted fundamentally to G. R. H. Wright under whose critical eye he made his first attempt at surveying and drafting at Shechem in 1962. The chapter was read in rough draft by William Ellinger and Thomas Schaub of the Albright Institute in Jerusalem, to whom thanks are due for valuable criticisms. Of course, none of these is to be held responsible in detail for the views expressed here.

Chapter VII

ARCHAEOLOGICAL PHOTOGRAPHY

Robert B. Wright

"The overriding difficulty of the archaeological photographer
is to induce his camera to tell the truth." Mortimer Wheeler

I

THE ARCHAEOLOGIST AS PHOTOGRAPHER AND THE PHOTOGRAPHER AS ARCHAEOLOGIST

It is the customary pattern in archaeology for the archaeologist to
take pictures or for a photographer to aim his camera at the diggings.
On smaller excavations the archaeologist having received his photographic training at the Washington Monument, the Eiffel Tower, and the
Damascus Gate, assumes the role of photographic recorder. Larger
sites, which need a full-time photographer, have difficulty finding
budgetary support for a professional and usually locate "someone good
with a camera" and install him with film and tripod. Certainly some
archaeologists take good pictures, and some photographers have developed a keen archaeological eye; but the uneven quality preserved in
archaeological publications and in reports to the scholarly societies
testifies to the difficulties involved.

At Gezer our intent has been to train persons in both crafts: an
understanding and appreciation for the methods of excavation linked to
skill in scientific illustration. This chapter explains the way in
which this intent was pursued at Gezer by integrating a precisely controlled photographic procedure into the recording system of the excavation.

II

THE PLACE OF THE PHOTOGRAPH IN ARCHAEOLOGY

Photographs had three uses in archaeology at Gezer: as part of the
recording system; as slides for lectures and for reports to the scholarly community; and as illustrations in preliminary and final reports.
The second and third of these uses are well known and need not be
elaborated upon. The integration of photography into the overall
recording control system was unique at Gezer.

Control was maintained over excavation by a well-developed system
of surveying, three-dimensional recording, top-plans, locus identification and architect's drawings, methods of which are explained in this
manual. At Gezer, the photographic recording was incorporated into
this continuous recording system and provided another control over the
progress and history of the digging. Photographs were understood to be

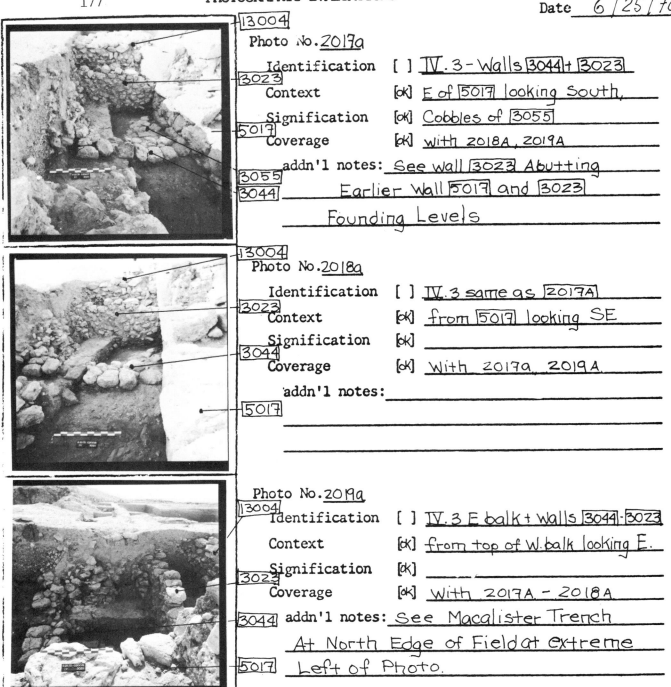

Photo No. 2017a

Identification [ ] IV.3 - Walls 3044 + 3023

Context [OK] E of 5017 looking South.

Signification [OK] Cobbles of 3055

Coverage [OK] with 2018A, 2019A

addn'l notes: See Wall 3023 Abutting

Earlier Wall 5017 and 3023

Founding Levels

Photo No. 2018a

Identification [ ] IV.3 same as 2017A

Context [OK] from 5017 looking SE

Signification [OK] _____

Coverage [OK] With 2017a, 2019A

addn'l notes: _____

Photo No. 2019a

Identification [ ] IV.3 E balk + walls 3044 · 3023

Context [OK] from top of W. balk looking E.

Signification [OK] _____

Coverage [OK] With 2017A - 2018A

addn'l notes: See Macalister Trench

At North Edge of Field at extreme

Left of Photo.

EVALUATION QUESTIONS:

1. Identification: Do the photos clearly illustrate the form, outline, and texture of the subject clear? Are all of the features which constitute the character of the subject present?

2. Context: Do the photos clearly indicate the contextual relationships between the subject and the total area?

3. Signification: Have any modifications in the information about identity and importance of the subject been made to that given in the field?

4. Coverage: Have enough photographs of the subject been taken? Have all the photos necessary for Total Context Coverage been made?

Figure 1. Photographic evaluation sheet from Area Supervisor's fieldbook.

an additional recording tool with their own advantages and limitations. As they were added to the field notebooks each evening, photos provided a record of the day's work and, when reviewed over a period of days, offered a sequence of the excavation's progress.

For the photographic record to be successful, we found it important that the photos be studied and evaluated continuously throughout the season. Without a constant review one is no better off than those who wait until they get home to see what they have. The supervisors had to be certain that the prints in the notebooks showed everything necessary for a complete record before excavation continued and corrections by additional photos were impossible. Photos were dry-mounted on cards and distributed to supervisors to be added to field notebooks. Many Area Supervisors marked locus numbers directly on the photos, indicating significant features by arrows (Fig. 1). Four questions were to be asked of each group of photographs:

1. Identification - Do the photos clearly illustrate what the object is? Is the form, outline and texture of the object apparent? Are all the features which constitute the character of the object present?

2. Context - Do the photos clearly indicate the contextual relationships between the subject and the surrounding area?

3. Significance - Has the information about the identity and importance of the object changed since the photographs were made?

4. Coverage - Have enough photographs of the subject been made?

III

AREA SUPERVISORS AND PHOTOGRAPHY

Supervisors are intent on getting their Areas dug well and recorded carefully, with as much progress to show for the season as possible, consistent with good methods. These legitimate goals tend, however, to make the supervisor impatient with the time-consuming work of making photographs. He does not like to see his workers idle; he wants to get on with the digging, to get that object out of the earth and into the basket and notebook. Yet supervisors had to come to grips with the plain fact that photography slows down excavation. Allowance had to be made for photography in planning and in the expectation of the schedule.

Supervisors were encouraged to direct the excavation with photography in mind. Each phase should emerge together. Quite apart from

179

being good archaeological method, this is important for the making of photographs if they are to be clear and unambiguous. One photograph should not need "a thousand words" of interpretation. The whole square should be ready when the subject is ready. Occasionally critical preparation of a friable object was upset because the surrounding context was not ready at the same time.

To maintain quality and direct attention to the overall goals we found it necessary at Gezer to provide control on the flow of photographs. Photos were requested by Field Supervisors, many times at the suggestion of Area Supervisors, and were scheduled after determining the preparation needed of the area, optimum time of day, light and other factors. Using a specially prepared Photo Request Form, supervisors would identify the Field, Area, subject, and indicate the prime locus and special features (Fig. 2). This form had space for a small

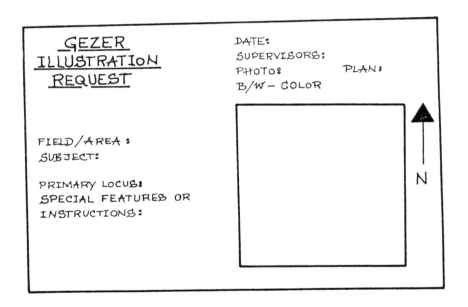

Figure 2. Photo request form.

sketch of the orientation and coverage of the subject. A judgment of the ultimate use of the photo was asked with the choice between a Record photo and a Publishable illustration. The photo request form did two things: First, it encouraged supervisors to "think photographically," that is, to pre-visualize the subject, examining it for the best angle, light, context and preparation. This improved the quality of the photographs because the supervisors were forced to be concerned with these matters, and it speeded up the schedule as much of the analysis had been done before the photographer reached the field.

Second, the tendency of some supervisors to call for a photograph after each rock is lifted or sherd is turned was substantially reduced, partially, one suspects, by the trouble necessary to fill out a request form. The initial complaints about "unnecessary paperwork" and "bureaucracy" soon subsided and the request form worked well. A balance was very soon struck between recording and excavation.

IV

DETERMINING SUBJECT MATTER

The final determination of subject selection rested with the Field Supervisor and the Director. However, there were certain basic subjects which normally were included in a comprehensive photographic coverage:

A. <u>Beginning and end of season</u>. Before digging began photos of every excavation area were made to record the condition of the field after the winter season. At the conclusion of the excavating season final photos were made to record the last phase of digging and to define the starting place during the next year's clearing.

B. <u>Complete strata</u>. Whenever an entire archaeological stratum had been cleared, it was prepared for full photographic recording. As major divisions of archaeological history, strata required careful documentation.

C. <u>Structures</u>. Independent structures and structural complexes were photographed at each phase of their building or use. As with strata, full phases were spread before the camera. Unless good archaeological method demanded otherwise, we were hesitant about allowing the camera to record more than one occupational level or phase of construction in a single photograph. Careful advance planning was necessary to keep the whole phase together and to have all of it ready for photography.

D. <u>Installations</u>. As was the case with structures, preparation of most kinds of installations included the surrounding phase or occupational level. Again, following accepted archaeological method, dismantling of the installation paralleled reduction of the occupation levels to which it was related.

E. <u>Significant objects</u>. Important objects discovered in the course of an excavation were, of course, photographed <u>in situ</u>, within their context. If they were sufficiently unique or characteristic, they were later photographed more formally.

F. <u>End-of-day photos</u>. At the conclusion of the excavating day, each Area was photographed whether or not photos were made of the Area that day. End-of-day photos provided a continuous record of the progress of the excavations at regular intervals. These photos did not require the same advance preparation of the site since they were not normally for publication.

Every subject was described by a complete complement of photographs. To fulfill this goal, two criteria of identification and context had to be satisfied:

G. <u>Identification</u>. The subject had to be presented in such a way that it was clearly identifiable. All characteristic features which made the subject what it was were to be revealed. The form of the subject was to be clearly defined and to be distinct from its background.

H. <u>Context</u>. No subject could appear in an archaeological vacuum. The horizontal and vertical contexts had to be demonstrated as clearly as possible. Its relationship to surrounding objects, the full Area, and the total archaeological context were demonstrated.

This "Total Context Coverage" principle applied to field technique as a series of photographs were made which included the following:

- The subject itself showing all characteristic detail.

- The relationships to other objects in context.

- The section of the Area containing the subject, with balks and major structures in association with the subject. If there was a direct connection between the subject and a main balk, or indirect connection through a secondary balk, this was shown in a photograph.

- The full Area being excavated from several perspectives. A minimum of two photos were made from 180° or the diagonals, plus a vertical view, if possible. If the subject was a stratum or a phase, the quantity of full-area photos was increased as necessary.

- The Field, or section of the Field, in which the Area was located. For small objects and installations it was necessary only that there be available a photo of the general part of the Field. For major installations and structures, however, a photo of the entire Field at that stage of excavations was necessary.

At the time of photography, the following information was requested of Area Supervisors:

1. <u>Identification of subject</u> - What are the characteristic features which must be shown in the photo? Also, locus number, stratum, phase (name and number of stratum and phase).

2. <u>Significance of the subject</u> - Why is the subject worth photographing?

3. <u>Contextual relationships</u> - Vertical to what has preceded; horizontal to other objects and structures and to the whole Area.

Requesting such information from Area Supervisors brought the photographers up to date with the progress of excavation and allowed the supervisor to sharpen his thinking about his Area.

V

PREPARATION FOR PHOTOGRAPHY

Preparation of an excavation area for photography had to be painstaking and thorough. Details often overlooked on the field stand out with glaring starkness in a photograph. Imperfections once recorded, with few exceptions, can never be removed. There are many photos which one wishes could be changed or cleaned up. For unknown reasons, the camera magnifies minor irregularities in the smoothest surfaces and makes any scene much "dirtier" than it actually is. This is especially true in monochromatic (black and white) photos, which depend only upon differences in texture and shades of gray to distinguish surfaces.

The different surfaces included within the camera's field of view each required a different degree of preparation:

A. <u>Excavated areas</u>. Before every photograph all Areas within the subject range of the camera were prepared.

Surfaces were cleaned of all debris and swept. Footprints, pebbles, roots, and other intrusive elements were removed.

Structures and installations were clearly defined. As necessary they were traced or undercut to exhibit a shadow-contrast outline. We had to be very careful only to emphasize, never to create, contrasts.

Balks had to be straight, clean, sharply cornered and evenly tagged. Lettering on balk tags was at least two inches high to be clearly legible in the photos.

In preparation we were careful not to create artificial structures. Half-balks and probe trenches that may be mistaken for structures or installations were avoided. The camera <u>can</u> be made to lie. Manufactured surfaces were likewise avoided. If a surface was not "real," it was left "evenly roughened" to indicate an intermediate stage of excavation.

If a surface was not of the same stratum as the primary subject, it was cleared of debris and roughened with a stiff brush. Likewise, if we wished to emphasize a locus and de-emphasize surrounding loci, judicious brush work was used.

B. <u>Non-excavated areas</u>. Balk tops, steps, and ground surrounding a square were cleared and then smoothed to eliminate footprints. Ground surrounding a square was cleaned to one meter and defined by a row of stones.

C. <u>Adjacent Areas and surrounding ground</u>. These Areas were "picked up"; people, tools, etc. were removed.

VI

THE PHOTOGRAPHIC TECHNIQUE USED AT GEZER

A. <u>Equipment</u>. Two camera systems were used at Gezer. For color slides several 35mm cameras were used, a Leica M-2, and two Nikkormats with 35, 50, 90 and 135 mm lenses. The well-discussed advantages and disadvantages of range-finder versus single-lens reflex cameras were apparent. The only special problems were those shared by all who insist in using cameras in that part of the world: heat and dust. Keeping the equipment shaded and protected from dirt was adequate precaution.

The 2-1/4 in.-square format was chosen for black-and-white photos because it provided contact prints large enough to avoid enlarging in the field and was a flexible format to allow freedom in cropping the final prints. A Hasselblad 500C with 50mm and 80mm lenses was used for the five seasons with good success. This single-lens reflex camera with interchangeable lenses and backs, a 45° prism finder, and a pistol grip handle proved a versatile and superior system for field photography. Prior warnings against subjecting good equipment to the hazards of the Mideast climate proved unfounded, for the equipment worked virtually flawlessly, given protection, frequent dusting, and bi-annual cleaning. (A complete inventory of equipment may be found in the Appendix.)

The field photographic laboratory was equipped to provide flexibility and capability for most photographic functions. The ambient environment was held at 75° F. (24° C.) at a relative humidity of about 25% by an air conditioner. The lab contained an eight-foot epoxy-lined sink, work tables, and storage areas. A drying cabinet had a separate forced-air environment which drew warm filtered air across prints and films. Equipment included an automated film processor, a stabilization print processor, and a dry mounting press.

In the field, equipment was carried in specially modified cases. Substantial tripods were used and a seven-meter photographic tower provided the elevated perspective especially used for recording large structures which extended through several areas. A five-by-three-meter opaque cloth was used to provide artificial shade when necessary. A special set of "meter-sticks" was designed for Gezer. They were made triangular in section so that they could always be braced in such a way as to present a surface parallel to the film plane. They were made in various lengths and marked in 10 cm. increments by staggered white and red plastic (or Formica) panels. The construction protected them against unsightly nicks and ground-in dirt and facilitated cleaning as well.

B. <u>Technical Control</u>. Photography has always depended upon several variables inherent in the system--changing exposure, development, and printing time--to work the creativity of the cameraman. At Gezer, given the aims of archaeological recording, we established a procedure to standardize the entire photographic procedure, to reduce the variables as far as possible, and to collate those remaining into a working whole.

Implementing a procedure devised by Minor White of M.I.T., based on the "Zone System" of Ansel Adams,[1] we began each season by recalibrating the shutter speed, film speed, meter readings, developing time, and printing time together. A working film speed was calculated, which often differed from the printed ASA, an exact development time was established for the particular combination of film and chemicals used, and a standard negative print time was found for which all negatives for the season could be printed.

With the initial integration of the equipment and processes, procedures were used which would protect these calibrations. Exposures were made from a standard 18% gray card with a spot meter. A stabilization print processor assured that print development time was uniform.

This procedure of technique and processes afforded precise control over the whole photographic procedure and assured maintenance of high quality prints and slides. As an example of the degree of control we were able to maintain, we regularly printed an entire roll of twelve exposures of different scenes together at a print timer setting held the same throughout the season, and all of the prints would be properly exposed.

C. <u>Light and Contrast</u>. In Near Eastern archaeology the most formidable problem in photography is light. One must control the extremes of contrast present in scenes where the chromatic elements of the subject are gray-on-gray, but where the tonal range between subjects in bright sunlight and those in shadow is three times as great as that normally encountered. Leafing through archaeological reports documents the problem clearly. I suspect the classic photo appears in Mortimer Wheeler's manual, <u>Archaeology from the Earth</u>, in which a shadow engulfing three-quarters of the photo is identified as "Sir Flinders Petrie in the courtyard of the School in Jerusalem."[2]

After several years' experimentation, in which we contributed our share of high-contrast pictures, we limited our photography to the morning hours, when the areas were in full shadow. From first light until the direct sun hit the excavation areas, usually from about 5:15 to 7:30 a.m., the soft light of these early hours gave us the modeling texture definition we wanted without the harsh contrast of the direct sun. When an unexpected find required recording which could not be scheduled at these times, the shade cloth was used to produce a shadow over the spot to be photographed.

Most of the procedures for good quality camera and lab work are applicable to archaeological photography, but some were found especially important. In composing a scene, the balance between concentration on the prime subject and necessity of context was important. Supervisors who were disappointed with a photo often discovered that what they had seen disappeared in the print because they had been viewing the scene with binocular vision; and the camera, which has but monocular capability, failed to distinguish adequately between subtleties of depth. Usually a shift of perspective corrected the problem.

With some three hundred rolls of film running through our cameras in a six- or seven-week season, control over this flow had to be maintained. We developed a photo identification board with movable numbers which displayed the important data; this was included at the lower edge of each photograph in such a way that it could be cropped out in printing. Approximately 10 cm. by 30 cm., it recorded the date, a sequential negative number, the Field, Area, and prime locus. The negative number was cross-referenced to the supervisors' field notebooks and to a record book kept by the photographic staff.

D. <u>Laboratory Operation</u>. Whether processed by hand, with the continuous agitator, or by the automatic processor, we used Eastman Kodak Microdol-X developer, diluted 3:1 and discarded after one use to assure fresh chemicals and repeatable performance. The processor was a custom designed, electronically controlled programmed unit which carried film from dry roll through final wash. The continuous agitator device rotated film processing cans on their sides and the chemicals were changed manually. Both of these devices used about one-third the usual amount of developer which brought the chemicals closer to the point of exhaustion and so were more economical than standard methods. Hypo eliminator and hurricane washing devices were regularly used to reduce processing time. Chemicals were stored in collapsible plastic containers which increased the useful life of the chemicals to near shelf life.

Contact prints were made with a print frame which printed a roll of twelve exposures on a single eight-by-ten-inch sheet of polycontrast paper. Stabilization processing decreased processing time, eliminated another variable, and withstood dry mounting and field conditions well. Permanent prints were fixed and washed.

Films and prints were dried in the cabinet. Negatives were filed by sequential number. One set of prints was mounted on the field notebook cards and the other mounted and added to the sequential print file. After the excavating season enlargements were made commercially, and a second file arranged by field and area was created.

VII

SMALL OBJECT PHOTOGRAPHY

Small object photography is an area of archaeological photography which has generally been done less than well. Perhaps this is because there are more variables to control or because most persons have little experience in this specialized form of photography.

If we can assume that the problems of film and light color balance are in hand and that control over light intensity can be maintained with an accurate meter and gray card, there are two factors which must be understood for success in photographing small objects. First, one must be able to identify the significant characteristics of the object --the outline shape, rim stance and shape, the handle configuration and base structure; the texture of the surface; the separation of planes of a linear object, and the incisions of a decoration or inscription. These significant characteristics must be isolated and understood. Second, one must master the use of light, its position and intensity, to preserve and project these characteristics in the final photograph.

Usually there is one camera position which is optimum. From that angle the object displays its characteristic features. Various backgrounds may be used, but the background must not compete with the object. A technique which we used with some success employed a sheet of translucent plastic bent to form the background. From behind colored light was projected onto the plastic providing both background color and wiping out shadows. The light came from a small slide projector with colored plastic squares in the slide chamber.

Lighting is the tool of small object photography, and control of its powers and uses is fundamental to good photographs. Artificial light attempts to duplicate nature, and the best photos work with this deception. A single source of light, high and to the left, is psychologically regarded as "natural," at least the illusion that there is a single light so placed. There may be more than one light (often there are three or more), but there must be only one shadow. The shadow must be placed naturally, but it must not obscure essential features of the object. The photo manuals suggest the classic light positions: main light high and 45° to the left, a fill-light beside the camera half as bright. This classic arrangement will give satisfactory pictures for most objects and is recommended (Fig. 3).

Figure 3.

To move from the classic lighting, one must be aware of what light can do and what one wants it to do. Round objects and jars, bowls, or lamps require attention to modeling to convey their roundness in a flat photograph. Modeling suggests substance and form and is usually achieved by moving the main light away from the camera. Light coming only from immediately beside the camera, as a flash bulb, flattens out the subject, because all surfaces receive the same amount of light (Fig. 4). Moving the light away from the camera varies the intensity of the light reflected from the object: it is brightest on the side in the direction of the light and diminishing to the side away from the light. This difference in light conveys the feeling of substance, or modeling (Fig. 5).

Texture is also revealed by moving the light to the side, as texture is the modeling of the macro-elements of the surface (Fig. 6).

A recurring problem in photographing jars, juglets, and bowls is what is termed rim collapse, when the front rim of the object and the inside or back rim are not discrete and the rim disappears. The solution is the same: vary the amount of light to distinguish between elements. The answer here is to cut down on the light inside the jar to increase the contrast between the rim and its background. This can most easily be done by lowering the fill-in light so that none of it falls inside the jar. The inside will be illuminated only by the main light; the outside rim will receive light from both main and fill-in sources (Fig. 7).

Angular objects require special care to preserve the several planes or surfaces. Each separate surface must be given a different level of illumination so that it is distinguished from the others (Figs. 8 and 9).

Objects with incised patterns or inscriptions are usually lit from the side, with a long, raking shadow to provide enough contrast for the incisions. The position of the light is important, for if the pattern of incisions is irregular, as in writing, lines parallel to the light will disappear. A lamp position must be found which preserves as much of the pattern as possible.

Transparent and translucent objects are many times best illuminated from below through a glass sheet, to allow the light to reflect from internal planes and imperfections. Sunlight striking a dirty window at certain angles clearly shows where it needs cleaning--a similar angle helps to give a transparent object substance.

Given control of color balance, illumination level, and background, the only real tool one has is the position of the lights. If one is concerned with mastering this tool, there can be no better exercise than to invest an afternoon and several rolls of film. The following procedure will be found useful: set up an object, a juglet perhaps, on a pleasing background, position the camera on a sturdy tripod, and keep the object, the camera, and the background fixed throughout the session. The lights should be the only variable element. They should be on stands or tripods to be moved easily into a wide variety of posi-

189

Figure 4.

Figure 5.

Figure 6.

Figure 7.

Figure 8.

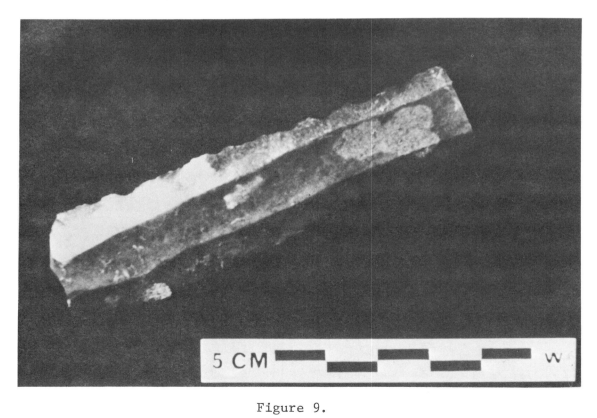

Figure 9.

tions. A detailed notebook should be kept, recording the exposure number, the positions of the lights, including angle and height, the illumination level at the object from each light source (read from a gray card), and the particular aspect of the problem one is concentrating upon. Use color slide film, or if available, Polaroid.

Identify the characteristic elements of the object, and one by one attempt to concentrate upon and isolate each of them, recording each position and exposure carefully in the notebook. Make some attempts at combining attention on several elements of the object, trading off where necessary to achieve a balanced and well-lit composition.

When the photographs are processed, spend another afternoon slowly and carefully examining the results, identifying from the notebook the reasons why a particular photo is good or bad and noting suggestions on ways to correct and improve. A second session, with a plan based on a critical evaluation of the results of the first, would be useful.

NOTES

1. Minor White, Zone System Manual (2nd ed., New York: Morgan & Morgan, 1970).

2. (London: Penguin Books, 1956), Photo 24b, opposite p. 29.

Appendix

INVENTORY OF PHOTOGRAPHIC EQUIPMENT

The photographic work at Gezer was made possible only by the encouragement and support of the administration of the project and the generous budget supplied by the Smithsonian Institution (see Preface). It is doubtful whether anything approaching the results could have succeeded without such support.

This Appendix contains an inventory of equipment and supplies used in the photographic operation at Gezer.

1. Cameras and Accessories

    Hasselblad 500C
    80mm normal lens
    50mm wide-angle lens
    (2) interchangeable film backs
    45° prism viewfinder
    Handle, rapid wind crank, strap
    12" x 15" foam-lined aluminum case

    (2) Nikkormat FTN
    35mm, 50mm and 135mm lenses

    Honeywell 1° spot meter, case

2. Photographic Lab Facilities

    8' epoxy-lined sink
    Film- and print-drying cabinet with filtered forced-air system
    Electrical converting and stabilizing equipment (220v and 110v
        available)
    Safe- and white-light systems
    Light-trap entranceway
    Air conditioner

3. Film Processing equipment

    Chemical containers: collapsible plastic inside, rigid outer
        cases 4 five-gallon, 3 one-gallon
    Water filter
    120 and 35 mm steel film-processing tanks and reels
    Miller Hurricane film-washer (adapted for 4 No. 120 reels)

Timing clock
Graduates, trays, thermometers, etc.
Continuous agitator for film tanks

4. Printing Equipment

Enlarger (light source for contact prints and enlargements)
Timer
120 and 35 mm print-frames
Kodak Ektamatic stabilization processor
Paper-safe, cutter
Dry-mount press, tacking iron
Polycontrast filters
Enlarging focus viewer
Negative and print files

5. Annual Supplies (six-week season)

 200 rolls EK Plus-X Pan Professional 120
 100 rolls EK Kodachrome-II
  20 rolls EK Kodachrome-II-A Professional, 120 mailers
  20 rolls EK Panatomic-X
1000 sheets EK Ektamatic paper, 8 x 10
  12 quarts each, Activator and Stabilizer
   5 gallons EK Microdol-X film developer
  15 gallons EK indicator stop
Hypo-check
  10 quarts Perma Wash hypo clearing agent
  15 gallons EK fixer
Miscellaneous chemicals

Chapter VIII

GEOLOGY IN FIELD ARCHAEOLOGY

Reuben G. Bullard

"The science of geology treats the crust of the earth in much the same way that archaeology considers strata of human occupation."

This discussion seeks to explore the parallel relationship of geology and archaeology and to examine some aspects of excavation in which questions arise that apply to areas of specialty for geologists. The writer is aware of the problem of terminology which may be unfamiliar to the non-geologist, so minimal definitions are included in the discussion.[1]

Field study for this chapter was carried out on the site of Gezer. The aim of the investigation conducted during the excavations has been a broader understanding of the relationship between Gezer's inhabitants and their environment during the city's history. Certain areas of inquiry have proved useful in the initial phases of this research. A survey of the local and regional geology made from field studies and from the growing literature has provided information about the nature and origin of the rocks and minerals encountered in excavation. Exposed soils and clays within five kilometers of Gezer were systematically sampled and analyzed for mineral and trace element content. Potential temper sources such as local stream channel and terrace deposits and Pleistocene and Recent sands of the Coastal Plain were studied mineralogically.[2] Randomly sampled discards from the daily pottery calls, together with oven wall fragments and mud brick remnants, were collected. This material was analyzed for clay mineral content, firing history, and temper. A growing catalogue of ceramic groups and temper suites is being assembled.

Stratigraphic relations and sedimentalogical data are areas of specialization for geologists who can contribute measurably to the understanding of the history of occupation at a site. Petrologic study of regional and local bedrock materials is providing a preliminary basis for determining the provenance of numerous igneous, sedimentary, and metamorphic lithic artifacts and building materials found in the historical phasing of a city-site.

I

REGIONAL AND LOCAL GEOLOGY

The topographic features of the earth's surface take their form mostly from the effects of bedrock composition, configuration, and climate. The location of mountains and hills, valleys and plains, rivers and streams, the ground water supply, the occurence of caves, the nature of the soil and the wealth of mineral resources are all governed by geological factors (Fig. 1).

Figure 1.   Aerial photograph of Tell Gezer
at the end of the 1968 season.

A division of the southern Levant into geomorphic or physiographic
provinces is relevant to the work of the archaeologist and the historian.   This is because each province is defined on the basis of topographic or surface relief features which are caused by geological
conditions in the crust of the earth.   Local environmental variation in
each province has a significant effect on the inhabitants even to the
extent of affecting their way of life.   The inhabitants of the Coastal
Plain, for example, lacked the hard rock sources for wall and house
construction which the Shephelah and Judean hill areas had in abundance.
Southeastern Galilee abounds with basalt surface rock which is a highly
durable grindstone material and stands in marked contrast with the soft
chalk and brittle chert rock sources of the Shephelah.   The high

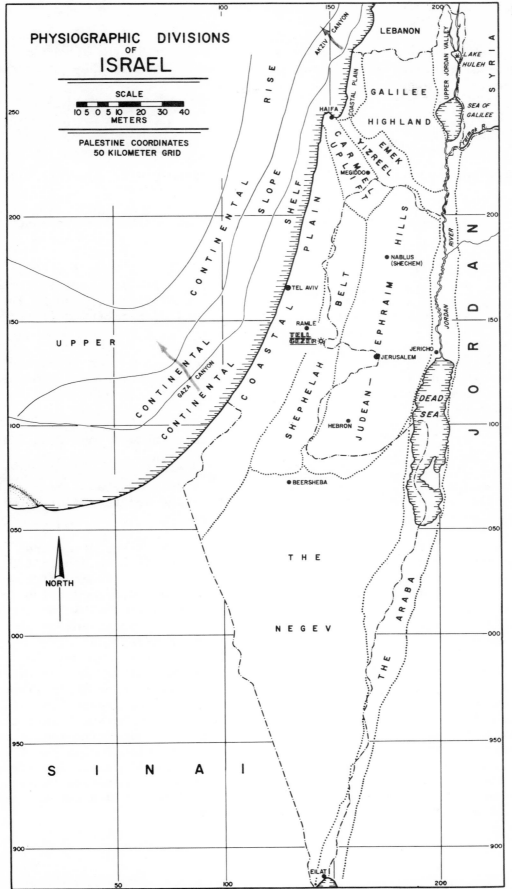

Figure 2. Physiographic provinces of Israel.

frequency of basalt grindstones at Gezer means that the inhabitants traded or traveled some distance to secure a material they preferred above local resources.

II

THE PHYSIOGRAPHIC PROVINCES OF THE SOUTHERN LEVANT (See Fig. 2).[3]

1. <u>The Negev</u>. This portion of Isreal extending from Beersheba to the Gulf of Aqaba is bounded by Sinai on the west and the Araba on the east.

2. <u>The Araba - Dead Sea - Jordan Valley</u>. The rift valley between Israel and Transjordan is a long (400 cm.) and narrow (10-30 km.) tectonic depression (crustal deformation) extending from the Gulf of Aqaba (Eilat) to the foothills of Mt. Hermon.

3. <u>The Emek Yizreel</u> (biblical Esdraelon). A graben structure (down-faulted block of the earth's crust) trends northwest from the central Jordan valley in the region of Beth-shan (Beisan) about 30 kilometers.

4. <u>Galilee Highland</u>. Galilee is situated between the Emek Yizreel on the south and the Lebanon border on the north.

5. <u>The Carmel Uplift</u>. Mt. Carmel is a folded upwarp which is a structural continuity with the Megiddo syncline and the Um el-Fahm anticline extending into the West Bank area.[4]

6. <u>The Judean - Ephraim Mountains</u>. "The backbone of central Palestine" is the northward trending anticlinical mountain belt with three north-northeast <u>en echelon</u> (off-set parallel) structural components: the Hebron mountains, on the south, the Judean mountains in the central area, and the Ephraim mountains on the north. This mountain system is bounded in the east by the rift valley faults and on the west by the dip of the bedrock (about 30°) under the Shephelah.

7. <u>The Coastal Plain</u>. The province extends along the eastern shore of the Mediterranean sea from the borders of Sinai on the south to the Lebanon border near Rosh ha-Niqra. It is punctuated only by the cape which is the result of the Carmel uplift. Below the Carmel promontory, the coastal area is subdivided into the Philistine plain on the south and the plain of Sharon on the north. Longitudinally the Coastal plain west of Gezer is marked with kurkar ridges (fossilized or cemented sand dunes) and hamra (deeply weathered Pleistocene red sands). The swamps the Romans began to drain have all been given outlets to the sea in modern times leaving swamp-deposits.

8. <u>The Continental Shelf</u>. This submarine extension of the coastal area of the eastern Mediterranean has a maximum width of about 15 kilometers. It exhibits numerous rock outcrops regarded as submerged kurkar. From the shoreline the area slopes gently westward to the shelf-break point at about the 110 meter depth west of the coast of Israel.

9. <u>The Shephelah</u>.

> "Over the Plain, as you come up from the coast, you see
> a sloping moorland break into scalps and ridges of rock,
> and over these a loose gathering of chalk and limestone
> hills, round and featureless, with an occasional bastion
> flung out in front of them. This is the Shephelah - a
> famous theatre of the history of Palestine - debatable
> ground between Israel and the Philistines, the Maccabees
> and the Syrians, Saladin and the Crusaders."[5]

"Shephelah" means <u>lowland</u>, or the subtle rolling foothill area bordered on the east by the Judean and Ephraim mountains and on the west by the Coastal plain. Morphologically the foothills province extends from the Carmel uplift in the north on Cretaceous limestones to the vicinity of Gezer from which it extends southward mostly on Eocene chalks and limestones to the northern Negev. Topographic highs persist under a protective armor of a caliche-like weathered residual bedrock crust termed <u>nari</u>.

It is upon such a topographic high that the city of Gezer was built, giving it a commanding position over the coastal road (the <u>Via Maris</u>) which lay toward the eastern margin of the Coastal plain because of the swamp land to the west. In addition Gezer was suitably situated to control traffic to the Judean mountains along the route through the Aijalon valley lying to the north and northeast of the city. Moreover, the inhabitants of Gezer were conditioned by the economic geological aspects of the central Shephelah, sometimes near, sometimes far: tools, building materials, weapons, and the raw materials for various enterprises and commodities.

III

SOILS AND SOIL CLAY MINERALOGY

The term soil has been used with a variety of meanings by farmers, civil engineers, archaeologists and geologists. Soil scientists regard soil as that earth material which has been acted upon by physical, chemical, and biological agents to the extent that it will support rooted plants. Archaeologists sometimes use the term for any very fine-grained sediment in the excavation which has color as its only distinguishing feature. In this discussion we are considering a soil to be the weathered material on or at the earth's surface representing the naturally altered parent rock material. Weathering processes change the minerals of the bedrock which were formed under different conditions into minerals which are stable in the environment of the existing climate. Soils may be residual (existing on the parent rock from which they are derived) or transported (moved elsewhere by natural agencies).[6]

The composition of soils varies with different parent rock sources and with different climate regimes. In Israel bedrock characteristics and climate have produced two dominant soil types in the region about Gezer. The dense crystalline limestones of the Judean-Ephraim mountains weather to terra rossa soils[7] containing some clay components and especially iron oxide, which imparts the distinctive deep red coloration. The softer chalks and marls which underlie the central and southern Shephelah give rise to a brown soil containing clay, oxides of iron and manganese mixed with calcium carbonate residues--a rendzinate soil.[8] Local soil clays are frequently concentrated in the floodplain deposits of the streams in that area (see Fig. 3). At Gezer rendzinate soils and clays found use as floor surfacing, wine or olive press wall surfacing, sub-plaster stone wall filling, oven walls, terra cottas, and unfired and fired mud brick material.

A surprising discovery in the soil and clay studies of the Gezer environment is the occurrence of insoluble tests or shells of Eocene foraminifera in the soil derived from the parent chalk (Fig. 4).

Originally composed of calcium carbonate, these silica-replaced fossils occur in the rendzinate soil produced by the weathering of the rock under local climatic conditions (see Fig. 5). They are entrained in the soil clay matrix and become a part of any mud brick or pottery materials made from it. The occurrence of such fossil foraminifera in statistically high numbers provides evidence for the locality as understood by the area of outcrop where a particular fossil bearing bedrock formation occurs. In Israel such areas may vary from one physiographic province to another (see Fig. 6).

Figure 3. Outcrop of a soil profile developed on the alluvial sediments of the Aijalon Valley north of Gezer.

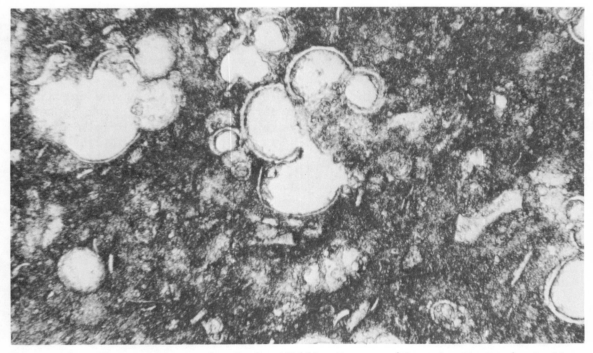

Figure 4. Photomicrograph of the Middle Eocene (Maresha Member) chalk which constitutes the uppermost bedrock strata underlying Gezer and the Shephelah to the south.

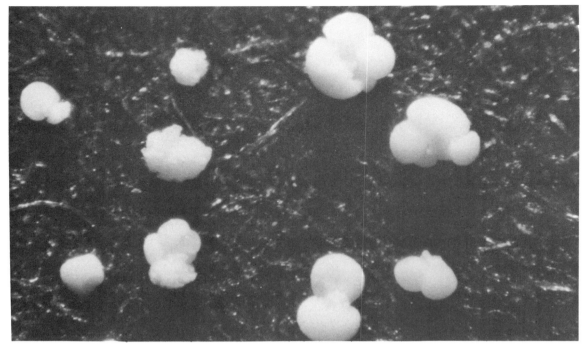

Figure 5.   Silicified foraminiferal tests which resisted the soil-weath-
ering process; they are residual within the clays developed
in the alteration of the chalk bedrock and become entrained
in mudbrick and pottery materials.

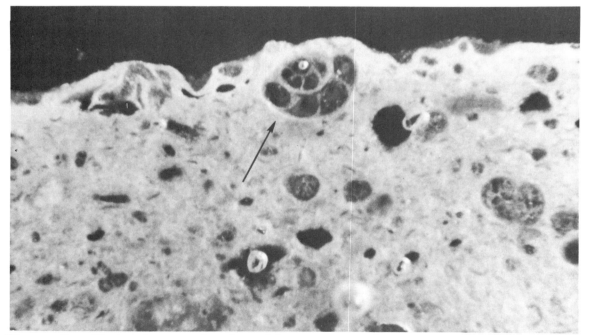

Figure 6.   Photomicrograph of a thin section of Type II-A Hellenistic
pottery (magnified 16X). The cut shows an equatorial section
of foraminiferal remains, of the species Rotalia trochidiformis
Lamarc (arrow), known from the Middle Eocene of the Gezer area.

IV

CERAMICS

Inasmuch as pottery may be considered the most durable and widely distributed packaging medium of antiquity, those shapes which were used over broad geographical areas become a valuable means of chronological interpretation. Pottery, from the viewpoint of a petrologist, is essentially a man-made (or in a special sense, a metamorphic) rock and is practically indestructible after its primary purpose is met. As such it is composed of heat-altered clays having a peculiar trace element chemistry along with temper (sand-size particles or straw) added by potters to give the mixture properties to resist failure during drying and firing.

The non-organic portion of soils of most importance to pottery makers is the clay mineral content. While potters knew nothing more about clays than whether they were plastic when wet and would become durable in shape when fired, we are in a position to understand just why some clays made fine pottery, some poor pottery, and some clays simply failed. Clays are natural fine-grain, earthy materials which become plastic when combined with water. Chemical analyses show that clays are composed of silica, alumina, and water and may also contain iron, alkalis, and alkaline earths. X-ray diffraction studies reveal that clay minerals are usually platy or fibrous in atomic structure, with groups of atoms repeating themselves to form layered crystalline sequences.

The plasticity exhibited by clays is the result of very thin films of water held on and between sub-microscopic plates or fibers. The slippery property of clays is a glide effect of these minute platelets on surface water. This response is the clay behavior sought by potters for workability in hand and on the wheel. After his vessel is shaped, the potter allows this "surface water" to evaporate during which the plastic effects diminish to the point where the vessel becomes "leather hard." Cohesion and electrostatic charges bond the clay mineral platelets and fibers together and the vessel is ready for firing.

The effect of heat is to remove internal water from the platelets and fibers. This is the point at which the potter found the answer to the critical question about his clay vessel--will it crack? Trial and error (with good luck) led him to realize that certain clays would not crack and that the addition of temper would lessen the tendency to do so of those which did. We know that kaolinite, illite, montmorillonite, palygorskite (attapulgite), and sepiolite are the dominant clay minerals present in southern Levantine sources. These minerals seldom occur naturally in high purity except in isolated environments. Only the first two may yield a fine ceramic when available in the quantities used by the makers of certain Cypriot and Greek wares. While some local sources in stream deposits contain varying amounts of kaolinite and/or illite, Gezer potters learned that most local soil clay sources (because they are rich in palygorskite--a fibrous clay) required tempering additives to prevent vessel failure during drying and firing.

Pottery temper was found by potters in the sands of local beaches, in the stream beds of local wadis and from recent and geologically older sand dune sources. In the case of most mud bricks and some terra cottas (sarcophagi, baking oven walls, and a few storage jar handles and walls), straw and grass tempers were utilized. The mineralogy of sand tempers varies with the place of origin, and, assuming ancient potters did not transport their temper raw materials from considerable distances, the composition may yield information about the probable locality of origin.

The activity of a modern potter shows the importance of good clay sources, but it is probably not typical for ancient potters because of transportation limitations. In 1968 a Palestinian potter at the Balâṭah refugee camp obtained his clay from the Moza Marl, which outcrops on the surface near el-Jib. He drove to the Mediterranean beach and dune sands near Natanyah for his temper materials. The Gezer studies do not show such a wide ranging combination in the same ware.

The Gezer staff recognized that the subjective nature of color values in ceramic description and study required the standardization of some recognized system from the beginning of the current excavations. We have adopted the Munsell Soil Color Charts for this purpose. Regardless of the nature of the illumination, essential color data are recorded for chroma, hue, and lightness value, using numbered terminology along with the designated common color name; for example, 5YR 5/2, reddish gray.[9] This system has been the reference standard for field geologists and pedologists for a number of years in the United States. Color plates, not possible here, are highly desirable in comparative ceramic study.

We can observe in the illustrations below distinct variations in gross temper compositions. Some of the areas where such sources occur today have been recorded, and we can say something about the probability of these sources being used in antiquity. Those categories appearing at the beginning of the list below are most likely materials made at Gezer from sources available very close to the city. All but the last two are very probably produced in what is Israel today from materials in the areas noted. Exotic or foreign ceramic materials are usually recognized on stylistic grounds, but analytic data can be useful here too, especially in the discovery of local copies.

V

PROPOSED PROVENANCE FOR THE GEZER CERAMICS

A combination of clay texture, clay mineral and trace element content,[10] and temper data has led to a tentative proposal for the origin of the Gezer pottery materials. We have added analytical data from unfired and fired mud and clay structures found throughout the excavation providing a high degree of certainty about local clay materials available to Gezer potters--if they desired to use them--in the past. We have grouped the pottery into categories which matched the preliminary data derived from natural clay and temper occurrences. A neutral designation termed "Type I," "Type II," etc. was used in the initial phase of the research.

The categories are as follows:

Type I Pottery (and mud bricks). The immediate area around Gezer with the local residual, colluvial and alluvial soil clays originating on the Sor'a formation (Middle and Lower Eocene). It includes material available today on the topographic saddle and on the foothills immediately to the south.[11]

Type II Pottery (and mud bricks). Residual, colluvial and alluvial soils derived from the Taqiye, Ghareb and Menuha Formations which underlie the lowlands immediately north and east of Gezer.

Type III Pottery. Soils and clays produced from the Turonian and Cenomanian (i.e., the Judean group) lithic strata which underlie the Shephelah to the north and the Judean mountains to the east.

Type IV Pottery. Residual, colluvial and alluvial soils produced by weathering of basalt flows such as in Galilee.

Type V Pottery. A category at present somewhat general, but initial data suggest the following: alluvial soils and clays from the Aijalon valley, the Yarkon river valley and the Sorek valley together with associated lake and swamp deposits through which these streams cut on the Coastal plain in their courses to the Mediterranean.

Type VI Pottery. The Coastal plain with lake clays and hamra sands and silts and the Recent dunal sands.

Type VII Pottery. Possibly the Golan, as the clays show relic shards (volcanic tephra) in the ceramic paste. Pyroclastic deposits from the late Neogene cindercones observed on the Golan (and the Hauran) are a possible source. Data incomplete.

Type VIII Pottery. Exotic clays and tempers, the physical, mineral, and trace element chemistry of which are totally unrelated to that which is known in the literature, e.g., Cypriot, Aegean or otherwise.

We are proposing these tentative categories as a basis for discussion and refinement. They represent only a beginning in the study of Gezer materials.

VI

SOME EXAMPLES OF GEZER CERAMIC PASTE AND TEMPER

A maximum surface area of a potsherd may be obtained by cutting a section tangential to the curvature of the vessel so that the longest and intermediate particle dimensions tend to be exposed (see Fig. 7). Type I pottery is illustrated in this example. The clay mineral content and trace element chemistry compares closely with that of the central Shephelah. Chalk and nari temper are available in the sediment load deposits in the valley of the wadi just east of Gezer. The particles are subangular to rounded as a consequence of stream transport abrasion. Chert and siliceous chalk are present in minor amounts.

An unusual combination of clay mineral variation and temper technique is shown in a Late Bronze vessel (see Fig. 8). Type II clay is produced on the Paleocene marls (Taqiye Formation) underlying the lowlands east and north of Gezer. The temper used occurs in the wadi just east of Gezer and contains partially silicified Eocene faunal assemblages. The attached handle portion of this potsherd (A) is an example of straw temper usage which was added to the temper used in the body portion (B). A significant difference was noted in the trace element content between (A) and (B): The handle paste (A) gives values in the range of that observed for the rendzinate soil formed on the Eocene chalks higher in the local geologic stratification on the flanks to the tell and on the Shephelah to the south (Type I conditions). The body portion gave trace element values comparable to those found for Type II ceramics. Only a few examples of this unusual combination of materials have been found. The Gezer potters may have found that the straw temper made the palygorskite-rich soil clays more amenable to handle construction.

A number of examples were observed in which the pottery raw material was probably obtained from the local neighborhood to the north or east of the city, but in combination with a temper similar in composition to the sediments occuring in stream sorted deposits along the Aijalon valley. North of Gezer this valley contains sediments which are eroded from the dark burnt lime deposits of kilns which were observed in considerable number along one of the local tributaries (see Fig. 9).

Figure 7. Tangential ceramic section cut to give maximum surface expression of the temper, in this case moderately rounded, sorted sediment, the result of its transportation history in a stream.

Figure 8. Equatorial section of a Late Bronze body sherd with attached handle; analysis shows that the potter used different clays for the body and the handle, adding straw temper to that for the handle (B).

The appearance of lime kiln dross in pottery tempers may serve as an indication of the beginning of the firing of carbonate lithologies to make lime. Ancient kilns were observed along a stream where erosion had exposed limestone bedrock more suitable for firing than the local nari (see Fig. 10). This uninhabited valley occurs just west of the pre-1967 "No-Man's Land" where twenty-two remnants of kilns of various ages were counted. Some of the kilns consisted of nothing more than mass-wasted piles of rubble. Outcrops of hard Turonian limestone had been exploited by the kiln operators along the wadi which drains this "kiln valley." The channel of this wadi, a tributary to the Aijalon valley, was choked almost to its banks with considerable quantities of fine sand-size to angular pebble-size dross fragments. Here the activity of water as a transporting, rounding, and sorting agent is impressed upon the sediment. This temper source, when incorporated in ceramics for the first time, would offer a basis from which to infer the existence of lime burning operations and the use of lime at the time the pottery was made. The data are incomplete, but late Early Bronze materials are the earliest ceramic evidence for this temper supply encountered at this point in the research.

A temper found frequently in the Gezer pottery is the red hamra sands which compose the highest Pleistocene transgressive deposits in the Coastal plain west of Gezer (see Fig. 11). Hamra is composed of sand-size quartz grains coated with the sesquioxides of iron and aluminum as a result of lateritic weathering and has the appearance of terra rossa.

Tempers exotic to the Gezer area are calcite (see Fig. 12) and basalt (see Fig. 13). A frequent occurrence of calcite temper may be expected in ceramics originating in such areas as the Ephraim mountains where veins of calcite twelve centimeters thick were observed in Cenomanian formations. The calcite tempered examples tend to show a mineral and trace element content distribution of Type III ware. Ceramic materials (Type IV) which arise in areas where alkaline-olivine basalt flows constitute the bedrock (e.g., southeastern Galilee) usually show values which compare with data found for the soil clays which weather from this rock. These clays usually have a montmorillonite content and trace element chemistry which sets them apart from soil clays formed on limestone in Israel. Basalt tempers are available in the sediments of streams which flow across the basaltic lava rock.

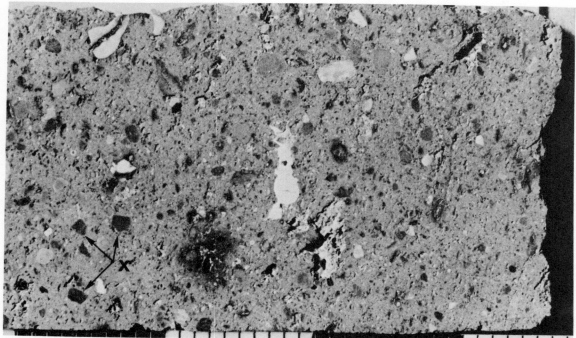

Figure 9. Ceramic section cut tangential to the wheel direction of a Late Bronze body sherd, showing Paleocene marl clays from the lowlands near Gezer, temper of sediments in the Aijalon Valley, and some kiln dross.

Figure 10. "Kiln Valley," a tributary to the Aijalon Valley; the remains of twenty-two kilns, ancient and modern, were counted in this outcrop area of crystalline Turonian limestone.

Figure 11. Ceramic section of an Iron I jug handle composed of local clays nearly saturated with fine red (hamra) sand temper.

Figure 12. Cut section of an Early Bronze sherd; the abundant calcite temper is characterized by the random sectioning of cleavage rhombs.

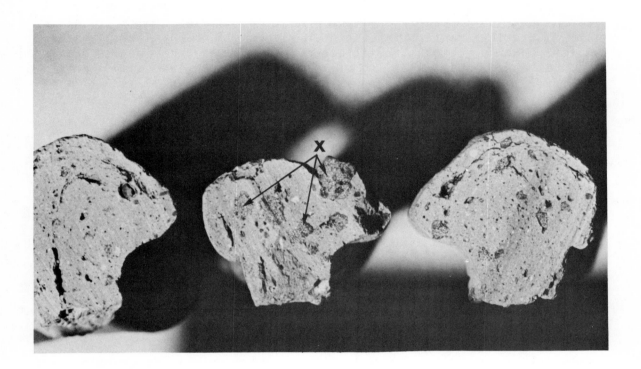

Figure 13.   Ceramic section of an "exotic" Iron I rim sherd, composed of
a paste having a montmorillonite content and trace element
concentration comparable to that found in soild formed on
Galilean basalt.

VII

STRATIFICATION AND SEDIMENTATION

The task of interpreting the history of stratified remains from
antiquity involves considerably more than the interpretation of the
ceramic evidence. It goes beyond the recognition of the layered or
stratified levels and the careful delineation of their geometry. This
vital and highly important facet to the understanding of the history of

a city which is undergoing excavation involves the examination of the sediments and the meaning of the configuration in which they are found.

"Digging is destruction." Even the casual observer of the glaring, gray-white dust which comes up under the trowel of the excavator is acutely aware of the fact that these deposits can tell their story only once. Afterward, they become refuse or spoil in actual fact. Geological research at an excavation is not the work of a laboratory technician whose job is merely analyzing those curiosities brought to him by the archaeologists from the field in the confines of research quarters. In the context of work done at Gezer (and also at Shechem) the research task is essentially a new way of looking at stratified sediments in historical deposits. This approach to the history of accumulation of sediments in ancient cities is that which has traditionally concerned the sedimentologist. Sedimentary petrologists add to the task of rock description that broader concern of understanding the geological history of a stratified unit, i.e., the mode of origin. The student of archaeology in similar manner stands to gain much by adding to description all the genetic data he can assemble.

Attention is directed to those processes in the confines of the regime of human activity which produced the sedimentation of the archaeological context. Our primary aim or purpose here is an elucidation of human history by means of those methods proven successful in the hands of the earth scientist. The ultimate goal we seek is an understanding of the ecology controlling the life of the Gezer inhabitant and his dependency upon the environment in which he lived.

The problems of major concern in the course of this research were: (1) the primary composition of the sediment; (2) the manner or mode of deposition; and (3) the agency which was responsible for the occurrence of the sediment in the context in which it was found. Vital to this concept is the observation by the specialist of the sediments in their stratified position. Facies relationships[12] exist within each stratigraphic entity in the same real sense they do in the sedimentary basins within the geological regime of sedimentary environments, whether continental or marine.

There are a number of ways to study sediments. The central concern of this research has been to present the data in such a meaningful and significant way that it is useful to the archaeologist and historian in the integrated synthesis of the primary material. We made arrangements to obtain our own samples, observing the lateral and vertical relationships of that which was being cleared. Documentation included photographic recording of the deposits in situ.

We set up a field laboratory in the dig house at Gezer. This consisted of a work bench with north light in the staff room, a binocular stereoscopic microscope and standard sieves. A suite of reagents was prepared for special treatment such as the solution of carbonates, spot and stain tests for dolomite, potassium, phosphates, copper, tin, and silver. Other tools considered as basic to mineralogists were also included in the equipment.

Sedimentary analysis at Gezer involved the recording of the texture, considering particle size, shape and roundness, surface texture, porosity and permeability, and the packing and fabric. Mineral composition was determined. Analysis of primary and secondary mechanical structures such as bedding, bedding planes, irregularities, deformation, disruption and truncation, and distortion.

VIII

CLASSIFICATION OF SEDIMENTS FOR THE ARCHAEOLOGIST

Inasmuch as human history is the ultimate goal of the study of these materials, the primary objective and determining principle in this classification is a genetically meaningful designation of the sediments studied. We have used the following classification as a preliminary framework:

A. Occupational structures and associated sediments.

1. Features cut or hewn into the bedrock which provide evidence of their primary usage (hence they become models for understanding their constructional counterparts).

   a. Rooms or dwelling places cut in the bedrock, wine and olive presses.

   b. Storage vats, silos, magazines, drainage channels, cisterns, and water tunnels.

2. Primary structures built in each of the successive cities.

   a. City walls and gates, streets, and drains.

   b. The structures which make up the courtyards of houses (with associated sediments) along with plastered walls, wine presses, cisterns, cooking ovens, quarters for livestock, and refuse pits.

   c. House interior structures (where they can be distinguished from b. above): wall and roof materials, doorway structures, floor sequences with ovens, hearths, cooking stoves (some have been observed having a fired clay composition), refuse pits, infant burials, and other debris from human activity within the confines of such dwellings.

d. Structures associated with crafts and with industrial activities such as pottery and lime manufacture, tools, and weapon manufacture with typical sediments.

e. Structures built for cultic and ceremonial practices and associated sediments.

f. Buildings serving man's aesthetic propensities, such as the arts: theaters and circuses.

3. Primary sediments left _in situ_ in surfaces as a result of human activity in the city as outlined in the contexts above. The composition and fabric of the accumulation and its subsurface make up. Consideration of the specific origin or agent of deposition.

B. Exotic (non-local) pottery, lithic objects, and mineral artifacts.

1. Mills, grinders, pounders, ballistae and stone and metal tools and weapons.

2. Semi-precious and precious minerals and gemstones.

3. Vessels fabricated from special rock and mineral materials, e.g., alabaster and basalt.

C. Destructional deposition.

1. Debris resulting from the falling of structures.

a. The collapse of walls, the filling of cisterns and water supplies, the destruction of cooking facilities.

b. Skeletal remains of occupants and animals.

2. Debris resulting from the burning of structures.

a. House roofs, the beams of which have burned with resultant structural failure.

b. Carbonate fortifications such as gate areas composed of limestone or nari which have been calcined by the use of fire.

3. See E. below, from which these may be inseparable.

D. Occupational hiatus.

1. A minor occupational lapse within the city (may be explained on the basis of a plague or famine or a migration of a city's population or a destruction of the city which was locally incomplete--more data needed).

   a. Sand, silt, and clay deposits from sheetwash and ponding on surfaces which are sites of normal occupational sedimentation.

   b. Air-borne deposits which would normally be eroded by normal occupational activities.

2. A major occupational gap.

   a. The development of an incipient soil on domestic sediment or destructional debris by natural processes of weathering.

   b. The erosion of strata by natural processes (see below). Stratigraphic truncation and angular unconformities may occur.

   c. The blanketing of streets and structures by loess (wind-borne silt) and sand (in semi-arid regions).

E. The processes or erosion which may remove any one or all of the above.

1. Mass wasting (downslope movement of material under the influence of gravity).

2. Running water.

3. Deflation by wind (wind erosion).

F. Naturally induced destructive agencies.

1. Earthquakes.

2. Volcanic eruptions with ash falls, mudflows, <u>nuée ardente</u> (hot dense gas clouds), caldera explosions (such as in the case of Thera).

3. Earthquake tidal waves.

4. Raising of sea level upon coastal sites.

5. Floods.

IX

SEDIMENTATION STUDIES AT GEZER

A. _A profile of virgin soil._

As the soft carbonates of the Central Shephelah undergo decomposition during weathering, an insoluble residue known as rendzinate soil is formed. The preservation of this soil is rare in the area of Gezer inasmuch as subaerial denudation (topsoil removal by erosion) has taken place since removal of the vegetable cover by man and animals, for example through possible deforestation. As a consequence, a residual profile of undisturbed or virgin soil was keenly anticipated in the excavations.

Such soil was in fact encountered first in the excavation of the MB IIC glacis and the LB I "Outer Wall" structures (see Fig. 14). In this area as much as one meter of virgin soil was found undisturbed on the nari bedrock below. The position of this quantity of virgin soil points to the fact that this thickness was preserved when the glacis and the LB wall were constructed in an area ideally situated for mass-wasting processes. Such soil retention may suggest the presence of some manner of plant anchoring of the regolith (weathered bedrock and soil). If climatic conditions were very little different from that of today, arboreal retention probably would be required to hold the soil in place. Deforestation of the Shephelah, therefore, may have taken place after the Late Bronze age, if indeed the area was ever under forest cover. Pollen and charcoal studies are being undertaken to understand the nature of the floral population.

Study of the MB II glacis constitutes another application of geological techniques to field archaeology. The section exposed by the Gezer Field I excavation trench is illustrated in Figure 15 (see also Fig. 14). The glacis was used as a defensive structure during the Hyksos period (Middle Bronze IIB and C). Gezer has an example of this structure which may prove to be classic. Its location between the massive inner wall (No. 4 on Fig. 15) and the outer wall has prevented mass wasting from causing significant deterioration in its stratification.

The glacis represents massive amounts of earth movement. The striking interfingering of the relatively clean, unweathered chalk with that of occupational and destructional debris and quarried bedrock marks out a pertinent chapter in the ecology of Gezer. Stratigraphic relationships show a dark brown (10 YR 3/2, Munsell) virgin soil with shallow cultural intrusion on the nari-bedrock. Above this is a lens of Taqiye

Figure 14.   Section of the inner face of the Late Bronze Age "Outer Wall" constructed on virgin soil which lies on the bedrock, the upper portions of which have weathered to <u>nari</u>.

FIELD I, AREA 8, TELL GEZER

1966 & 1967 EXCAVATIONS

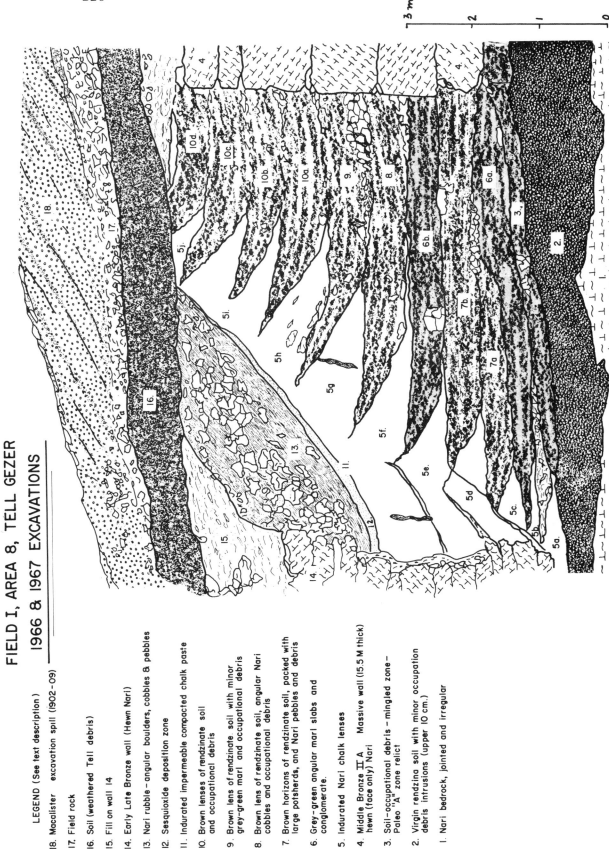

LEGEND (See text description)

18. Macalister excavation spill (1902-09)

17. Field rock

16. Soil (weathered Tell debris)

15. Fill on wall 14

14. Early Late Bronze wall (Hewn Nari)

13. Nari rubble – angular boulders, cobbles & pebbles

12. Sesquioxide deposition zone

11. Indurated impermeable compacted chalk paste

10. Brown lenses of rendzinate soil and occupational debris

9. Brown lens of rendzinate. soil with minor grey-green marl and occupational debris

8. Brown lens of rendzinate soil, angular Nari cobbles and occupational debris

7. Brown horizons of rendzinate soil, packed with large potsherds, and Nari pebbles and debris

6. Grey-green angular marl slabs and conglomerate.

5. Indurated Nari chalk lenses

4. Middle Bronze II A   Massive wall (15.5 M thick) hewn (face only) Nari

3. Soil–occupational debris – mingled zone – Paleo "A" zone relict

2. Virgin rendzina soil with minor occupation debris intrusions (upper 10 cm.)

1. Nari bedrock, jointed and irregular

Figure 15.   Glacis stratification south of the Middle Bronze Age "Inner Wall," on virgin soil with a post-Roman incipient soil developed on the occupation debris (16).

marl (No. 6a on Figure 15) distinguished by the Paleocene foraminifera, _Globoconusa_ sp., a light gray-green color (5 Y 6/2), and "limonite concretions" pseudomorphic after goethite. This marl outcrops to the east and north around the lowest parts of the hill upon which Gezer is situated. Lenses 7a and 7b are surface rendzinate soil derivations of the Eocene mingled with occupational debris. After another lens of Taqiye marl, local surface soil materials (No. 8-10d) were used to back-fill in front of the massive MB II nari wall.

The surface of the glacis gives evidence of the care used in the preparation of this defensive structure. The surface and supporting lenses (wedges) are composed of unweathered chalk quarried from the Maresha formation (contains Middle Eocene cocolithophoridae and foraminifera). The freshly quarried chalk was tightly packed to achieve a high degree of hardening. At the surface the chalk was worked into a paste giving it a firm smooth surface that has been virtually impermeable to ground water; as the water ran down the slope of the glacis it deposited about two to four inches of sesquioxide concentration of iron and aluminum (No. 12) immediately above the chalk paste (No. 11).

It is important to realize that this degree of impermeability could be achieved only with the use of unweathered chalk materials, always in short supply because of the nari crust which locally attains a thickness of three meters. Moreover, siliceous chalk bedrock horizons were useless since the quarried aggregate of this material could not be packed hard and would easily be scaled by assaulting enemy soldiers. The construction of this sloping chalk apron about the city demanded a supply of fresh chalk which could be supplied by a nearby quarry. This material was available only from the excavation of such features as tombs, cisterns, rooms, and water tunnels. The relative inaccessibility of unweathered chalk created an economic supply problem that forced the glacis builders to go to the base of the local Shephelah to quarry raw material required for the surface.

B.   The stratigraphic hiatus.

Criteria which distinguish sedimentary processes other than those regarded as occupational accumulation or destruction sediment are as follows: (1) a stratified weathered zone in which there is gradational enrichment of clay mineral content vertically; (2) sediment of a clearly loessic character (wind-blown silt in the 0.03-0.08 mm. size range); (3) sheet wash deposits or ponded sediments across broad areas of the site. These deposits, occurring within the stratification of a tell, are usually devoid of facies which exhibit an occupational or destructional sedimentary character in their inherent fabric.

C. Weathering and soil zones.

An occupational hiatus permits natural processes controlled by the climate to produce physical and chemical changes within the upper levels of exposed occupational features in destruction debris. Weathering has been estimated to proceed in the eastern Mediterranean area at the rate of 10 centimeters in 1000 years.[13] Anticipation of changes in abandoned cultural contexts is therefore not unreasonable. Soils in the true pedogenic sense of the word within the local stratification were encountered in an incipient state.

An example horizon with known vertical control may be observed in Figure 15. The latest pottery found on top of the MB II wall (No. 4) was Roman. No later contexts were found above this level. Macalister dump (No. 18) is seen above the "soil" with the characteristic sorting of his tip lines. Samples were taken at five centimeter intervals throughout this stratum. Minor yet significant increases formed during the 1700 years of weathering were noted in the clay mineral content upward in this unit. Changes in the clay mineral composition show an increase in palygorskite, a mineral released by the action of weathering, over illite, a major component of the unfired mud brick debris that reflects mineral concentrations of the alluvial clays of the Aijalon valley. This study of a "paleosoil" is intended as a model designed to serve as the basis for understanding the meaning of stratified sediment of this nature.

D. The occurrence of loess.

No better place to observe the cessation of normal occupational activity in a city may be found than the street environment (see Fig. 16). Street surfaces inward through the entrance of the south-central gate have been delineated in the step-like demonstration of successive street surfacings utilized by the excavators. This surface distinction may be made partly on the basis of the relative hardness or resistance of the street sediment to the trowel. A deposit of an unusual nature was discovered in the excavation of these street surfaces: A locally variable sixteen-centimeter thickness of finely divided sediment uniformly in the silt size range of .03-.08 mm. blanketed the area observed. Sieved portions of this stratum showed the absence of the usual occupational sediment ingredients: charcoal flecks, unweathered chalk particles, nari, pottery fragments of various sizes, and the field soil clay which is usually mixed with the street surface material.

Figure 16.   Stepped street surfaces cleared in the area of the Gezer
             Solomonic gate (Field III).   The stratum marked X is com-
             posed of wind-blown sediment termed "loess," signifying a
             hiatus in the occupation or use of the gate.

Figure 17.   Section of a depression-fill sediment illustrating succes-
             sive rainstorm deposit in a typical graded bedding sequence.

Comparative analysis with loessic samples taken on field trips in the Beersheba area revealed a striking comparison of particle sizes in the concentration ranges typical of that of loess. An occupational hiatus of this form can be missed by anyone who is scraping only for hard surfaces.

E. Precipitation (rainfall) runoff.

While the subject of surface water drainage is one familiar to students of geology, these features may not be initially recognized by untrained eyes. This form of sedimentation has been observed in a number of stratified contexts.

Areas where local ponding occurs give rise to a peculiar sediment known as graded bedding. A coarse to fine particle deposition occurs where surface water runoff cannot find an outlet. Sequences of graded bedding (coarse particles grading upward into finer sediments) imply repeated rainstorms which carry a sediment load to a local base-level in which the coarse particles settle out more rapidly that the fine (see Fig. 17). One can actually count the number of rainstorms from the graded couplets in the example from Field I excavated by Joe D. Seger of the Gezer staff.

F. Occupational sedimentation: mudbrick debris.

Mudbricks have been observed with various compositions in varying states of preservation. The history of the use of mudbricks is documented in an unusual way in a section cut through the Middle Bronze Age gate structure. An interesting chapter on the history of the southern fortifications is suggested in Figure 18.

The sediment is compositionally different in the various types of mudbricks used for the construction of the defensive wall and its gate. The frequency and distribution of the bricks serves to illustrate the fact that certain compositions played a key role in the structural stability of the walls.

The higher clay content of the Aijalon floodplain colluvial, alluvial, and residual soils provided a greater structural strength than the residual rendzinate soil materials nearby. The wall, however, is an illustration of structural failure; for the inhabitants of the city found it necessary to add to the fired brick structure (A), brick material of a far less competent composition (B). Several different compositions of debris brick material were used.

Figure 18.   Balk section of a portion of the mudbrick construction of
the Middle Bronze IIC "South Gate" (Field IV), showing
repair with inferior materials (A).

Figure 19.   Megascopic photograph of the "High Place" sediments from
the chalk pavement, showing burnt and fractured bone fragments, tooth fragments (X), and scorched nari fragments
from a free ash and fire-fall context.

The effects of mass wasting and slump may be observed not only in the crescentic slip-plane scar (at arrow) observable on the surface above the wall but also in the lobate flow structures at the toe of the slip. Whether this represents a failure in the fortification structures or whether it is a subsequent failure of the wall, it took place before internal destruction afforded a buttress to prevent the inward slumping of the wall structure.

The two phases of wall construction signify different types of fortification activity: an orderly construction of a defensive wall built of the best materials available and prepared carefully to produce a durable structure (Locus 3012), followed by hasty additions to this well-conceived structure from occupational debris sediment (3020) taken from inside the city to repair or strengthen the former construction. The use of low strength occupational debris sediment in the construction of the brick defensive wall may have been an ill-conceived last resort to bolster a failing structure by means of materials available to the inhabitants of the city within the confines of their defenses. This section is an illustration of a potentially tragic incident in the history of the wall near the southwest gate.

G. Occupational sedimentation: domestic surfaces.

During times of continuous occupational sedimentation in those areas where houses exist as structural entities through long periods of time, thick occupational sequences have been found. This takes the form of slow accretionary floor surfaces in domestic quarters. These sediments have been observed as thin layers composed of sand, silt, and clay-sized particles of chalk, nari, ash, pottery and field soil clay into which have been pressed olive pits, small bone fragments, and potsherds (usually with convex surface upwards).

Important differences in the nature of the occupational sediment exist as it is laid down in the dwelling floor context. The significant features to be noted are: (1) specially prepared flooring which may be composed of field soil or chalk and nari layers; (2) ash layers which are a facies continuum from a cooking or a baking area; (3) the dust and sediment from the human and animal activity in the environment of a courtyard. This last may include animal pens, ovens, grinding implements such as saddle querns and mortars, and grain and water storage containers, along with refuse pits. The walls of these structures commonly were found to be composed of easily worked nari and rarely of siliceous chalk and limestone. Unfired mudbricks have been recorded for courtyard walls. Calcined lime with straw binder, occasionally layered from multiple redressing is characteristic of roofing construction which was supported with half-beam timbers. Specially prepared flooring materials include crushed chalk paste (some examples featured minor straw binder), crushed nari with a rendzinate soil matrix, fitted cobble/pebble stone floors, compacted field clay, hamra sand and bimodal[14] recent beach sands. Specialized features constructed into these flooring surfaces were hearth depressions and store-jar receptacles (especially in Middle Bronze houses).

H. Destructional sediment: defense structure failure.

Among the means used to breach defensive structures was a form of attack which was quite effective against carbonate lithologies. This was a "breaching fire." Since the gate structures were probably the most assailable of all the defensive fortifications of the ancient city, this area usually came under attack. Such an incident may be recorded in the archaeological stratification of Gezer in the area of the Iron Age gate in Field III. This kind of assault could be very effective. Decomposition of the nari gatehouse structure resulted with the nari blocks being reduced to calcium oxide in a failure of the outside and part of the inside wall. Ceramic evidence found sealed in charcoal beneath the calcined wall rock material enables the probable date of deposition to be assigned to the time of Pharaoh Shishak, ca. 918 B.C., whose Palestinian conquests are recorded in the literature.

I. Ceremonial practice sedimentation.

Macalister had excavated the Gezer "High Place" area in his campaigns early in this century. Very little of the original sediment of this interesting area was left for the modern excavator to examine. Macalister did, however, leave the stratification immediately underlying the pillars untouched. This presented an excellent opportunity for the application of the critical analysis of modern stratigraphic technique. These small remnants of the original stratification held the only remaining information which could tell a more accurate story concerning the events of man's activity in this place. The sediment was washed to remove the masking effect of fine silt and clay size material and sorted with a five millimeter, 250, and 74 micron sieve sequence so that the particles could be studied according to size category and composition.

The "High Place" was excavated in 1968 under the supervision of Anita Walker. Initial phases of the excavation made clear that any structures connected with the use of this area had been destroyed.

Speculations about the function of this area ranged from that of a burial and mortuary center in the city to that of an area of sacrifice (either animal or human).

Analysis of the deposits of the area near the "laver" or hollowed stone block determined that the sediments were of a unique character (see Fig. 19). Compositions of this nature were not observed in any other context of this or other excavations in which the writer has taken part. A typical excerpt from the field lab notebook follows:

G.68 7/31
V.7.188
LOC.7006 (soil under plaster surface next to basin)
      556 gm. sample

This material is composed of fine pebble to fine sand size nari, burned nari, scorched and burned bone splinters and fragments, burned teeth fragments (indicated by "X" in Fig. 19), pottery fragments, terrestrial gastropod fragments, fine sand size clear quartz grains, and calcite fragments. Proportions were: unburned nari and chalk 50%; burned and blackened nari 30%; burned bone and teeth fragments 15%; pottery and miscellaneous 5%.

The nature of the sediment on this plaster surface connects the use of that level with burning in which there has been free ash and fire fall in the production of burned nari and burned and scorched bones. The fire was not that of a hearth, but burned in such a way that its coals fell away from the point of burning before the nari was calcined and the bone material consumed. The burned teeth (four fragments showing enamel and dentine) show strong burning, together with the other bone fragments, suggesting that the animal involved in the burning included the head part(s) of (a) carcass(es). The pavement was made up of a chalk and nari pebble chip aggregate in a nari and chalk paste.

The presence of burned nari and bone in this chip pavement surface is atypical of any paved surfaces observed, including the streets of Field III (the Solomonic gate) and the floor and court paving surfaces in the makeup of Field I (domestic quarters) including MB and EB levels. A different kind of activity yielded the sediment of this area. Certainly a ceremonial/sacrificial explanation is possible.

As a further commentary on the sediment of the "High Place," analysis of the pillars is pertinent. The composition of these materials is nari, the partially weathered bedrock material amply available to Gezer inhabitants on the flanks of the Shephelah about the tell (see the rock outcrops which show surface morphology atypical of natural weathering and mass wasting activity in Fig. 1). The nature of one of these mono-

liths, No. 7, is exotic to the central Shephelah. It contains Upper
Cretaceous, Campanian or Turonian megascopic shallow marine fauna.
This facies of limestone is not locally expressed in the Turonian exposed in the Nesher Cement Quarry to the north of Gezer. The nearest
available source known to the writer is the western flank of the Judean
anticline.

A channeling not characteristic of natural solution has been cut
into this pillar. The depth and position of this surface feature could
afford a rope hold by which the stone was dragged to its present position.

J. Sedimentary structures and facies relationships.

Lateral relationships within each stratum must be examined from the
standpoint of facies relationships: the lateral variation within a
given stratum of sediment caused by synchronous deposition of polyge-
netic agencies. This concept should be constantly in the mind of the
excavator for whom it is critical to recognize the nature of each
facies of a stratum or phase as it is being dug. Sedimentary structures may be recognized primarily on the basis of fabric and texture of
the sediment body in addition to the mineral composition. Thus study
of these features is critical while they are being dug.

K. Sedimentary description.

Analysis of the sediments in archaeological stratification is a
vital feature of the historical elucidation of the data. A practice
common among excavators involves a concise description of the sediment
bodies shown in profile or section drawings of the stratification exposed along a trench face or balk. Here the genetic significance is
almost completely lost unless otherwise described. The use of such
color texture terms as "sticky black burnt," "green bricky," and "dark
brown stony," is not only imprecise but unacceptable. Where color is a
natural function of a deposit and germane to an understanding of its
nature and function, a standardized reference term should be used in
locus descriptions along with the correctly designated popular color
name.

Each sedimentary entity should be carefully studied and analyzed to
record not only the composition of its material, but also the agency,
insofar as it can be determined, by which it was deposited. Notation
essential to this aspect of description is a standardized size reference table (see Fig. 20). The use of such terms as "egg," "fist," and

Modified Wentworth Size Class		Metric Measure		U.S. Standard Sieve Mesh #	Microns
BOULDER	Large	409.6	cm		
	Medium	102.4	cm		
	Small				
		25.6	cm		
COBBLE	Large				
	Medium	15.0	cm		
	Small				
		6.4	cm		
PEBBLE	Large				
	Medium	1.6	cm		
	Small				
		4.0	mm	5	
GRANULE	Large	3.36	mm	6	
	Medium	2.83	mm	7	
	Small				
VERY COARSE SAND		2.00	mm	10	
		1.68	mm	12	
		1.41	mm	14	
		1.19	mm	16	
COARSE SAND		1.00	mm	18	
		0.84	mm	20	
		0.71	mm	25	
		0.59	mm	30	
1/2		0.50	mm	35	500
MEDIUM SAND		0.42	mm	40	420
		0.35	mm	45	350
		0.30	mm	50	300
1/4		0.25	mm	60	250
FINE SAND		0.21	mm	70	210
		0.177	mm	80	177
		0.149	mm	100	149
1/8		0.125	mm	120	125
VERY FINE SAND		0.105	mm	140	105
		0.088	mm	170	88
		0.074	mm	200	74
1/16		0.0625	mm	230	62.5
COARSE SILT		0.053	mm	270	53
		0.044	mm	325	44
		0.037	mm		37
1/32		0.031	mm		31
MEDIUM SILT	1/64	0.0156	mm		15.6
FINE SILT	1/128	0.0078	mm		7.8
VERY FINE SILT	1/256	0.0039	mm		3.9
		0.0020	mm	Analyzed by Pipette or Hydrometer	2.0
		0.00098	mm		0.98
		0.00049	mm		0.49
CLAY		0.00024	mm		0.24
		0.00012	mm		0.12
		0.00006	mm		0.06

Figure 20. Grain size scales for sediments.

"melon," size is to be discouraged. As in sedimentology, particle sorting, size, composition and fabric are important properties of deposits which are characteristic of given agencies in the total cultural activities of man. In the absence of the activities of man, i.e., in a stratigraphic hiatus, the depositional agencies of natural processes are quite distinctive. Destructive events of man are recorded in a fashion readily discernible to most observers. Chaotic fabrics, surfaces bearing shattered pottery, smothered and charred combustibles, collapsed roofs, and out-of-plumb wall remnants are some of the destruction facies encountered.

L. The Petrology of Artifacts.

The role of tools and weapons in the occupational activity of the inhabitants of Gezer is one of considerable significance. It shows the extent of man's utilization of raw materials of his immediate and remote neighborhood. It is a reflection of his dependence upon economic geology, sometimes close, sometimes remote from the immediate environment of his way of life.

This phase of research concerns the petrology of the artifacts as a means directed to the understanding of the provenance of each of these entities. Petrographic study, the purely descriptive aspect of petrology, is relevant in two aspects of this discussion: (1) to ascertain the reason why a particular rock type or mineral was used for a specific function as a tool or a weapon, i.e., the essence of the physical properties, hardness, luster, fracture, cleavage, color, and ability to take a polish; (2) to suggest a potential provenance.

Consideration of the grinding stones used by the Gezer inhabitants constitutes a case in point. The unsuitability of the local bedrock is a critical issue. Chalk has neither the hardness nor cohesiveness required for this function. Chert (often referred to as flint), a nodular component of the local chalk (see Fig. 21), is far too brittle and unworkable to be shaped into a suitable grinding vessel. Some limestone mortars and a few kurkar saddle querns have appeared in the stratification. There is a far greater number of basalt saddle querns at Gezer; obviously the inhabitants preferred this material, brought from a distance, for even mundane domestic activities (see Fig. 22).

232

Figure 21.

Figure 22.

233

In summary, the provenance of the rocks and minerals recorded at Gezer ranged from the chert (flint) available in the nodules which occur in the Middle Eocene horizons within the Gezer water tunnel to such very exotic materials as acid pumice (see Fig. 23) which may have floated from an Aegean explosive source to the shores of Israel. The lithic catalogue is growing with each additional season of excavation.

The contribution of a geologist to the success of any archaeological excavation is proportional to his awareness of the petrology of the region of the site(s) he is working. Study in this area is far from complete, but an initial foundation has been laid upon which future research may be structured.[15]

Figure 23.

NOTES

1. A handbook and glossary of field terms for archaeologists is in preparation. An inexpensive useful source is the American Geological Institute, <u>Dictionary of Geological Terms</u> (1962).

2. Residual soils are those formed from weathered bedrock <u>in situ</u>. The soil now exists in place of the rock from which it was formed. Colluvial soils and clays are those which have moved downslope from the place of origin under the influence of gravity. Alluvial soil clays are those eroded, transported, and deposited by the running water of streams. Temper is any coarse material added to pottery clay to prevent failure of the vessel. Geological time-rock terms, e.g., Pleistocene, may be found in any introductory text.

3. See especially M. W. Ball and D. Ball, <u>American Association of Petroleum Geologists</u>, Bulletin 37, No. 1.

4. A syncline is a fold in the rocks in which both sides dip inward toward an axis. An anticline is also a fold structure, but instead both sides dip outward from an axis.

5. G. A. Smith, <u>The Historical Geography of the Holy Land</u> (1966), p. 143.

6. Residual soil is considered virgin when there is no significant cultural material found on it. Transported soils are not found where they are formed but where they are redeposited by some agency of sediment movement, for example mass wasting down slope or running water.

7. M. Gal, <u>Proceedings of the International Clay Conference</u> (1967), Vol. II.

8. <u>Ibid</u>. and D. H. K. Amiran <u>et al</u>., <u>Israel Atlas</u> (Jerusalem: Carta, 1955).

9. The Munsell Color Company, Inc., 2441 North Calvert Street, Baltimore, Maryland 21218, publishes soil and rock color charts.

10. Trace elements are those present in minor amounts in the earth's crust. Those used in this study are zirconium, strontium, nickel, titanium, copper, manganese. Iron and calcium were also recorded.

11. The bedrock formations outcropping in the vicinity of Gezer are in sequence, older to younger, the Bi'na limestone, Turonian in age; the Menuha formation, Senonian age; Ghareb formation, Maastrictian age; Taqiye formation, Paleocene age; and the Zor'a formation, Lower-Middle Eocene.

12. A lateral (synchronous) subdivision of a stratified unit; it may be a change of agency of deposition, e.g., a street surface sediment is a facies of the courtyard sediment, both of which were deposited at the same time.

13. D. H. Yaalon, Bulletin of the Research Council of Israel, IIG, No. 3 (1963).

14. Bimodal sediment has two principal size categories derived from two sources and/or agencies contributing to its make up. Coastal sands of Israel contain both quartz sand grains (from the Nile) and larger waveworn marine mollusk shell fragments. Wind-blown sands are better sorted and exhibit a narrow range of size variation.

15. This chapter is reprinted with minor changes from The Biblical Archaeologist, Vol. XXXIII:4 (Dec. 1970), pp. 98-132, by permission of the author and the American Schools of Oriental Research.

INDEX